Reformer in Modern China

Chang Chien, 1853-1926

Studies of the East Asian Institute
COLUMBIA UNIVERSITY

Chang Chien, 1853-1926

Chu, Ch'ang-ling

SAMUEL C. CHU

Reformer in Modern China

Chang Chien, 1853-1926

COLUMBIA UNIVERSITY PRESS
New York and London, 1965

Samuel C. Chu is Associate Professor of History at the University of Pittsburgh.

Library of Congress Catalog Card Number : 65-10541
Printed in the United States of America

The East Asian Institute of Columbia University

THE EAST ASIAN INSTITUTE was established by Columbia University in 1949 to prepare graduate students for careers dealing with East Asia, and to aid research and publication on East Asia during the modern period. The research program of the East Asian Institute is conducted or directed by faculty members of the University, by other scholars invited to participate in the program of the Institute, and by candidates for the Certificate of the Institute or the degree of Doctor of Philosophy. Some of the products of the research program are published as Studies of the East Asian Institute. The faculty of the Institute, without necessarily agreeing with the conclusions reached in the Studies, hope with their publication to perform a national service by increasing American understanding of the peoples of East Asia, the development of their societies, and their current problems.

The Faculty of the East Asian Institute are grateful to the Rockefeller Foundation and the Ford Foundation for the financial assistance which they have given to the program of research and publication.

Dedicated in loving appreciation to my parents
Shih-Ming Chu and Grace Zia Chu

Foreword

VERY FEW scholarly biographies of Chinese leaders are available in Western languages. Chang Chien, the subject of Professor Chu's fascinating study, was a most unusual Chinese: a truly transitional figure standing astride the late imperial era and the modern day. Although eminently fitted for a distinguished official career, he forsook officialdom to become a modern entrepreneur. Yet he was a most unusual entrepreneur in devoting the profits from his successful businesses to the modernization of his native community. With an excellent traditional education, he devoted most of his talents to the problems of bringing his country into the modern world.

Chang Chien's active career was almost equally divided between the nineteenth and the twentieth centuries and between national and local problems. He moved with equal ease among officials, merchants, and scholars; in the "examination world" of imperial days as in the world of assemblies and cabinets of the early republican era. In his efforts to provide public primary schools, good roads, or a modern hospital for his native district he acted in the best traditions of the Chinese gentry. In struggling to cope with the periodic flooding of the Huai River or to rationalize the national salt administration he devoted himself to problems which have concerned public-spirited Chinese officials for centuries. In his efforts to modernize Chinese education or to inaugurate a Chinese-owned modern textile industry he was actuated by motives of recent-day patriotism.

Chang Chien was, in short, the all-round Chinese scholar-leader, characteristic of the best his culture produced, yet highly individualistic in his interests and style. A product of his age, he also left his mark upon it through many pioneering enterprises.

Fortunately a great deal of primary information on Chang Chien and his environment is available in Chinese. Professor Chu, a graduate of the East Asian Institute and a Ph. D. in history at Columbia, has used this material most effectively to present a well-rounded, analytic biography of this man of many parts. Students of China's modernization may draw from this study an appreciation of the difficulties confronting a late Ch'ing entrepreneur. An illuminating example is the unbelievable difficulties Chang Chien encountered in accumulating the capital to start his first cotton-spinning mill, despite his national reputation and excellent connections with sponsoring officials. For another example, in the attempt to create a modern local school system he had to start at the very beginning—to establish China's first modern normal school. Student's of traditional Chinese society should find the account of Chang Chien's education, his encounters with the examination system, and his apprenticeship as a personal secretary to a high official very revealing.

This study, like those before it in the East Asian Institute Series, was in large part done at Columbia University using the resources of Columbia's East Asian Library.

C. MARTIN WILBUR

September, 1964

Professor of Chinese History
Columbia University

Preface

THE ACTIVE LIFE of Chang Chien as a modernizer, spanning an eventful quarter century from the last few years of the nineteenth century to the early 1920s, is still recent enough to be recalled by many of the older living Chinese of today. Even those of his countrymen who had no personal knowledge of him have heard of him by reputation. Within the past decade several Chinese studies of various aspects of Chang Chien have also appeared. Outside China (and the neighboring country of Japan), however, he is virtually unknown. In fact, only in the last few years has there been any mention of him in Western-language study of modern China. My primary purpose then, is to make him better known to the world at large. There is, however, a related purpose. Where Chang Chien is at all mentioned, he is referred to primarily as an industrialist.[1] Hence I have felt it appropriate to trace his career in some detail, in order to bring out his other important roles of educator, conservationist, and public benefactor. In tracing his career, I have made an attempt also to sketch in the history and the particular characteristics of the institutions with which he was dealing, such as the educational system and the salt administration, wherever such information would contribute to a clearer understanding of Chang Chien's role in these fields of endeavor.

As a result this study is at once a biography but also something less. It is a biography because the actions and thoughts of the central figure dominate the discussion at every one of its stages. It also follows a generally chronological sequence. Yet it is something less than a full biography because certain facets of Chang Chien's life have been regarded as largely irrelevant to an understanding of his career as a modernizer, and therefore slighted or omitted altogether. For instance, his reputation as an essayist, poet, and calligrapher is acknowledged, but no attempt is made to describe his activities in the literary field, or to assess his literary ability. Similarly, his collected writings contain numerous correspondences which he carried on with various warlords and national political figures after 1915, when his active work was virtually confined to his native district of Nan-t'ung. These writings have also been ignored, on the ground that they actually accomplished little, and are not essential to our understanding of the man or his times. A full-length biography should also include as full as possible a treatment of the subject's childhood and young manhood (which in Chang Chien's case extended to his forty-second year). Since this study concentrates on Chang Chien the modernizer, it draws upon his earlier years only where certain experiences seem to bear directly upon his later career. Finally, Chang Chien's private life and personal idiosyncrecies are probably better known than most of his contemporaries, but details of his personal life have been included only where they contribute to our understanding of his actions and motivations.

It is my hope that what emerges from this study would be an account of the public career of a most unusual man, not only for China of his time, but in the world at large as well. His career, while it can in no sense be considered typical of men of his gentry background and scholarly tradition, still reflects enough of his class status and training so that this study is no mere isolated account of a single individual. In a sense it can be regarded as a case study of the potentialities and limitations of one man's effort to transform the life pattern of a single region, given the benefit of certain favorable factors, but also operating within certain self-imposed and external restraints. In a specific sense Chang Chien the modernizer represents the pragmatic Confucian who personally made a distinction between what was essential in Confucianism and what was not, sloughing off the latter to pursue a highly unorthodox course of action, yet holding true to the former throughout his life.

In the pursuit of this study I have benefitted from a great many persons, to whom my public acknowledgment of gratitude has long been overdue. The study was originally suggested by Professor Franklin L. Ho, and completed as a doctoral dissertation under the joint guidance of Professor C. Martin Wilbur and Professor Ho. My debt to my two *lao-shih* can never be fully acknowledged. I am grateful also to Professor Shepard Clough and the late Professor J. Bartlet Brebner for greatly widening my mental horizons in the latter stages of this study. The kind interest shown to the study by professors L. S. Yang, Mary Wright, and Howard Boorman at various times have helped to sustain me in my labors. A special note of thanks is due to Mr. King-kong Wong, who, quite unbeknownst to me (and I to him), completed an independent study of Chang Chien as a master's thesis at the University of Washington. By checking my study with Mr. Wong's, I have strengthened both its factual content and interpretations. Whenever more than a word or phrase have been altered as a direct result of this process, I have noted the fact by citing the appropriate section of Mr. Wong's study in my notes. Of the staff of the East Asian Library (Columbia), Library of Congress, Chinese and Japanese Library (Harvard), Sterling Library (Yale), and the Hoover Institute, who have generously aided my efforts, I would like to single out Mr. Howard Linton and Dr. T. K. Tong of Columbia, Dr. K. T. Wu and Dr. Osamu Shimizu of the Library of Congress, and Mr. Eugene Wu of Hoover Institute for special thanks. I am also the beneficiary of a number of mentors, colleagues, and friends who have kindly gone over the draft in whole or in part. Among these are Knight Biggerstaff, S. H. Chou, K. C. Hsiao, Chang-tu Hu, K. C. Liu, T. K. Tong, and L. S. Yang, all of whom have helped me to remove errors of fact and interpretation, leaving the remaining imperfections as my sole responsibility. In addition, I am grateful to Mr. T. W. Chang and his son, William Chang, for their cordial support of my efforts to study their illustrious kinsman, and to the following persons for favoring me with remembrances and interviews: Mr. K. P. Fengson, Dr. and Mrs. George L. Hagman, Dr. P. W. Kuo, Mrs. N. C. Lee Pien, and Mr. H. S. Sung. To the usual inadequate words of thanks which an author accords his wife, I would like to add that my wife acted as a secretary-proofreader throughout the writing of this study. Finally, I am grateful to the East Asian Institute of Columbia University, and to Professor Herschel Webb, Chairman of the Institute Publications Committee, for the generous grant which made the publication of this study possible.

SAMUEL C. CHU

January, 1965
Pittsburgh, Pennsylvania

Contents

A Note on Romanization

I have made it a general practice to follow the Wade-Giles system of romanization as much as possible. Two types of general exceptions to this practice, however, should be noted. Wherever a geographic term is more commonly known in another form (e.g. Shanghai, Szechwan), I have used this generally accepted form. Also, wherever one of Chang Chien's industries and enterprises already had an English equivalent name (e.g. Dah Sun, instead of Ta Sheng), it seems entirely too pedantic to insist on the Wade-Giles romanization, and I have refrained from so insisting. I might add that all Chinese and Japanese personal names are given in their natural order, with surnames first.

VALUE OF ONE HAIKWAN TAEL

(1 haikwan tael = 1.4 yuan)

Year	*Equivalent to U.S.* $
1880	1.41
1881	1.35
1882	1.39
1883	1.37
1884	1.36
1885	1.29
1886	1.22
1887	1.18
1888	1.14
1889	1.15
1890	1.27
1891	1.20
1892	1.06
1893	.96
1894	.78
1895	.80
1896	.81
1897	.73
1898	.70
1899	.33
1900	.75
1901	.72
1902	.63
1903	.64
1904	.66
1905	.73
1906	.80
1907	.79
1908	.65
1909	.63
1910	.66
1911	.65
1912	.74
1913	.73
1914	.67

Source: Odell, Ralph M. *Cotton Goods in China.* Department of Commerce. Bureau of Foreign and Domestic Commerce. Special Agents Series, No. 107. Washington, 1916. P. 26.

Reformer in Modern China

CHAPTER ONE

Introduction

CHINA IN THE latter part of the nineteenth century was caught up in a world-wide process of cultural confrontation, the magnitude of which the participants were only fragmentarily aware. The dynamic, expansive West had thrust itself insistently into every corner of the civilized world, calling forth responses varying from ultimate resignation, the experience of most of the African continent, to viralent resistence on the West's own terms, such as occurred in Japan. The Japanese experience demonstrates the fact that, for every nation which would meet the West on the same level as the West, that nation would have to undergo, to a greater or lesser extent, a process of industrialization, social change, and reevaluation in cultural values; in a word, modernization. The Chinese experience was no exception. In China, as in many other countries, responsible men were forced by events to realize that the traditional Chinese civilization could not withstand the dynamic West without undergoing change. For these men the degree of change was the crux of the problem, with various school of thought, ranging from those who wished only the most superficial of changes, to those who would see the wholesale replacement of Chinese culture by Western culture. Between these two extremes stood a group of men who advocated a substantive program of modernization for China, but one which was to be based on the traditional culture.

One of the most successful yet least known among the last group of these men was Chang Chien. Born of humble background in 1853, known as a classical scholar of high reputation, he successively undertook the establishment of cotton mills, the founding of schools, the reclamation of unproductive land, the championing of a constitutional government, the advocacy of salt reform and river conservation, and, by the time of his death in 1926, the transformation of one of the more backward areas of Kiangsu Province into a nationally known, model district. The career and accomplishments of Chang Chien illustrate concretely the interaction between the forces of progress and reaction at work in China in the later nineteenth and early twentieth centuries. In a larger sense they also reflect the problems faced by modernizers in all parts of the world confronted by the West.

Chang Chien's life spans a transitional period in his country's history, a period which was anything but propitious. China was then approaching the nadir of her decline, from hegemony in a world of her own to being a near-vacuum fought over by the Western powers. The causes of her decline were many, and lay back over long stretches of time. In the hundred or so years from mid-eighteenth century to mid-nineteenth century alone, China's population underwent a threefold increase, from in excess of 143 million to slightly less than 430 million.[1] The problem of feeding this vast population was complicated by recurrent natural disasters, the consequences of which increased in severity as the public works efforts of the imperial government declined. The Manchu rulers of the Ch'ing dynasty had held sway over China through the greater part of the seventeenth and eighteenth centuries. During this period, the Imperial Court, pursuing a policy that was characterized by extreme conservatism and a dynastic rather than national outlook, managed to hold the Chinese officialdom in check by maintaining ruling power while dividing responsible positions between Manchus and Chinese. By the middle of the nineteenth century the regime had become so effete that a succession of large-scale rebellions—the most serious of which were the T'ai-p'ing Rebellion (1851–64) and the Muslim revolts in the outlying southwestern and northwestern parts of China (1855–73)—were pacified with difficulty, largely through the efforts of regional Chinese armies. With the subsequent rise of the regional officials, a trend toward decentralization of power occurred which the Imperial Court was never able to reverse thereafter.

Into this recognizable pattern of dynastic decline entered the new element of Western intrusion. Contact between China and the West had been largely peaceful until the nineteenth century, but the opening shots of the Opium War (1839–42) between Great Britain and China signified a new era of Sino-Western relationship. Henceforth contact with the West increasingly came to mean pressure from the West. The latter held the trump card of military superiority because of its own advanced technology and the decadence of the Chinese military machine. Whenever China resorted to arms against the West, she was always bested, as was the case in the Opium War, the "Arrow" War (1856–60) against an alliance of Great Britain and France, and resistance against the French in Annam (1884–85). These defeats cost China her suzerainty over Burma and Indo-China among her more important vessal states, on top of which she was forced to pay large sums of indemnities. She also had to open a number of ports to foreign trade—among which were Canton, Shanghai, and Hankow—and suffered further indignities in the loss of control over her import trade and the granting of territorial concessions. Politically and economically China seemed to be following the path of India in approaching the point where she would no longer be master of her own house.

In the face of these Western pressures, China was forced to take certain steps in the hope of redressing the disparity between herself and the West. The most obvious of China's weaknesses was in military strength. Accordingly, the first efforts of such outstanding officials as Tseng Kuo-fan, Li Hung-chang, and Tso Tsung-t'ang was in the improvement of the country's defenses. In 1855, while he was fighting the T'ai-p'ing forces, Tseng Kuo-fan established a small arsenal in Kiangsi Province. Ten years later Tseng Kuo-fan and Li Hung-chang founded the Kiangnan Arsenal at Shanghai, which was by far the largest arsenal in China then and for many years thereafter. Meanwhile Tso Tsung-t'ang had established a shipyard near Foochow in Fukien Province. These three men were at the forefront of Chinese efforts to match Western military superiority by the establishment of arsenals and shipyards.

While military advancements occupied the chief attention of the most progressive elements of the Chinese officialdom, a modest beginning was also made in the field of education. A small school created in 1862 to train interpreters, the T'ung-wen Kuan, became the antecedent of China's first modern institution of higher education. A program to train students abroad was instituted a decade later, largely through the efforts of Yung Wing, the first Chinese to be educated in America. These measures fitted in well with the movement for *tzu-ch'iang*, self-strengthening, which at that time was pushed by Li Hung-chang and others. The narrow scope of the movement for self-strengthening slowly evolved to cover more than just the making of arms and the training of students. In the field of communications, lively debate arose over the advantage of building railroads in China. There was less opposition to the erection of telegraph lines, and the first line, established between Tientsin and its port of Taku, went into service in 1879. In the field of general industry, the establishment of a cotton mill in Shanghai was planned in 1882, but it did not materialize until a decade later. In all these efforts, Li Hung-chang played a leading role.

The course of China's reaction to Western pressure was determined by a number of factors, the chief among which was that of leadership. In contrast to Japan, which, among other factors, benefitted from the rise of a group of able and energetic leaders in her efforts toward modernization, China suffered from a lack of unified leadership working toward reform and modernization. To be sure, scattered individuals did see the need for China to modernize herself along Western lines. Aside from those already mentioned, we need only single out such men as Feng Kuei-fen, Kuo Sung-tao, Hsüeh Fu-ch'eng, and Cheng Kuan-ying.[2] Yet the contributions of these few stood out precisely because they were exceptional rather than representing the norm. The vast majority of the ruling official-gentry class was conservative in outlook and regarded innovations as possible threats to the basis upon which its privileged position in Chinese society was founded. Consequently, the efforts of the progressive officials were sporadic at best, and every reform was pushed through against determined opposition on the part of conservative elements among the official-gentry class.

Western pressure and Chinese reaction were both greatly intensified in the last years of the nineteenth century and the opening decades of the twentieth. Import trade through the treaty ports increased in volume by leaps and bounds. Whereas in the early nineteenth century opium was just about the only item which the West could sell to the self-sufficient Chinese in any quantity, decades of exposure to Western commerce had created in the Chinese an appetite for factory-made goods. Cotton and cotton cloths were in the lead among the items imported, but kerosene, sugar, flour, and other consumer goods were not far behind. The increasing sale of foreign goods in China seemed to bear out the contention held by many Westerners that China was a vast untapped market. This estimation further whetted the appetite of the Western powers to get a share of this market.

China's slowness in adjusting herself to Western pressure was the more glaring when contrasted with the course of action taken by Japan. That island kingdom, in many ways even more isolated from Western influence before the arrival of Commodore Perry in 1853 than China was before the Opium War, had rapidly come to terms with the new situation. By 1890 Japan had promulgated her constitution, and thereby served notice to China and the West alike that she could no longer be regarded as a backward Asiatic country. Meanwhile her continual efforts to enlarge her influence in the adjacent lands, particularly in Korea, had brought her into conflict with China on a number of occasions. The two countries finally went to war over a minor incident in Korea in 1894. Events on sea and land rapidly proved the superiority of the Japanese in every phase of modern warfare. The outcome of the war was soon evident.

With her victory Japan became one more aggressive power scrambling for concessions in China. The latter's inability to best even a small non-Western power so lately opened to modernization proved the failure of China's self-strengthening movement. China was revealed to the world for what she was: a helpless hulk completely open to the plunder of all who wished to despoil her. And the reaction was immediate. In the three years following the signing of the Treaty of Shimonoseki ending the Sino-Japanese War in 1895, France, Russia, Great Britain, and Germany successively wrested important territorial and economic concessions from her. The day of China's dissolution seemed imminent.

Faced with the dire situation, those elements in China which had been working for gradual reform and modernization were thrust aside by what might be termed "the activists." Led by the brilliant but intemperate K'ang Yu-wei, a small band of reformers in 1898 managed to obtain the ear of Kuang-hsü, the reigning emperor. There occurred what came to be known as the "Hundred-day Reform." In a little over three months edict after edict came from the Imperial Throne, embodying many drastic political and administrative reforms. This seeming success for the activists, however, was short-lived. Before any of the reform edicts could be put into effect, a palace revolution took place and the powerful and conservative Empress Dowager Tz'u-hsi resumed the imperial power which she had permitted the Emperor to exercise for the few years prior to 1898. Six of the reformers were executed, and K'ang Yu-wei himself had to flee for his life.

Although the activists failed in their attempt to reform China, the basic cause of their action, the desire to strengthen China and rid her of the "accursed foreigners," remained. Two years after the failure of the Hundred-day Reform, it was the populace that had its chance to attempt direct action. This came in the form of a mystical patriotic group known as the Boxers. They were aided by the conservative elements among the officials, who accepted their claim of being able to drive the foreigners bodily out of China by force. With little real understanding of the Westerner's source of strength, the Boxers embarked on a campaign of arson and murder, which soon brought swift retribution. The upshot was China's ultimate humiliation at the hands of the joint forces of eight nations, to which China was forced to pay a staggering indemnity of 450 million taels.

The Boxer debacle proved to even the most conservative elements within the Chinese officialdom that some reform was absolutely necessary. The Empress Dowager herself, sobered by her precipitous flight to the interior to avoid capture by the joint expeditionary force, called for reform proposals from the officialdom. A number of leading officials came to the fore with their ideas. Of these officials none was more progressive or influential than the two governor-generals Chang Chih-tung and Liu K'un-i, whose jurisdictions spanned almost the entire Yangtze valley.

During the decade from the end of the Boxer debacle to the Revolution of 1911, forces of reform were definitely making headway. They were further encouraged by the victory of Japan in the Russo-Japanese War of 1904–05, which they interpreted as a victory for a constitutional Asiatic country over an autocratic European power. When in 1908 both the Empress Dowager and the Kuang-hsü Emperor died, there were high hopes within the ranks of the reformers that orderly and gradual reform under the aegis of the Manchu reigning house was just around the corner.

That this was not to be can in part be blamed on the basic conservatism of the Manchus, who were not genuinely willing to institute reform measures which threatened their own privileged position over the Chinese. A more decisive factor was the revolutionaries, who were independent of both the conservatives and the moderate reformers. As early as 1885, Sun Yat-sen, the future revolutionary leader of China, had already expressed his conviction that the fall of the dynasty was an inevitable prerequisite to the successful transformation of China, but his words then made little impression upon the majority of the Chinese at home and abroad.

The successive disasters from 1894 to 1900, however, definitely strengthened the revolutionaries' hand, and from 1901 onwards they increasingly had the sympathies of a large segment of the overseas Chinese, from whom thcy obtained both financial aid and moral support.

When the revolution came, it succeeded like most major revolutions in the world: unplanned, haphazard, and benefitting from a number of accidental factors. In some four months' time the Manchu imperial house relinquished all power, a provisional government was set up, and the first Chinese republic came into being.

Those who expected the downfall of the empire to mark an upswing in China's modernization were soon doomed to disappointment. Instead of a strong and united government working toward the reconstruction of the country, there came the scourge of warlordism, which kept the country divided and irresolute. Republicanism seemed to suffer yet another blow when, during the course of World War I, Yüan Shih-k'ai, the first President of the Republic, sought to add imperial trimmings to his already dictatorial powers. In this he failed, and died soon after. The death of Yüan virtually ended all attempts to revive the throne, but while World War I was going on the cause of constructive republicanism in China seemed as futile as ever. The only good China derived from the war was the respite she enjoyed from Western political and economic penetration. Although politically Japan's aggressive designs more than made up for the preoccupation of Western powers in Europe, economically China's infant industries, especially her light consumer-goods industries, enjoyed a rapid growth with the slackening of foreign competition. Meanwhile all kinds of Western ideas were making their impacts on China. The end of the war saw China still in a political chaos, but socially and economically she was no longer the China of the 1890s.

It was against this backdrop of events that Chang Chien carried out his career. His achievements as a modernizer was directly related to these events, and as he progressed in his career, he in turn came to play a part in shaping the contemporary history of his country.

CHAPTER TWO

Early Life

CHANG CHIEN was born in the village of Ch'ang-lo in the district of Hai-men on July 1, 1853.[1] His family, however, had resided for many generations in the adjacent district of Nan-t'ung, to which Chang Chien soon returned as a child. Located on the north bank of the Yangtze River near its mouth in Kiangsu Province, Nan-t'ung was situated within the alluvial delta area of the Yangtze and was quite flat, with the exception of five hills on the riverbank: Chün Shan (Army Hill), Lang Shan (Wolf Hill), and three lesser hills. The people of Nan-t'ung were characterized by one writer of local history as industrious, persevering, with strong kinship ties, but conservative and superstitious.[2] Most of them made their living from the cultivation of cotton, as well as the staple crops of rice and wheat. Generally speaking Nan-t'ung and other districts north of the Yangtze River were much less well endowed in climate, fertility of soil, and communications than the localities on the south bank of the Yangtze.

Chang Chien's father, Chang P'eng-nien, had two wives, who between them bore him five sons. The elder Mrs. Chang, nee Kuo, gave birth to the oldest son, Chang Yü, and the youngest, Chang Ching. Between them there were Chang Mo, Chang Ch'a, and Chang Chien, all born to the younger Mrs. Chang, nee Chin. Chang Mo died at the age of nine of accidental drowning while playing with the neighboring boys. Chang Ching and Chang Yü died in 1902 and 1914 respectively. Chang Ch'a alone survived Chang Chien's death, by six years. Of his four brothers, Chang Chien was on intimate terms with only his third brother, Chang Ch'a. But the warm and close relationship between the two, which grew up through years of close collaboration in many projects, was something which sustained Chang Chien throughout his life.

Chang Chien's family had been illiterate farmers for generations. His father broke the pattern of the family by acquiring a moderate education. Chang P'eng-nien became a farmer of some local importance. His education, however, did not go far enough to permit him to qualify for the civil service examinations.[3] Chang Chien early showed high intelligence and became the favorite of his father, who initiated his schooling when he was three years old. Throughout his childhood he studied under a succession of tutors, first together with his brothers and later alone. He was to spend most of his early mature years in study and in the taking of various civil service examinations.

Chang Chien competed in his first examination in 1868, at the age of fifteen. It was then necessary for promising youths whose ancestors in the three previous generations had not been scholars to have guarantors and co-guarantors among the local gentry or in his own clan in order to qualify for the examination. Since Chang Chien's family came of farming stock, he had to comply. There was no lack of willing guarantors, but his father trusted his tutor, Sung P'u-chai, explicitly. And when the latter suggested that Chang Chien would do well to take the examinations under an assumed relationship with a certain Chang Chiung in the neighboring town of Ju-kao, Chang P'eng-nien agreed to the deception. Chang Chien therefore took his early examinations in Ju-kao under the name of Chang Yu-ts'ai. Chang Chiung turned out to be a completely unscrupulous individual, and, with the connivance of venal officials, blackmailed Chang Chien's family out of large sums of money and caused it no end of trouble. At one point Chang Chien had to leave Ju-kao in the middle of a dark, rainy night to avoid the possibility of being imprisoned. Fortunately there came to the aid of the hard-pressed father and son several staunch friends, among whom were Chang Chien's new tutor, Chao P'eng-yüan, and magistrate Sun Yün-chin. It was largely through their efforts that Chang Chien was allowed to regain his own rightful name and registration. The whole unpleasant affair dragged on over a period of five years and made a lasting impression upon Chang Chien.[4]

These early difficulties, however, did not prevent him from attaining the *hsiu-ts'ai* degree on his first try. He successfully passed through the *hsien*, *chou*, and *yüan* examinations, placing twenty-sixth in the latter, and was classified a *fu-sheng*.[5] In 1870 he tried for *chü-jen* for the first time, and succeeded in placing sixteenth in the *k'o* examination but failed to pass the provincial examination. He was to repeat this pattern of succeeding in the *k'o* examination and failing in the provincial examinations four more times, in 1873, 1875, 1876, and 1879. These repeated failures were especially galling to

Chang Chien, since he won the top position in both the Kiangsu *k'o* examination of 1876 and 1879, advancing from the classification of *fu-sheng* to that of *lin-sheng* in 1876. Also during this same period he successively came through as the top man in the examinations of two local academies (1874), and *sui* examination of 1877, and the examinations of three special academies (1879). The degree of *chü-jen*, however, continued to elude him until 1885, when, having traveled to Peking and taken the examination of the Imperial Academy, once more coming out on top, he competed in the provincial examination at the capital and succeeded in placing second highest among those who passed. He was then thirty-two.[6]

By this time he had already achieved considerable reputation as a scholar. Nevertheless he was to find the road to *chin-shih* no less difficult than the path to *chü-jen*. This in spite of the fact that he had won the confidence of such influential men as P'an Tsu-yin, President of the Board of Works, and Weng T'ung-ho, the imperial tutor, who were the examiners on various occasions and who did everything they could to help him. Some of these instances of help were noted by Chang Chien in his personal record. In his second attempt at the *chin-shih* degree in 1889, for instance, P'an, in the capacity of the chief examiner, tried to include his paper among the ones who passed, but failed to locate it. In 1890 the examiner for his section forwarded his paper to the final selection, presided over by Weng. Again it failed to pass and another candidate's paper was adjudged the best. The extreme irony occurred in Chang Chien's fourth attempt in 1892. Once more Weng T'ung-ho was the chief examiner. He was determined to see that not only would Chang Chien pass, but that he would get the top prize as well. When the papers were all in, he and his colleagues went through the best papers with care, trying to pick out Chang Chien's paper by its style and content. Finally they settled on one as the most likely. Yet when the names of the successful candidates were posted, Chang Chien's name again failed to be included. A postexamination search revealed that his paper had been eliminated in the early rounds by an assistant examiner because of minor stylistic errors. Weng was deeply chagrined. Chang Chien himself was no less disappointed.[7] By this time he was approaching forty years of age and had devoted twenty-four years of his life to the examination grind. By his own calculation he had spent a total of some 120 days in examination stalls. He was overwhelmed by the futility of any further attempts and resolved to "put away the examination paraphanalia."

Two years later, however, in 1894, Chang Chien once more took the metropolitan examination, at the insistence of his older brother. When the list was posted he did not even trouble to be present. This time his name was found in the sixtieth position. He improved on this in the reexamination by placing tenth, and when the palace examination was over, he was chosen to be the *chuang-yüan*, the highest of all. He was duly appointed a Compiler of the First Class in the Hanlin Academy. It may be of interest to note that the name of his friend, Weng T'ung-ho, was not among the examiners in the first two of these examinations but was included on the eight-men board of examiners for the final examination.[8]

During this long struggle up the ladder of scholastic achievement Chang Chien had married and had also proven his abilities in areas other than the civil service examination. He was betrothed to his wife, nee Hsü, as early as 1870, when Chang Chien was seventeen, but circumstances delayed their marriage until four years later. Soon after Chang Chien's marriage he entered the employment of Sun Yün-chin in Nanking, who in his previous capacity as the magistrate of Nan-t'ung had befriended Chang Chien. Though nominally a secretary, he was placed in an academy with Sun's own sons and ordered to devote his time to study. This first of a long line of Chang Chien's benefactors remained one of his staunchest supporters for many years and was instrumental in giving Chang Chien early opportunities to gain experience in international affairs and in water conservancy. Through Sun's recommendation in 1876, Chang Chien transferred into the service of Wu Ch'ang-ch'ing, who was then the garrison commander at P'u-k'ou, across the Yangtze from Nanking, but who was soon after transferred to Teng-chou in Shantung Province. He took Chang Chien with him to his new post. General Wu had a number of promising young men under his patronage. Among them were Yüan Shih-k'ai, the future first President of China, Hsüeh Fu-ch'eng, later ambassador to England and France, and Ho Ssu-k'un, later a prominent associate of Chang Chien's. All were treated with consideration. Chang Chien's duties were made light so that he had ample leisure to devote himself to study. These circumstances, together with his growing maturity, no doubt played a part in his obtaining the top ranking in several of his examinations at this time.

Chang Chien's connection with Wu Ch'ang-ch'ing led to his taking part in the Korean episode of 1882. Relations between China and Japan in the modern era had begun in 1870, when Japan first attempted to negotiate a commercial treaty with China. Li Hung-chang and Minister Soejima Taneomi eventually came to an agreement in 1873. In 1874, however, Japanese activities in sending a "punitive expedition" to Formosa and the subsequent controversy between China and Japan over the Liu-ch'iu Islands (Ryukyus) indicated that the two countries had many areas of potential conflict. Among these potential danger spots Korea loomed large in the eyes of both China and Japan.

Aware of her own precarious position in Korea, China, in the person of Li Hung-chang, pursued a policy of balancing one danger off with another. English support was counted on against possible Russian designs, and to cope with Japanese ambitions, the Korean king was prevailed upon to sign commercial treaties with other powers, especially with the United States. Li did not have an easy task, however, as the Korean king himself was caught between factions, the most powerful of which were the radical faction of the queen and the reactionary faction of the Tai-wen-kun, father and ex-regent to the young king. Furthermore, nearly the entire country was opposed to any kind of connection to the foreigners. Under the circumstances it was much to Li's credit that a commercial treaty was signed between Korea and the United States in the early part of 1882. Other powers quickly followed suit, and Korea signed similar treaties with England, France, and Germany.[9]

In July, 1882, ultranationalist rebels, of the Tai-wen-kun's faction, surrounded the Japanese Legation, killed and wounded several Japanese, and forced the Japanese minister, Hanabusa Yoshitada, to flee to an English ship for safety. Acting Governor-general Chang Shu-sheng of Chihli Province, in charge during Li Hung-chang's absence at home to observe the traditional mourning period, at once dispatched Admiral Ting Ju-ch'ang and Ma Chien-chung to Korea.[10] The army of General Wu Ch'ang-ch'ing was ordered to mobilize and to leave for Korea forthwith. Upon receiving this order on August 9, General Wu, who had come to recognize Chang Chien's ability during the six years the latter served under him, placed him in a position equivalent to a modern chief-of-staff for the entire campaign. Chang Chien was then twenty-nine years of age.

His very first task, the mobilization of troops in Teng-chou, proved to be a stiff challenge, since the army had to be in Korea within twelve days. Because of the fact that many of General Wu's protegees had gone back to their respective provinces for the triennial provincial examination, Chang Chien found himself carrying the entire burden of the administrative work with an undersized staff. Fortunately he had the able assistance of Yüan Shih-k'ai, Hsüeh Fu-ch'eng, and Ho Ssu-k'un. Even then, Chang Chien worked practically round the clock to get the army ready for embarkation by the assigned date.[11]

On August 16 the army was ready to move. The following day it left Cheeloo on board four ships for Korea. Due to efficient advance planning the ships reached Masan on the assigned date of August 21, even with a one-day delay at Wei-hai-wei occasioned by inclement weather. The landing in Korea gave Yüan Shih-k'ai, who was placed by Chang Chien at the head of the advanced group, a chance to display his coolness and courage under adverse conditions. On August 25 the Chinese army crossed the Han River and encamped two miles from Seoul.[12]

At this point in the campaign the Chinese resorted to a strategem to deprive the Korean rebel faction of its head. After consulting with Ting Ju-ch'ang and Ma Chien-chung, General Wu paid the Tai-wen-kun a courtesy call on the morning of the twenty-sixth. Confident of Chinese good will, the Tai-wen-kun returned the courtesy that afternoon, at which time he was politely but firmly detained and given to understand he had been acting contrary to the will of the Chinese Emperor. He was immediately escorted to the troopships at Masan and taken to Tientsin. Chinese troops attacked and surrounded the main body of the rebels on the twenty-ninth. Without their leader, the rebels were speedily defeated.

After fighting had ceased Chang Chien noticed that many of the rebels seemed to have fought only out of family loyalty and personal considerations. He persuaded General Wu to hold the prisoners and await the arrival of loyal Korean officials, and to punish only those adjudged guilty of leading the uprising. Thus there was no indiscriminate slaughter of the rebel forces. Afterward both the Korean king and General Wu freely praised Chang Chien for his part in the whole affair. The King awarded him a ceremonial robe, and General Wu, in accordance with a previous promise he had made to reward those who did the most to bring success to the expedition, sent a thousand taels to the Chang family in Nan-t'ung.[13] Chang Chien returned from Korea in 1884. Later that same year Wu Ch'ang-ch'ing died and his protegees were scattered.

The decade following his return from Korea was a comparatively quiet one for Chang Chien. He continued to make slow progress in the civil service examinations. He aided his father in the latter's plan to promote silk production in Nan-t'ung. His literary reputation had gained sufficient renown so that he was invited to write local histories for several neighboring districts. As we have seen, he finally succeeded in gaining the first position in the highest examination in 1894 at the age of forty-one. But the satisfaction he must have felt in reaching the long-sought-for goal was made hollow by the death of his father that same year. Also in 1894 China and Japan went to war over Korea. The war swiftly proved to the world China's utter incapacity to defend her interests. The treaty concluded at Shimonoseki on April 17, 1895, was generally regarded as a national disgrace. It came as a deep personal shock to Chang Chien. He forthwith made the decision to forego all active governmental service and returned to his native district of Nan-t'ung.

In the light of Chang Chien's subsequent career as a modernizer it does not seem unreasonable to surmise that his long struggle as an examination candidate and his personal experience in Korea had a direct bearing upon his outlook toward governmental service and his decision to abandon that career. Chang Hsiao-jo, in his biography of his father, has stated that the main factors which led Chang Chien to turn away from an official career were his concern for the weakness of China, his desire to break through the stereotyped conception of the uselessness of scholars in practical affairs, and his realization that even high officials were at the mercy and whim of the Throne. The last point was made vividly clear to Chang Chien in one specific episode. He was present in Peking one rainy day when the palanquin of the Empress Dowager returned to the capital. The officials meeting Tz'u-hsi all kneeled in the mud by the roadside, as court etiquette required them to do. They presented a most ridiculous sight, especially so since the Empress Dowager did not even deign to acknowledge their homage.[14]

The reasons given above can be considered the overt factors, but his long and frustrating experience with the civil service examination and his stay in Korea probably contributed to the underlying motivations. His early difficulties in the examinations and his refusal to knuckle under to them illustrate a certain stubborness and dogged perseverance in his makeup which was to be evident again later on, notably when he was working to raise funds for Dah Sun Cotton Mill. His later disappointments served to open his eyes to the supposed desirability of an official career. By the time he finally succeeded in the examinations, he was already in his forties and had acquired some fame through exploits outside of the traditional and prescribed course of scholarly advancement. Under the circumstances it should not be too surprising that the prospect of a slow advancement through the official hierarchy held little attraction for him.

Chang Chien's experience in Korea also left a decided impression upon him. The successful outcome of the affair of 1882 convinced him that only by pursuing a vigorous policy in Korea would China be able to check the Japanese threat there. He wrote three treatises on the Korean question, all existing copies of which have been lost. From his other writings, however, we can piece together his recommended course of action in Korea. He proposed the reiteration of existing treaties, clearly proclaiming China's suzerainty over Korea, and the stationing of troops at the strategic northern Korean city of Pyongyang.[15] He further advocated: (1) following the precedent of the Han Dynasty in incorporating northern Korea within China's boundaries; (2) placing a Chinese resident-general and troops in Korea to bolster her external defenses and to supervise her internal reforms; or as an alternative (3) encouraging Korea to put her own house in order, modernize her armed forces, and act in conjunction with Chinese troops in Manchuria.[16] Chang Chien was not blind to the likelihood of antagonizing Japan with such a forward policy. In fact he wished to see China take the initiative of forcing Japan either to accept Chinese terms or to commit herself as an open aggressor. These bellicose proposals arose from his conviction that a determined China might lose Korea temporarily but could never be beaten in the long run. He was not alone in his opinion, as other officials cherished similar sentiments, notably Teng Ch'eng-hsiu and Chang P'ei-lun. These suggestions, however, were overruled by the Throne in favor of Li Hung-chang's policy, that of peaceful penetration in Korea and the balancing of one power by another. Yet although Chang Chien's specific recommendations failed to be adopted, they demonstrate clearly that he was vividly aware of the threat represented by Japan. It was the same fear of Japan later on that in part prompted him to forego the regular career of an official in favor of doing something concrete to modernize his country.

For Chang Chien the signing of the treaty of Shimonoseki really marked the end of his scholarly life. Thereafter he was to devote his time and energies to the cause of a whole series of problems related to the modernization of China. These included industrial growth, constitutional government, modern education, land reclamation, salt reform, river conservancy, and civic and philanthropic projects. The Chang Chien of the pre-1894 era was virtually indistinguishable from the scores of "bright young men" turned out by the traditional civil service examinations system, perhaps more capable and worldly-wise than most, but certainly no less patriotic and no less steeped in Confucian classics. The Chang Chien of the post-1894 era retained much of the old moral core, but added to this was the man of foresight, action, and achievement, a man who was at the forefront of those who showed China the way out of the old centuries into the new. This is the Chang Chien on whom our attention will be primarily centered.

CHAPTER THREE

Dah Sun and Nan-t'ung Industries

THE SUCCESS of Chang Chien in the palace examination of 1894 gave him a great natural advantage over others when he decided to devote his life outside the regular official career. In a country like China, where education was the *sine qua non* of social position, power, and prestige, his obtaining the rank of *chuang-yüan*—highest of the highest—counted for a great deal in any field he chose to enter. Added to the fact that no native of Nan-t'ung had ever been designated that rank in its recorded history, the magnitude of Chang Chien's prestige in Nan-t'ung and in Kiangsu can well be imagined.

Having decided to abandon all thought of pursuing an official career so that he would be able to devote himself to some concrete means of helping his country, Chang Chien cast about for the best way to achieve his goal. He was convinced that, in the long run, the introduction of modern education must underlie all reforms, but he did not have the necessary funds to introduce educational reforms, even on a limited scale. Furthermore, he saw another matter which was more pressing for China at the moment: the need to do something about the tide of factory-made goods which was flowing into China.[1] More and more his thoughts settled upon the idea of establishing a cotton mill in his native district of Nan-t'ung.

A number of factors helped channel his thinking. Nan-t'ung was located in the sector of Kiangsu long famous for its cotton. Cotton was grown together with rice and wheat as one of the staple crops of the area. Nan-t'ung cotton was sought after by neighboring localities because of the greater length of its fiber and its superior texture.[2] Thus there was an existing commodity which commanded a ready market in Chang Chien's native district. Hitherto a great deal of the cotton sold locally was used in hand spinning, but with the acceptance of cheap, machine-made yarn from abroad, handicraft workers generally concentrated on weaving, so that conditions for the establishment of a cotton mill became favorable.[3] Another factor which impinged on his thinking was the signing of the treaty of Shimonoseki in 1895, with the stipulation that the Japanese should enjoy the right to establish factories in the interior of China. Under the most-favored-nation clause of treaties with all the powers, this meant that countries like England, Germany, and other Western powers would receive the same right. Chang Chien was already aware of the deep inroads in China's economy made by the increasing import of cotton yarn and cloth from such countries as England and India. He hated to think of the prospect of seeing foreign-owned factories established in China, on top of what was already taking place.[4]

Rise of Imports of Cotton Textile Products

The single most remarkable fact in the picture of China's imports in the last third of the nineteenth century was the phenomenal rise in the import of cotton goods. This was particularly true of cotton yarn. Whereas only 33,507 piculs (2,234 tons, as 15 piculs equal a ton) of yarn were imported in 1867, 2,748,644 piculs were imported in 1899, an eighty-twofold increase.[5] In the decade of 1882–91 alone, cotton yarn import jumped from 184,940 piculs to 1,212,922 piculs.[6] Much of the jump during this decade was accounted for by the great increase in the import of Indian yarn. "The Indian cotton goods trade and its growth," stated Commissioner of Customs R. E. Bredon of Shanghai in 1891, "are the leading features of the last few years' trade in Shanghai. . . . From 1 million taels [$1,290,000] worth in 1885 the trade grew to be worth 10 millions in 1891, and this, too, without in any way cutting into the trade in English and Dutch yarn."[7] Following 1891, the import of Japanese yarn had an even more spectacular rise than did Indian yarn the decade before. Through the port of Shanghai alone, it jumped from a nominal worth of 1,760 taels in 1891 to 6,303,346 taels by 1901. Meanwhile the value of Indian yarn imported through Shanghai also rose from 10 to 21 million taels during the same period.[8] A measure of the increasing importance of cotton among the imports of China during the decade of 1882–91 can be seen when more than sixfold increase in the amount of cotton yarn imported is contrasted with the increase in the value of all imports (from 79.5 million taels to 136 million).[9] From this it is clear that import of cotton goods, especially cotton yarn, was rapidly assuming the dominant position among the commodities imported into China in the late nineteenth century, comparable to a position once occupied by opium.

Development of the Cotton Industry in China

The great increase in the import of cotton yarn during the decade of 1882–91 showed that there was a ready market in China for machine-spun yarn. At the same time, the Treaty of Shimonoseki merely confirmed a trend which could not be long delayed in any case—the desire of foreign interests to establish factories in China. Chang Chien was not the first person to realize the dangerous implications of this trend. Only a handful of cotton mills, however, were in existence prior to the establishment of Dah Sun.

The establishment of a modern cotton industry in China occurred over a relatively short period of time. Despite the fact that China had long been one of the leading cotton-producing countries of the world, the bulk of her raw cotton was consumed by the hand-looms of the cottage industry, while the rest went for such modest uses as padding for winter clothing and quilts. Modern machine processing of cotton did not come into being in China until 1890. Although the efforts of the progressive officials played a large part in the development of the cotton industry, the initial impetus in the establishment of the first cotton mill in Shanghai was supplied by a private merchant named P'eng Chi-chih.[10] In 1878 P'eng approached Li Hung-chang and Shen Pao-chen, the commissioners of trade for northern and southern China respectively, with a scheme to set up a weaving mill. Li Hung-chang was very much in favor of the scheme, and recommended Cheng Kuan-ying to P'eng as the official representative in the venture. Spring of 1879 saw a disagreement among the directors of the enterprise. Thereafter P'eng severed all relationship with the enterprise and Cheng Kuan-ying took an increasingly active role in its affairs.[11]

Cheng Kuan-ying came from an educated family, but chose to enter a business career, to which he devoted most of his mature life. He anticipated much of the later developments of the modernization in China in his book, *Sheng-shih Wei-yen* (*Warnings to the Seemingly Prosperous Age*), written in the 1880s, which, among other things, advocated the creation of a cotton industry to check the drain of wealth through import of cotton goods. After he had assumed the direction of the embryonic enterprise, he made strenuous efforts to make sure the venture would not fail through the lack of thorough preparation. There were then a number of factors which had to be taken into consideration, among them the lack of any reliable data concerning the applicability of China-grown cotton for machine spinning and weaving, the hostility engendered by the project among the majority of the merchants and officials, and the inconstancy and incapacity among the executives, Cheng himself included. During this period of experimentation and delay, Cheng obtained from Li Hung-chang the guarantee of a monopoly in machine manufacturing of cotton cloth for ten years. Li took an active interest in the venture, and largely took over from Cheng in getting the weaving mill finally out of the planning stage. The Shanghai Weaving Bureau commenced production in 1890, and the success of the enterprise became immediately apparent; so much so that Li was not daunted by the outbreak of a disastrous fire which reduced the enterprise to a complete ruin. Subsequently the enterprise was reestablished as Hua Sheng Cotton Mill under the direction of Sheng Hsüan-huai and had a history of varied successes.[12]

The establishment of the Shanghai Weaving Bureau marked the beginning of a decade which saw a continuing growth in the establishment of cotton mills. Without going into details, we may enumerate the ones which preceded Dah Sun. The locality with the largest number of mills was Shanghai, and most of the early mills were Chinese-owned. Among these were Hua Hsin (1891), Yü Yüan (1894), Yü Chin, Ta Shun (both 1895), and Yü T'ung (1898). Other Chinese-owned mills were found in Wu-ch'ang (Hupeh Weaving Bureau in 1892 and Hupeh Spinning Bureau in 1898), Ningpo (T'ung Chiu Yüan in 1894), Wusih (Yeh Ch'in in 1897), Soochow (Su Lun in 1897), Hangchow (T'ung Yi Kung in 1897), and Hsiao-shan in the province of Chekiang (T'ung Hui Kung in 1899). Beginning with 1897, foreign interests also established a number of cotton mills. That year saw the founding of two English-owned mills, Laou-Kung-Mow and Ewo, while German interests established Soy-Chee and American interests started the International Cotton Manufacturing Company (Hung Yüan).[13] Japanese interests were not far behind, but the period of Japanese domination did not arrive until after the turn of the century, when many of the early ventures, ruined by undercapitalization or mismanagement, fell into Japanese hands.

The Founding of Dah Sun

Chang Chien was at home in mourning for his father in 1895 when Governor-general Chang Chih-tung was assigned to the Liang-Kiang post, temporarily replacing Liu K'un-i, in the face of possible Japanese threat to the Yangtze delta area. The two Changs found each other congenial. Governor-general Chang commissioned Chang Chien, along with Shen Yün-p'ei, to raise and train a corp of militiamen to guard the northern approaches to the mouth of the Yangtze River.[14] The defeat of China by Japan removed the necessity of such a step, but Shimonoseki posed the greater threat of the specter of foreign mills being established on Chinese soil. Governor-general Chang took the initiative in urging local officials and gentry members to initiate industrial enterprises.[15] In October, 1895, he requested Chang Chien, Lu Jun-hsiang, and Ting Li-ying, all outstanding members of the Kiangsu gentry, to accept the posts of directors of commerce bureaus and to start cotton mills in Nan-t'ung, Soochow, and Chinkiang respectively.[16] On Chang Chien's part, he accepted the dual responsibilities for Nan-t'ung only after much hesitation.[17]

He succeeded in persuading six men to become the promoters of the Nan-t'ung cotton mill: P'an Hua-mou, Kuo Hsün, Fan Fen, Liu Kuei-hsin, Shen Hsieh-chün, and Ch'en Wei-yung. P'an, a Cantonese, Kuo, a Fukienese, and Fan, who came from Ningpo, were active businessmen from Shanghai, while the other three were all natives of Nan-t'ung and Hai-men.[18] Assured of adequate support from the group, Governor-general Chang Chih-tung made public an announcement on January 15, 1896, of his intention to encourage the investment of private capital in cotton mills. This was followed shortly afterwards by an announcement designating the six men, with the help of Chang Chien, as the appointed group to undertake the setting up of the Nan-t'ung cotton mill.[19]

The promoters went to Nanking and conferred with Governor-general Chang on tax exemptions, receiving his promise that all necessary assistance would be rendered by the incumbent magistrates of Nan-t'ung, Wang Shu-t'ang, and of Hai-men, Wang Ping.[20] The governor-general further gave his approval to the detailed arrangements of the newly named Dah Sun Cotton Mill.[21] An initial capital of 600,000 taels was to be raised, with the Shanghai group of promoters, headed by P'an Hua-mou, responsible for 400,000 taels, and Shen Hsieh-chün and the rest of the Nan-t'ung group responsible for the remaining 200,000 taels.[22] P'an and Kuo Hsün were put in charge of the funds to be collected. Chang Chien was to serve as the liaison man between the promoters and the government.[23] The factory was to be located five miles northwest of the city of Nan-t'ung at T'ang-chia-cha, where land had already been bought for the purpose. Machinery with a total capacity of 20,000 spindles and the power plant necessary for its operation were to be purchased, which would produce an expected 150 piculs (20,000 pounds) of yarn per day. Raw materials were to be bought locally, and the finished products were primarily to be sold locally also. The provincial government kept the taxes on the products low to encourage growth of the enterprise, and other official aids were stipulated.[24] On February 11, 1896, a memorial from Governor-general Chang to the Court at Peking announced the initiation of the venture and paved the way for official approval of the enterprise.[25]

In the spring of 1896 the Court ordered Chang Chih-tung and Liu K'un-i to return to their former posts of Hu-Kwang and Liang-Kiang respectively. Governor-general Liu affirmed his willingness to abide by the wishes of Governor-general Chang on the matter of establishing Dah Sun, except for minor modifications in taxes.[26]

In August, 1896, two of the original six promoters, Fan Fen and Ch'en Wei-yung, backed out.[27] Of the remaining promoters, P'an Hua-mou was especially wary of taking chances and cautioned the others to proceed slowly. Then a new factor entered the picture, the possibility of acquiring some cotton-spinning machinery which was already in Shanghai. This was the machinery which Governor-general Chang Chih-tung had bought from England. In his previous tour of duty as the governor-general of Hu-Kwang, Chang Chih-tung had been instrumental in establishing the Hupeh Weaving Bureau in Wu-ch'ang. Subsequently he had ordered from England machinery with a capacity of 40,700 spindles to enlarge the productive capacity of the enterprise. When he was shifted to the Liang-Kiang post in 1894, the machinery was sent to Shanghai, along with an English engineer named Thomas, who was responsible for the installation of the machinery. Governor-general Chang entrusted it to Huang Tsun-hsien, an official, and to Wu Hsi-ling, a merchant, to be used in a mill under joint official-private auspices. Then when Governor-general Chang was recalled to his Hu-Kwang post at the end of 1895, he felt it inadvisable, with himself about to be absent, to continue the arrangement in Shanghai. Accordingly, he requested Lu Jun-hsiang, the director of the Soochow Commerce Bureau, to make use of the machinery in the cotton mill which the latter was planning to set up.[28] But Lu, fearing that the machinery would prove to be unsuitable, bought new machinery directly from England for his Su Lun mill. In February, 1896, Governor-general Chang entrusted the machinery to the director of the Kiang-ning (Nanking) Commerce Bureau, Kuei Sung-ch'ing, with instruction to sell it if possible.[29] Director Kuei apparently indicated the availability of the machinery to the Dah Sun group, tentatively setting the price at 500,000 taels.

The possibility of acquiring this machinery gave the Dah Sun venture new impetus. On September 14, 1896, P'an Hua-mou and Kuo Hsün wrote to Chang Chien, advising that the machinery, which had been left on open docks in Shanghai for some time, be checked for possible damages sustained. Moreover, they urged getting from the government assurances of complete private control of the machinery before purchasing it.[30] Subsequently the machinery was found to be in tolerable condition. Director Kuei Sung-ch'ing, no doubt anxious to close the deal, was willing to sell the machinery even if the asking price was not paid all at once. Through his representative, he further told P'an and Kuo that the provincial government would be willing to assist the private buyers if necessary.[31] Chang Chien now conceived of the idea of changing the enterprise to a joint official-private venture, with the government contributing the machinery and the private backers raising a matching sum of 500,000 taels.[32]

On November 2, Kuo Hsün came to Nan-t'ung to inspect the factory site. Chang Chien broached the matter of the new arrangement. Kuo demurred, saying that it still would be difficult to raise money from private sources. Chang Chien informed Kuo that he had found Chiang Hsi-shen and Kao Ch'ing in Nan-t'ung to replace the departed Fan and Chen. Kuo returned to Shanghai.[33] Two days later, P'an and Kuo wrote to Chang Chien, suggesting that the project of the mill be postponed for a year.[34] They cited the unfavorable business conditions of Shanghai as grounds for delay, but their real reason may well have been reluctance to enter into the new arrangement. As Chang Chien was to recall later, the day he received this letter, he "was beset by doubts and worries and paced the floor the entire night through."[35] He wrote to P'an and Kuo, urging them not to despair.[36] Apparently he succeeded for the moment. P'an and Kuo agreed to let Liu Kuei-hsin, one of the original promoters, join the Shanghai group, with Chiang and Kao, the two new promoters, joining Shen Hsieh-chün to form the Nan-t'ung group, each group agreeing to raise 250,000 taels.[37]

On December 6, 1896, following Director Kuei's intimation of a possible government loan of 60,000 taels, an agreement was signed between the government and the six private promoters, pledging the government to contribute the necessary machinery with a capacity of 40,700 spindles, valued at 500,000 taels, providing that the private promoters raised a like amount. The government would retain only supervisory power, with all actual control remaining in the hands of the private group. All profit and losses were to be shared equally between the two parties. Kuei Sung-ch'ing signed for the government, while Chang Chien attached his signature to those of the six promoters.[38] On the occasion of the signing, P'an and Kuo again stated that it was virtually impossible to raise money in Shanghai. It was then agreed among the promoters that P'an and Kuo would each raise 80,000 taels; the remaining 340,000 taels would be the responsibility of the Nan-t'ung group. Liu Kuei-hsin now rejoined the latter group.[39]

On March 26, 1897, the six promoters and Chang Chien held a meeting in Shanghai. The Nan-t'ung group accounted for nearly 59,000 taels, which they had raised, while P'an and Kuo had raised only 20,000 taels.[40] At this meeting it was agreed that all would work toward the goal of reaching the 200,000 taels figure in the following three months.[41] But rumors of P'an and Kuo's dissatisfaction persisted, even reaching the ear of Governor-general Liu K'un-i.[42] P'an and Kuo now apparently felt that they would be at a disadvantage in the enterprise, to which complaint the Nan-t'ung group answered that the condition was of P'an and Kuo's own making, and that the two men could easily change the situation by assuming responsibility for raising a larger share of the funds than their self-imposed limit of 160,000 taels.[43]

In May, 1897, another business recession set in. The Nan-t'ung group petitioned the Kiang-ning Commerce Bureau for a loan of 100,000 taels, citing the bureau's loan of 600,000 taels to the Su Lun Mill of Soochow as precedent. In the petition they stated the cost of construction of Dah Sun to be 240,000 taels, of which only half was accounted for by the money already gathered.[44] This petition was unsuccessful, but it further worsened the relationship between the Nan-t'ung and the Shanghai groups. P'an now claimed that news of official involvement in the venture had led Shanghai investors to withdraw the 20,000 taels previously raised.[45] In July the Nan-t'ung promoters went to Shanghai and tried to have the Shanghai group produce at least 60,000 taels to match the 120,000 taels collected by the Nan-t'ung promoters, but P'an remained adamant.[46] Matters reached an impasse at this point. The Nan-t'ung promoters then requested Director Kuei to allow them to resign, but Kuei instead urged them to persevere in the venture.[47]

Chang Chien now looked to other quarters for financial resources. He began to approach Sheng Hsüan-huai, the noted official-entrepreneur who already controlled several cotton mills in Shanghai.[48] Chang Chien proposed that half of the government-contributed machinery be assigned to Sheng to establish a new mill in Shanghai, in exchange for which Sheng would help raise money for Dah Sun. In this effort Chang Chien had the encouragement of Director Kuei.[49] On August 16, 1897, an agreement was signed between Chang, Sheng, and the government, in which the main points were: (1) two mills, one at Nan-t'ung and one at Shanghai, to share equally the machinery of 40,700 spindles capacity; Chang and Sheng to raise 250,000 taels each from private sources to match the government contribution of the machinery; (2)Chang Chien in full charge of the Nan-t'ung mill, with Sheng getting a free hand at Shanghai; and (3) confirmation of the tax scheme set forth in the previous agreements with the government.[50] This agreement confirmed the main points of a private agreement signed by Chang and Sheng five days previously on August 11. The private agreement included the additional stipulation that, aside from his financial responsibility toward the projected Shanghai mill, Sheng would share responsibility in raising the 250,000 taels stipulated for the Nan-t'ung mill, plus an additional 150,000 taels. For these obligations, Sheng was given the option of appointing two of the department heads in Nan-t'ung.[51] The signing of these two agreements meant that in effect two factories were to be established in place of one, with Sheng assuming complete responsibility for the Shanghai mill and promising to back Chang Chien on Dah Sun. Upon hearing this drastic revision of the enterprise, P'an and Kuo tendered their resignations to Director Kuei and severed all further connections with Dah Sun.[52]

Within a month Sheng Hsüan-huai was informing Chang Chien of the difficulty of raising funds among Shanghai business circles because of the recent example of the joint official-private cotton mill at Wu-ch'ang being completely taken over by the government.[53] Chang Chien received assurances from Governor-general Liu K'un-i that private interests would have a complete free hand in managing Dah Sun,[54] but this apparently did not calm the doubts of prospective investors. Chang Chien himself went to Shanghai in November to try to raise more funds, but without success.[55]

In December, 1897, Chang Chien let out the contract for the building of the factory for the sum of 90,000 taels, payable in a few months' time,[56] and the foundation of the main plant was laid that month. Construction proceeded steadily through 1898. Not only was it necessary to build the main factory buildings and warehouses, but considerable work had to be done in building roads, bridges, river enbankments, and canal locks. Chang Chien's commitment to the contractors increased his financial worries. The seemingly advantageous agreement with Sheng Hsüan-huai became worthless when the latter failed to live up to his word. Faced with bad business conditions and mounting financial crises in his other business interests, Sheng never assumed his end of the responsibility toward either the projected Shanghai mill or Dah Sun.[57] Attempts by Chang Chien to secure government loans through Director Kuei were equally unavailing, despite the latter's earlier intimations.[58]

On April 17, 1898, Chang Chien sent an appeal to Governor-general Liu K'un-i, setting forth the desperate financial situation and stating that a minimum of 50,000 taels was needed in a month's time to meet commitments.[59] There is no evidence of Liu's response to this appeal. In the same letter Chang Chien also informed Liu of his prospective trip to Peking on other matters and his hopes of raising money there.[60] Leaving Shen Hsieh-chün in charge of Dah Sun, he went to Peking in June. There he tried to raise additional money, but once more met with failure.[61] At this time some 180,000 taels had been raised from private sources, but most of the money had already been used to pay the contractors.[62] By November Chang Chien was at his wit's end. He now sought to resign from both his position as director of Nan-t'ung Commerce Bureau and his responsibility toward Dah Sun, but Governor-general Liu persuaded him to stay on.[63] The governor-general, at least, was thoroughly sympathetic toward Chang Chien's efforts. He had tried to help in 1897 by urging various local officials to lend official funds to the venture, but without success.[64] Now in 1898 he tried again.[65] This time his appeals apparently succeeded in persuading customs and salt officials to lend Dah Sun 38,500 taels,[66] but still more funds were needed.

Chang Chien now swallowed his pride and once again approached Sheng Hsüan-huai. On December 26, 1898, he wrote to both Sheng and Governor-general Chang Chih-tung, informing them of his vain efforts to raise funds from other sources after Sheng had broken his word. Relying upon Governor-general Chang's support, he further proposed to Sheng that, assuming that Sheng had legitimate reasons for failing to uphold his end of the agreement, he should at least be willing to lend Chang Chien 100,000 taels, to be repaid within one year at 8 percent interest per annum.[67] Sheng's reply five days later contained the counterproposal that Chang Chien take over the direction of the four cotton mills Sheng already controlled in Shanghai at the time, and merge the financial needs of Dah Sun with those of the other mills.[68] Chang Chien's answer to this was a flat refusal.[69] In a letter dated January 11, 1899, he unburdened his frustrations to Governor-general Liu:

> I am writing with much shame. Do I not know the difficulties which you have encountered? In the past three years I have lost count of the times when I had to endure discouragement and sarcasm. I have had to associate with people whom I would not have associated with ordinarily, and I have done things I would not have done otherwise. My tongue is numb and my writing brush tattered. I have done things in the daytime which I regret at night. You probably did not know this. How could I have told you everything anyway?[70]

By the end of 1898 the factory was 90 percent completed.[71] Most of the machinery had been installed under the supervision of the original engineer, Mr. Thomas, but the financial situation remained desperate. Temporary aid came in the form of official loans. Responding to Governor-general Liu's appeal, the magistrates of Hai-men and Nan-t'ung lent the equivalent of 30,000 taels to Dah Sun, while the Likin Bureau lent 10,000 taels.[72] By this time Chang Chien realized that, to the original estimated sum of 250,000 taels, which had never been fully raised, another 250,000 taels must be added to ensure the possession of sufficient operating capital.[73] For this additional sum, he decided to negotiate a foreign loan. He found two Americans in Shanghai who agreed to raise the sum for him, payable in ten years at the interest rate of 6 percent per annum. They apparently promised more than they could deliver, for no further news came from them after their departure from China.[74] Then for a while it seemed that a private investor from Fukien was about to put 200,000 taels into the venture, but this prospect also came to nought.[75] Having exhausted all these possibilities, Chang Chien decided to begin production at Dah Sun while taking care of the most pressing debts by reselling a part of the 80,000 taels worth of raw cotton already bought.[76] The machinery was tested on May 8, 1899, and the first spool of Dah Sun yarn was produced on May 23.[77]

The beginning of production did not relieve Chang Chien of his financial difficulties. Of the 220,000 taels raised, 210,000 taels had already been spent in paying for construction cost and in payment for the guaranteed 8 percent dividend of invested sums.[78] In June, 1889, Chang Chien made another futile trip to Shanghai to raise funds.[79] While there he started negotiations with a group of Shanghai merchants to rent out Dah Sun for three years at the annual rent of 40,000 taels (equivalent to 8 percent of the assessed value of 500,000 taels). The negotiation first broke down over disagreements about the net worth of the enterprise, and foundered completely when Governor-general Liu refused to sanction such an arrangement.[80] Liu now tried to come to the aid of Chang Chien once again by telegraphing the magistrates of Shanghai, Chinkiang, Wu-hu, and Kiukiang to lend Chang Chien official funds. The local magistrates' reaction can be gauged by that of Yüan Shuang-ch'iu, the magistrate of Wu-hu, who, notwithstanding his old friendship with Chang Chien, stated that Chang Chien was foolish to get involved in the venture in the first place.[81] One official, however, did lend Dah Sun 200,000 taels.[82]

As this was still insufficient, Chang Chien borrowed from English and Japanese banks in Shanghai during August and September to keep going.[83] Yarn prices now began to rise sharply on the Shanghai market.[84] Chang Chien consulted with Shen Hsieh-chün, his closest business associate and one of the small band of loyal friends who stood by him throughout his difficult days. The two men jointly decided to take the gamble of increasing production at the risk of exhausting the limited supply of raw cotton even sooner.[85] This decision turned out to be fortunate. Dah Sun was able to replenish its cotton supply and continue production. By October, 1899, Chang Chien sent the first optimistic letter to Governor-general Liu since he began the project.[86] Thereafter Dah Sun was firmly established as a going concern.

Throughout the period of nearly five years during which Chang Chien persisted in trying to raise funds for Dah Sun, he had the greatest difficulty in convincing private investors that the project was financially sound. After Dah Sun became a joint official-private enterprise, he found it even harder to raise funds from private sources, and the venture was bailed out of difficulties several times only by opportune loans from official sources. The reluctance of private businessmen to invest in Chinese-owned cotton mills was not entirely without good reason. They knew of the fact that investors in one of the early mills had not received a cent of dividend in return for their money, and that the backers of the Su Lun Mill had succeeded in getting some dividends only after reluctant company officials were forced to pay them. It was in order to overcome such adverse circumstances that Dah Sun agreed to pay 8 percent guaranteed dividend (*kuan-li*) on all investments starting with 1896, the very first year of the venture, long before actual production.[87] The rate of 8 percent was also the highest among cotton mills, for 6 percent was considered high by Chinese mills in Shanghai, where the foreign mills were only paying dividends of 3 percent.[88] In spite of this inducement, it was still difficult to raise private funds. The persons closest to the venture had to risk even more. While the investors in Dah Sun were guaranteed a high return as soon as they contributed funds, Chang Chien and the other promoters received not a cent of salary during the three years before Dah Sun began production.[89]

With the enterprise finally on its way, the Boxer disturbance of 1900 caused only a minor setback. Thereafter Dah Sun followed a general pattern of increasing production and profits.[90] The continued success of Dah Sun led Chang Chien to think of expanding its operations by the establishment of branch mills. Accordingly, he applied in 1904 for official permission to open a branch mill in Ch'ung-ming, a large island in the Yangtze estuary south of Hai-men. In his petition he proposed to set up a mill with machinery of 20,000-spindles capacity on a capital of 800,000 taels. He cited the former Governor-general Chang Chih-tung as having given him the right to establish cotton mills in the general area of Nan-t'ung and Hai-men, which could be interpreted to include the territory of Ch'ung-ming. He further added that, due to the abundance of cotton in Ch'ung-ming, opening of one cotton mill there would not necessarily preclude the possibility of others setting up separate cotton mills.[91]

This last statement betrayed the real reason for Chang Chien's desire to establish a branch mill in Ch'ung-ming. He had heard rumors that certain Shanghai merchants were planning to establish their own mill either in Ch'ung-ming or Hai-men. If this took place, it would cut into the source of raw cotton available for Dah Sun, and it would place a rival mill directly in Dah Sun's own back yard. It was to forestall this possibility that Chang Chien made plans to push through the opening of a branch mill.[92]

His petition was duly approved, and raising 600,000 taels by early 1906, he was able to start operations by April, 1907.[93] Whereas forty-four months were required to start operations at the main mill, the branch will took only twenty-seven months from its inception to the time all buildings were erected and machinery installed.[94] In a number of ways the branch mill benefitted from the experience gained with the main mill, as for instance, many of its workers went through a period of training at Nan-t'ung before the opening of the branch mill.[95] For the first few years, however, the latter operated at a loss.[96] Chang Chien in his report on the tenth anniversary of the branch mill attributed the difference between the main mill's success and the branch mill's early difficulties to the fact that the main mill had the advantage of superior location, with better transportation facilities, a ready local market, and an adequate supply of skilled labor.[97] The branch mill's construction cost alone amounted to more than 700,000 taels,[98] which, together with 215,000 taels paid out as guaranteed dividend from 1904 to 1908, kept the branch mill in the red during that entire four-year period.[99]

The machinery for the branch mill came from two sources.

Machinery with the capacity of 12,000 spindles was obtained from the province of Shansi. It was originally ordered from England by the Shansi provincial government for a cotton mill, but the project was abandoned during the Boxer uprising. An additional 14,000 spindles were bought directly from the Howard & Bullough Company in England,[100] adding up to 26,000 spindles in all.

The establishment of the branch mill was followed shortly by the reorganization of the entire Dah Sun enterprise. Certain shareholders had launched rumors detrimental to Dah Sun in general and to Chang Chien in particular. As a result, Chang Chien called a shareholders meeting on August 31, 1907. [101] Some fifty shareholders and ten honored guests attended the meeting. At this meeting Cheng Hsiao-hsü, one of Chang Chien's earliest associates, proposed that Dah Sun be reorganized into a limited liability company, in accordance with the newly promulgated commercial laws of the country. Cheng's suggestion was accepted by the shareholders.[102] All essential personnel, however, remained unchanged.

Under the reorganization the branch mill was designated as Dah Sun Mill No. 2. In subsequent years Chang Chien had ambitious plans for further expansion. Eventually four Dah Sun mills were established, two in Nan-t'ung and one each in Ch'ung-ming and Hai-men, although plans for the founding of mills in Ju-kao, Tung-t'ai, Yen-ch'eng, and elsewhere in Kiangsu were never realized.[103]

The Growth of Dah Sun

The growth of Dah Sun can be traced in a number of ways.[104] Taking the most common yardstick for cotton mills, the number of spindles, we find that the original number of 20,350 was increased by another 20,350 in 1904. This was the other half of the machinery which was supposed to be used by Sheng Hsüan-huai in the Shanghai mill which he never established. In 1915 the total number of spindles at the Nan-t'ung mill stood at 60,700. This was raised to 74,700 by 1918. Meanwhile the branch mill had started in Ch'ung-ming in 1907 with 26,000 spindles. By 1925 its total stood at 35,000 spindles. In 1921 a third mill was established in Hai-men with 34,340 spindles. Yet another mill, originally planned as Mill No. 8, but later designated Mill No. 1B, was started in 1924, with

16,724 spindles. Thus by 1925 the combined number of spindles of Dah Sun's four mills was 177,488. To this figure should be added 1,342 looms in the weaving sections of three of the mills (Mill No. 1B had no looms).

Another measure of Dah Sun's phenomenal growth was in its total capitalization. Starting with 500,000 taels in 1899, the figure rose to 580,000 taels in 1901, 1,130,000 taels in 1903, and 1,802,490 taels in 1905. This latter amount included the capital for the establishment of Mill No. 2 at Ch'ung-ming. Further increases pushed capitalization figures to 1,919,390 by 1907 and to 1,995,790 the following year. In 1915, and again in 1918, further increases totaling 1,000,000 taels were authorized to pay for added machinery.[105] In the report made in 1925, the figure for Mill No. 1 was 2,500,000 taels, and for Mill No. 2, 1,194,390 taels (no figures were given for Mills No. 3 or 1B). Information available in 1929 gave the same figure for Mill No. 1, but increased that of Mill No. 2 to 1,416,390 taels, and added that Mill No. 3 had a capital of 3,000,000 (again figures for Mill No. 1B were not available). Thus the total capital for the three largest of the four Dah Sun mills in 1929 stood just shy of the 7,000,000 taels mark.

More indicative of Dah Sun's year-to-year growth, however, are the figures for the net profit earned. These can best be seen in table form, as in Table 1, which tabulates number of spindles and capitalization as well.

Suffice it here to point out only a few salient points. Figures available to us from 1899 to 1913 show that, starting with the figure of 52,369 taels in 1900, the upward trend of earnings received no substantial reversal until 1907, when, from the previous year's gain of more than 400,000 taels, it fell to less than 56,000 taels. In 1910 a second drop from more than 247,000 taels to about 75,000 taels occurred. But three years later, the figure had exceeded the previous peak of 1905. After 1913, earnings apparently jumped to fantastic heights. Although annual records are available only up to 1913, authoritative sources indicate that Dah Sun annual dividends reached the figure of 90 percent during World War I.[107] In the report to the stockholders issued in 1925, the total profits of Mills No. 1 and No. 2 since they came into operation were given as nearly 13,500,000 taels.[108]

The growth of Dah Sun from 1899 to the 1920s stands out in sharp contrast with the Chinese-owned sector of the cotton

Table 1

GROWTH OF DAH SUN[106]

Year	*Number of Spindles*	*Capital (in taels)*	*Net Profit (in taels)*
1899	20,350	500,000	—
1900	20,350	500,000	52,369
1901	20,350	580,000	105,978
1902	20,350	580,000	187,002
1903	20,350	1,130,000	255,134 (d)
1904	40,700	1,130,000	225,124 (d)
1905	40,700	1,802,490 (a)	483,070
1906	40,700	1,802,490	400,204
1907	66,700 (a)	1,919,390	55,904
1908	66,700	1,995,790	158,852
1909	66,700	1,995,790	247,447 (a)
1910	66,700	1,995,790	75,324
1911	66,700	1,995,790	172,216
1912	66,700	1,995,790	442,035
1913	66,700	1,995,790	530,231
1914	66,700	1,995,790	—
1915	86,700	2,495,790	—
1916	86,700	2,495,790	—
1917	86,700	2,495,790	—
1918	100,700	2,995,790	—
1919	100,700	2,995,790	—
1920	100,700	2,995,790	—
1921	135,040 (b)	3,295,790	—
1922	135,040	3,295,790	—
1923	135,040	3,295,790	—
1924	168,488 (c)	—	—
1925	177,488	—	—

(a) Totals of Dah Sun Nos. 1 and 2 hereafter.
(b) Totals of Dah Sun Nos. 1, 2, and 3 hereafter.
(c) Totals of Dah Sun Nos. 1, 2, 3, and 1b hereafter.
(d) Figures in Yen, *Chung-kuo Mien-yeh Chih Fa-chan*, 119, corrected by figures in primary sources in *TCLS* (1), 147.

industry as a whole. Out of a total of sixteen Chinese-owned cotton mills established between 1896 and 1913, all except Dah Sun either failed or changed ownership by the time of World War I.[109] The unique success of Dah Sun must be attributed to a number of factors. First, Dah Sun had the advantage of being located in the best cotton-growing district in China. It could count on an adequate supply of the superior Nan-t'ung cotton, which sold at a price 10 to 15 percent cheaper locally than in Shanghai, due in part to the saving in transportation cost.[110] Dah Sun effected further economy by buying directly from the field and ginning the cotton itself.[111] Second, there was a ready local market. The bulk of Dah Sun yarn was sold in the Nan-t'ung and Hai-men area.[112] This area had long had a flourishing handicraft weaving industry. The introduction of machine-spun yarn fitted in well with the needs of the local hand weavers. Third, because of the difference of living standards in Nan-t'ung as compared to Shanghai, for instance, Dah Sun wages were generally 10 to 20 percent lower than comparable wages in Shanghai. For example, Dah Sun paid its workers in the carding room a maximum daily wage of twenty fen (equivalent to approximately U.S. $0.08 in 1916),[113] while Soy-Chee and International Cotton, both foreignowned mills in Shanghai, paid their cardhands maximums of twenty-seven fen (about U.S. $0.11) and twenty-five fen (about U.S. $0.10) respectively.[114] Fourth, compared to the general run of Chinese-owned cotton mills of the time, Dah Sun was efficiently managed and economically operated.[115] Almost unique among its competitors, Dah Sun sought improvement in technology and administration.[116] The credit for this state of affairs does not belong to Chang Chien alone, but must be shared with several of his associates, notably Shen Hsieh-chün and Chang Ch'a, Chang Chien's older brother. Liu Hou-sheng, one of Dah Sun's officers, has stated that Chang Ch'a was a better businessman than his better-known younger brother.[117] Chang Ch'a was a successful local magistrate in Kiangsi in 1902 when he received an urgent call for help from his younger brother back home. After some hesitation, he returned to Nan-t'ung and began a lifelong association with Dah Sun, lasting some thirty years. Of his four brothers, Chang Chien was close only with Ch'a. The two had unbounded trust in each other. Chang Ch'a's business acumen admirably complemented his brother's tireless energy and organizing ability.[118]

Dah Sun's successes, culminating in the war years and immediately following postwar years of 1918–21, was unfortunately followed by a steady decline thereafter. This trend was true of Chinese industry in general, and Dah Sun was caught in the over-all business decline. This fact, however, does not totally exonerate Chang Chien from being at least partially responsible for Dah Sun's misfortunes.

At the time during World War I when Dah Sun's profit reached fantastic heights, Chang Chien was warned by one of his associates of the danger of declaring such high dividends in preference to plowing some of the profit back into the company, but he did not heed this warning.[119] Continued high profit inevitably attracted speculators from Shanghai and elsewhere to putting money into the company, thus accentuating even more unrealistically its apparent prosperity.[120] Meanwhile, Chang Chien used a part of Dah Sun's excess profits to support his numerous other Nan-t'ung projects,[121] without keeping the accounts absolutely clear.[122] The day of reckoning came soon after the end of the war-induced period of prosperity. The years following 1923 saw both Dah Sun No. 1 and No. 2 operating in the red, while No. 3 was barely in the black.[123] Now the stockholders of Dah Sun, long the beneficiaries of the company's success, turned on Chang Chien for its sudden failure. He was accused of permitting Dah Sun to lend 2,500,000 taels to various land reclamation companies, most of which were also failing in the general business decline.[124] Chang Chien was further accused of siphoning off 900,000 yuan (about 630,000 taels) from Dah Sun for the various Nan-t'ung projects.[125] That these charges were probably true can be seen in the fact that Chang Chien in self-defense merely argued that Dah Sun had a moral obligation to help out the Nan-t'ung projects, and he assured his critics that he would personally assume any debts incurred by Dah Sun to the projects.[126]

From 1923 on Dah Sun went further and further into debt. In 1924 Dah Sun No. 1 was already operating under a loan extended by a consortium of banks in Shanghai.[127] After Chang Chien's death in 1926 Dah Sun declined even faster. By 1935 Mill No. 2, owing the Bank of China and the Bank of Communications a total of 1,100,000 yuan, became the joint property of these two banks. Later it was sold to a Chinese company for less than 500,000 yuan.[128] A year later the Shanghai consortium lent another 4,000,000 yuan to Dah Sun No. 1 and 1,000,000 yuan to No. 1B.[129] The records are not complete beyond 1936, but it appears that the major units of Dah Sun had all become heavily indebted by the time of the Sino-Japanese conflict.

Other Nan-t'ung Industries

Dah Sun was fundamental to the industrial complex of Nan-t'ung because, with minor exceptions, all other enterprises founded by Chang Chien were either directly or indirectly connected with Dah Sun. Aside from the T'ung Hai Land Reclamation Company and the T'ung Jen T'ai Salt Company,[130] the other important Nan-t'ung enterprises were Kwan Sun Oil Mill, Dah Sing Flour Mill, Han Mu Lin Publishing House, Che Sun Waterways Company, Dah Ta Pier Company, Dah Ta Inland Navigation Company, Dah Sun Steamship Line, Fu Sun Sericulture Company, and Tze Sun Iron Works. Of these, only Han Mo Lin Publishing House, being primarily connected with the Nan-t'ung Normal School, was not a subsidiary of Dah Sun.

The first enterprise which grew directly out of Dah Sun was Kwan Sun Oil Mill. Strictly speaking, the mill was the result in the first instance of the desire of several cotton mills in Shanghai to set up a cottonseed-oil mill in the region of Nan-t'ung and Hai-men. All except Hua Sheng Cotton Mill soon dropped the scheme. Dah Sun and Hua Sheng joined forces in founding Kwan Sun. Most of the Kwan Sun machinery was originally ordered by Hua Sheng for the use of the Shansi provincial government. After the latter failed to carry through its end of the deal, it was sold to the German-owned Soy-Chee Cotton Mill. For the price of 10,000 taels, shared equally by Dah Sun and Hua Sheng, the machinery was bought back from Soy-Chee. It lacked, however, the boiler and the engine needed to power the machinery. Consequently it was arranged to locate Kwan Sun immediately adjacent to Dah Sun in T'ang-chia-cha so that the machinery could be operated by means of Dah Sun's power plant. Of the original capital of 50,000 taels, 10,000 came from the two cotton mills while the additional 40,000 were raised by Sha Yüan-pin, who became the manager of the enterprise.[131]

Kwan Sun began operation in 1903. Soon it was profitably converting cottonseed, formerly a waste product of Dah Sun, into useful by-products. By 1909 its capital had been raised to 213,000 taels and it had acquired its own power plant. That year the stockholders agreed to raise an additional 107,000 taels as a first step toward the eventual goal of 400,000 taels as the total capital.[132] Of this 107,000 taels, the original stockholders subscribed to 60,000 taels, with the remaining 47,000 taels to be raised on the open market in Shanghai.[133]

By 1915 further constructions had been added to the original two-storied brick structure to give it a capacity of 142 rooms. At that time it was earning a net profit of around 30,000 yuan (about 21,000 taels) in an average year.[134] By 1921 it was employing a total of over 400 workers under the general supervision of Sha Yüan-pin, who had been with the company ever since its inception. Cottonseed oil, which had many household and industrial uses, was the company's main product. It also produced cottonseed cake, cottonseed husks, and waste cotton as by-products. The cottonseed cake was a valuable fertilizer and found a market throughout the greater part of Kiangsu. Cottonseed husks and waste cotton were sold locally, the former for fuel and the latter for garment padding. Kwan Sun maintained sales outlets throughout Kiangsu and even in Japan, Europe, and the United States. The products of Kwan Sun consistently won prizes at various international and national expositions. There was no question as to the success of this first subsidiary enterprise of Dah Sun.[135]

Another enterprise which grew out of the fact that Dah Sun originally had more power than it could profitably use was the Dah Sing Flour Mill, later renamed Fuh Sing.[136] The enterprise was originally the brainchild of several officials of Kiangsu and Kiangsi, who initiated the venture as an adjunct of Dah Sun in February, 1901. It soon turned out that the available machinery had too limited a capacity for profitable production. As a result the enterprise was established as a separate entity from Dah Sun in 1902. Largely through the efforts of Hsü Shih-lin, one of the original Kiangsi officials, 40,000 taels were raised as capital and the necessary machinery purchased from the United States.[137]

The first two years of Dah Sing's existence it maintained a working agreement with Dah Sun. Not long after it severed all connection with the latter, it was forced to close up because of mismanagement. Its backers, in order to save the business from a total loss, entrusted it to Chang Chien and Chang Ch'a. Between them the Chang brothers managed to raise 100,000 taels, and the flour mill was reopened in June, 1909, under the new name of Fuh Sing.[138] In 1914, 50,000 taels were added to the capital. Finally in the spring of 1921 an additional 100,000 yuan (about 71,000 taels) were raised, bringing the total capital to 221,000 taels.[139]

Fuh Sing, like Dah Sun and Kwan Sun, was also located at T'ang-chia-cha. It occupied a three-storied structure as its main factory, with later additions of offices and dormitory space.[140] In 1921 it employed sixty men. The wheat used came mostly from Nan-t'ung and the surrounding districts in Kiangsu. The flour produced was sold in most of the important coastal ports, as far as Tientsin in the north and Foochow in the south, with one grade of flour exported even to Japan.[141] That Fuh Sing turned out to be a highly successful business can be seen from the net profit figure of 87,000 yuan (about 62,000 taels) in 1911. A decade later net profit jumped to a high of 250,000 yuan (about 179,000 taels) per year.[142] The business of Fuh Sing continued to expand into the 1930s. By 1933 it was processing 500,000 piculs (33,333 tons) of wheat yearly, a two-and-a-half time increase over the figure of 1920.[143]

Close as the connection between Kwan Sun, Fuh Sing, and Dah Sun was, the two steamshiplines, the pier, and the waterway companies were even more intimately linked with Dah Sun. The first of the steamship lines, also called Dah Sun, came about directly as a result of the effort to facilitate the shipment of raw materials and finished products between Nan-t'ung and Shanghai. For several months after Dah Sun Cotton Mill became a going concern in late 1899, the mill used the steamshipline operated by a Shanghai merchant named Chu Pao-san. As the business of Dah Sun increased, the arrangement became less suitable. Early in 1900 Chang Chien undertook to reorganize the steamshipline, renaming the line after the cotton mill and arranging with Chu to raise the capital to 32,000 yuan (about 23,000 taels), with the cotton mill responsible for 12,000 yuan.[144] Soon after the reorganization, the steamshipline began to carry passengers, which added to its income. By the end of 1901 Chang Chien found the partnership with Chu and other Shanghai backers still unsatisfactory. He began negotiations, which ended in August, 1902, with his buying out the Shanghai group for 14,000 yuan (10,000 taels), 70 percent of their share of the capital.[145] From 1902 until 1909, Dah Sun Steamship Line consistently showed a profit, to the extent that it could add a new ship to its fleet in 1906 at a cost of 26,000 taels without having to issue new stocks.[146]

The success of Dah Sun Steamship Line no doubt prompted Chang Chien to lay plans for a second line, plying between Nan-t'ung and some of the nearby localities. In 1903 the Chang brothers, together with Sha Yüan-pin, obtained official permission for the new line, under the name of Dah Ta Inland Navigation Company. With an original capital of 20,000 yuan (about 14,000 taels), the company, consisting of a single small steamer, began regular runs through the interior waterways between Chin-sha and Lü-ssu, located at the two extremeties of Nan-t'ung district. Just as Dah Sun Steamship Line came into being to facilitate the transportation of Dah Sun Cotton Mill's products to Shanghai, the bulk of Dah Ta's business was the transportation of raw cotton from the outlying parts of Nan-t'ung to the mill. Increasing demands of the cotton mill caused the expansion of Dah Ta.[147] In 1906 its capital was increased by 10,000 yuan (about 7,000 taels) and two more small steamers were added, to ply between Nan-t'ung and the neighboring districts of Tung-t'ai, Yen-ch'eng, and Hsing-hua.[148]

Because Dah Ta ships traveled the interior waterways which crisscrossed the Yangtze north-bank districts, a good deal of opposition was aroused by the appearance of these steamers, some from official sources. Opposition began even before the establishment of the company. A certain official Li of Nanking wrote to Governor-general Wei Kuang-tao his opposition to the granting of permission for the company on the following grounds: (1) the greater speed of the steamer would cause frequent collisions in the narrow waterways; (2) the steamers would eventually cause crews of native boats to lose their jobs, thereby either inciting them to attack the steamers or turning them into bandits; (3) some bridges spanning the waterways were too low; (4) sparks from steamers' funnels would endanger native boats loaded with fuel; and (5) constant battering by the wake of passing steamers would weaken the banks of the waterways.[149] That the viewpoint of official Li did not prevail is already indicated above by the granting of the permission to establish the company. Opposition, however, was not confined to one official alone. In 1904 the Liang-Huai salt commissioner ruled against the passage of steamers on certain salt waterways. Chang Chien protested this decision to Governor-general Wei in no uncertain terms, pointing out the special danger that, if Chinese shipping lines were hampered in their developments, they would soon be hard pressed by foreign competition permitted under the terms of the Treaty of Shimonoseki.[150] Apparently his protest was effective, as Dah Tah continued to operate on interior waterways for many years thereafter.

The success of Dah Ta is shown by the fact that by 1919 total capital reached the 80,000 yuan (about 57,000 taels) mark. Four years later it was doubled.[151] The three ships of 1906 were increased to thirteen by 1914, and two more ships were added in each of the three years of 1917, 1920, and 1921. By then the ships were plying on eight routes, connecting Yang-chou, Ju-kao, T'ai-chou, and others with the localities already mentioned.[152]

The activities of the two steamship lines made it necessary to set up two more enterprises. In 1904 Chang Chien applied for and received permission to organize the Dah Ta Pier Company in Shanghai. With 139,000 taels as capital, Dah Ta carried out the building and maintenance of a pier with warehousing facilities for the use of Dah Sun Cotton Mill and other Chinese enterprises. In his application Chang Chien emphasized the fact that existing piers were all foreign-owned and that the establishment of Dah Ta would be a great boost to Chinese prestige.[153]

In 1906 a pier with warehouses was built at T'ien-sheng Harbor in Nan-t'ung district, serving the needs of T'ang-chia-cha. The development of T'ien-sheng Harbor as the chief transportation center for the products of the various Nan-t'ung industries came full circle that same year with the setting up of the Che Sun Waterways Company, which took over the task of harbor improvement as well as improvement of the interior waterway between T'ien-sheng Harbor and T'ang-chia-cha.[154] By then T'ien-sheng was already handling nearly two million taels of business yearly and netting the provincial government a handsome revenue of nearly 12,000 taels in likin, the internal transit tax.[155]

With all these enterprises booming, it was inevitable that some kind of enterprise would be set up, capable of making the less complex machines needed in the various industries, as well as providing facilities for repairing them. Such an enterprise was established in 1905 by the Chang brothers, who raised 200,000 yuan (about 143,000 taels), largely from the reserves of Dah Sun Cotton Mill.[156] Named the Tze Sun Iron Works, the enterprise grew out of the pooling of the repair facilities of Dah Sun Cotton Mill, Kwan Sun Oil Mill, and Dah Sing Flour Mill. Its first manager was Chang Ching-ju, son of Chang Ch'a, who served capably until his early death in 1917. Under his management Tze Sun grew by 1915 into an industrial concern employing a total of 200 men. Its principal product was manually operated cotton gins, but it also made numerous other products, ranging all the way from household pots and pans to sizable river steamers. Most of the newer ships of Dah Ta Steamship Line were locally built by Tze Sun.[157] Unlike most of the other Nan-t'ung industries, Tze Sun generally operated at a loss, its deficit being made up by Dah Sun.[158]

Most of the enterprises described thus far follow the pattern of growing out of Dah Sun, and later becoming either important businesses in their own right or continuing to serve as subsidiaries of Dah Sun. Among the enterprises located in T'ang-chia-cha, however, was one company which began largely as a separate entity but later entered into the closest ties with Dah Sun. This was the Fu Sun Sericulture Company, which later became Fu Sun Weaving Mill. The germinating idea which led to the founding of Fu Sun antedated even the establishment of Dah Sun, for it was Chang Chien's father, Chang P'eng-nien, who first became interested in promoting sericulture in Nan-t'ung in the early 1890s. Chang Chien, having been associated with his father in this project, conceived at the time of the establishment of Dah Sun a two-prong textile program for Nan-t'ung, the development of cotton *and* silk. Until 1904, however, he had no chance to carry out the second part of his design. That year he, together with his brother and Kao Ch'ing, one of the chief backers of Dah Sun, founded the Fu Sun Sericulture Company. At first the activities of the company were limited to the raising of silkworms and the promotion of the planting of mulberry trees, efforts which could hardly be termed industrial. Sometime after the important meeting of stockholders of the Nan-t'ung industries in 1907, which linked all industries into one organization, Fu Sun was reorganized into a weaving mill, based on a capital of 100,000 taels.[159] Thereafter growth was steady. By 1926 Fu Sun occupied a large complex of buildings in T'ang-chia-cha and employed close to 400 men and women. It was organized into three departments, silk, cotton, and dyed fabrics, producing cotton cloth, silk fabrics, and dyed fabrics respectively.[160]

Of the enterprises in Nan-t'ung which were only indirectly connected with Dah Sun, the Yih Sun Distillery, founded in 1905, was originally located on the land of the T'ung Hai Land Reclamation Company and designed to use the wheat and kaoliang grown as subsidiary crops on reclaimed lands. After the typhoon of 1905 had badly affected crop production on the reclaimed land, the distillery was moved to Chang Chien's native village of Ch'ang-lo.

There it became a profitable enterprise, and its distilled spirits were good enough to win prizes at the International Exposition of Milan in 1906. By the 1930s it attained a productive capacity of 1,500 catties (2,000 pounds) yearly.[161]

Two other smaller enterprises were the Dah Lung Soap Factory and the Mao Sun Construction Company. The former came into being to utilize the waste products of Kwan Sun Oil Mill in the production of soap and fertilizers. The latter was organized when other private merchants, attracted by the facilities offered by T'ang-chia-cha, came to locate their own enterprises there. This created a need for the construction of new factory and office buildings. Mao Sun was founded specifically to answer that need.[162]

All of the enterprises mentioned above were amalgamated into one corporate entity in 1907. As a result of the reorganization of Dah Sun into a limited liability company that year, its previous arrangement of subsidizing all other Nan-t'ung enterprises, an arrangement which had reached a figure in excess of 400,000 taels by this time, was found to be incompatible with Dah Sun's new corporate structure.[163] Again at the suggestion of Cheng Hsiao-hsü, the Nan-t'ung Industrial Company was created.[164] Its capital of 600,000 taels came from Dah Sun's extra reserves (*kung-chieh yü-li*).[165]

Chang Chien as an Industrialist

Although Chang Chien did not come from a business background, and did not confine his activities solely to the industrial world, his involvement in establishing Dah Sun and his later industrial efforts inevitably call for us to examine him in the role of an industrialist. Just what did he do in regard to the operation of his numerous industrial enterprises? Did he personally run them on a day-to-day basis? Was he aware of the manifold repercussions of industrialization upon an agrarian country like China? How did he fit his industrial activities into the scheme of his total career? In short, what was his exact role in the industrial development of his district and his country, and how much was he conscious of the larger implications of his industrial efforts?

There are several ways in which we can examine Chang Chien the industrialist. The most obvious would be to assess him as the active manager of the various enterprises, the man who made the executive decisions. Unfortunately we are handicapped by the scarcity of pertinent sources. No such records as business memoranda, orders of purchase and sale, directives to department heads, or even private letters among the various Dah Sun executives have been left for us. Consequently we can get only a general idea of Chang Chien's duties and activities within Dah Sun. What little we know, however, does shed some light on Chang Chien as a business executive.

The single most important piece of evidence we have on Chang Chien's relations vis-a-vis the other executives at Dah Sun is a document called the "Factory Agreement," written either by Chang Chien or at his direction in December, 1897. It was modeled upon agreements of other cotton mills then operating in Shanghai.[166]

As contained in *T'ung-chou Hsing-pan Shih-yeh Chih Li-shih* (*History of the Establishment of Industries in Nan-t'ung*), the "Factory Agreement" is a document of some forty pages.[167] There is a brief preamble in which Chang Chien explains why he went into the cotton-spinning business and goes on to justify the need for such a document as the agreement. The main body of the agreement, composed of fifteen articles, begins with the definition of duties and responsibilities of Chang Chien himself, then those of the heads of each of the four departments: business, supervisory, general affairs, and accounting. The agreement goes on to state conditions of employment, salaries, bonuses, hours, and other minor matters, even including the type of meals which the junior executives were permitted to have while working at the plant.[168] These stipulations are applicable to only the office staff, and specific though they may seem, they are far surpassed in detail by the following section giving instructions and regulations applicable to the different stages of production. In what amounts to an appendix of some thirty-four pages, this section contains stipulations ranging from the one requiring all apprentices of the buying and selling departments to study English for two hours each day to those setting forth the daily production quotas of workers in the different stages of the cotton-spinning process. There are also detailed stipulations as to the exact duties of plant guards and as to what to do in case of fire.[169] In other words, all regular working conditions and emergency measures which could be foreseen were covered in the "Factory Agreement."

What are the implications of this detailed set of regulations?

There seem to be three. In the first place, the need for such a detailed set of regulations probably arose in part because the operation of Dah Sun was unfamiliar to the cotton workers of Nan-t'ung, who made up the labor force of the enterprise, and who knew cotton spinning only as a handicraft industry. Secondly, the fact that Chang Chien issued such a document demonstrated clearly that he was directly responsible in the first instance for every policy decision of the company down to the most minute matters. Finally, we must assume that not all of these regulations, formulated at a time before even a single spool of Dah Sun yarn was produced, stood the test of actual operations. Modifications must have been made as Dah Sun operations became more regular. Nevertheless, the fact that no written revisions of this agreement were ever made and that it appeared in print in the same detailed fashion ten years after Dah Sun commenced operations seems to imply that, broadly speaking, this agreement remained the "bible" for Dah Sun operations.

The impression that Chang Chien took it upon himself to exercise broad powers is further buttressed by the specific duties which he assigned to himself in the "Factory Agreement":

> It is my responsibility to act between the official and private promoters of the enterprise, to regulate profit, to overcome obstacles, to set regulations, to appoint and remove officers of the enterprise, to investigate into achievements and inefficiencies, to determine credits and faults, and to pass out awards and fines.[170]

Thus the conclusion that Chang Chien was the policy maker and at the same time overseer of actual operations is inescapable, but this must be qualified somewhat by the other scattered information at our disposal. From Chang Chien's report to the stockholders given in 1907, we learn that at the very start in 1896 six departments were contemplated for Dah Sun operations, each to be headed by one of the six original promoters in the enterprise. Then after the two Shanghai promoters P'an and Kuo withdrew, the departments were consolidated into four, with Shen Hsieh-chün heading business, and the other three promoters, now designated as directors (*tung-shih*), heading the remaining three departments.[171] During this early stage Shen Hsieh-chün shared many of the responsibilities of Chang Chien, and, as we have seen, the key decision in 1899 to increase production, which saved Dah Sun, was a joint decision on the part of the two men.[172] Soon afterward they were joined by Chiang Hsi-shen in actively directing the business. In 1902 Chang Chien's elder brother Chang Ch'a heeded the former's call for help by giving up his official post and returning to Nan-t'ung. Chang Ch'a's presence permitted Chang Chien to devote most of his time to the normal school and to his land reclamation projects. Two years later, after Chiang died and Shen retired, Chang Ch'a assumed sole responsibility for the over-all direction of Dah Sun.[173] From that time forward Chang Chien in effect occupied what amounted to the position of a board chairman in a Western-type corporation while Chang Ch'a was the chief executive of the enterprise.

There is another way in which we can examine Chang Chien the industrialist. That is to trace his economic views, particularly as they pertain to industrialization and the impact of machine manufacturing upon China. A number of Chinese scholars, in examining the economic thoughts of late-Ch'ing thinkers, have included Chang Chien.[174] The picture of Chang Chien the industrialist thus presented to us is a man of definite views, ranging from the advocacy of private enterprise, of the corporate structure of business enterprises, to championing a larger scheme of "cotton and iron policy" (*mien-t'ieh chu-i*). There is no question that Chang Chien was deeply convinced by the necessity for China to industrialize. Immediately upon the defeat of China at the hands of Japan in 1895, Chang Chien, presumably at the request of Governor-general Chang Chih-tung, drew up a long memorial which Governor-general Chang submitted to the Court in his own name. Among the many specific suggestions in the memorial, the following concerns the promotion of industry:

> People all say that foreign nations maintain themselves through commerce. This is a superficial view. They do not know that the basis of the foreign nations' riches and strength is industry. First they master chemistry and the other natural sciences, and become adapt at machine manufacturing, to the extent that the unprocessed become refined, the few become many, and the worthless, valuable. And then the merchants have the opportunity to make substantial gains through trade. In the *K'ao-kung Chi* of Chou times the crafts are considered as one of the six main vocations. Emperor Shun, in appointing nine officials to oversee universal affairs, had one in charge of industry. The *Analects* is one of the nine classics. It too mentioned the crafts as the source of wealth.

From this it can be seen that the three generations of ancient sages all agreed on this point. Later generations emphasized the scholar and the official and neglected the crafts and industry.

The goods sent from abroad into China are all machine-made of fine quality, with a value upwards of ten times the original material. Even such inexpensive items as coarse fabric, kerosene, dyes, firing clay, after they have been processed, become valuable. Take Japan for example. She has emphasized industry, organizing industrial promotion organizations along with commercial exhibitions, and singling out the superior products among the everyday objects produced by the people. This can be said to be following the examples of the West. Since the Japanese government rewards the maker of superior products to encourage excellence, the various crafts compete eagerly, thereby improving Japanese goods constantly and finding greater markets for them. Today Japan's natural resources are limited to things like seaweed and coal. Where she is able to gain great profit from China and the West is in her application of manpower and not in her natural resources.

China is densely populated. If she were to rely upon agriculture alone, she cannot survive. There will be no end of difficulties in the days to come. Therefore we must concentrate with single purpose [to promote industry]. Otherwise the country cannot provide for the millions of her uprooted people and recover the tens of millions [of taels] which she loses every year [to foreign nations]. Every province should be required to establish industrial bureaus to concentrate on the problem. They should search the customs office records for native products with the greatest market potential, then improve the quality and increase the production of such items in order to promote their sales [abroad]. Factories should be set up to produce items of foreign goods which have the greatest sale in China, in order to compete with the foreign items and check their sale. Such efforts should be in the fields of coal mining, iron production, the machine processing of silk, the planting of cotton, tea, and sugar cane, the processing of sugar and flour, ceremics, woolens, and foreign-style needles, nails, wine, and matches. These efforts would achieve the result of both promoting the sale of native products and resisting the import of foreign goods. It would be the responsibility of governor-generals and governors of every province to establish commercial bureaus, and proceed according to conditions of production and sales in each locality. Every province must accomplish some results, and the provincial officials from governor-generals down should be held accountable for their success and failures.

Moreover, officials heading groups of craftsmen should be dispatched abroad to learn from various industries. They should learn all they can in [improved] agriculture, manufacturing, textiles, [iron] refining, shipbuilding, armaments, roadbuilding, mining, and chemicals. After returning to China they should be put into industrial efforts, the officials responsible for theoretical planning and the craftsmen into actual execution.

China is the most populous country in the world. If we can only industrialize, what worries would we have? This is the way to care for the people and strengthen the nation. It is not designed merely to eliminate insults [from foreign nations], but it would achieve that result also.[175]

Ten years later, on the occasion of the founding of Tze Sun Iron Works, Chang Chien had this to say:

As stated in the *Shih Chi*, we Chinese depend on agriculture for our food . . . handicraft for our production, and commerce for our intercourse. Handicraft is indeed the central connection between agriculture and commerce. . . . In the West the people found handicraft too expensive; consequently they turned to machine manufacturing. At the least, what one machine produces is equivalent to that of several tens of workers, sometimes to that of several tens of animals, at the most, several hundreds or even a thousand heads of animals. The machine's efforts are even, consequently its quality is also superior. It can be in constant operation, so that its quantity is also large. It is by nature exact and economical. As a result its products can reach us and reap great profits. Today China is promoting industry without using machinery. This is comparable to trying to win a thousand *li* race while riding on a tortoise. And if we use machinery without seeking to make them ourselves, this is tantamount to be in perpetual dependence on others, taking the third position while delegating the top position to Western factories and the second position to the commercial middlemen. The products of our industries are only circulated in our own markets, thereby expropriating the profit of manual laborers. . . . This is not a desirable state of affairs.[176]

Thus, in spite of the fact that Chang Chien was not above citing precedents in Chinese history to justify his position, there is no denying that he saw clearly the basic advantages of machine manufacturing over handicraft industry, and the need for industrialization in China's attempt to save herself. We must still ask, however, whether he understood the theories and forms of modern industrial and business enterprises.

In his attempt to promote industrial development Chang Chien's career and pronouncements both betray his preference for private enterprise, but he did not clearly champion private enterprise as such. Rather he advocated gentry participation in business. Relying upon his own experience, he argued that the funds needed by the gentry for such activities as social welfare projects should legitimately come from business enterprises.[177] This was appealing to the gentry along practical grounds, but Chang Chien went further. Confronting the deep-seated tradition among the gentry that business careers were beneath their dignity, Chang Chien asserted that, on the contrary, the gaining of wealth through successful business ventures was "right and honorable."[178]

While Chang Chien steadfastly maintained the distinction between gentry and merchants, his championing of gentry involvement in business was in effect an argument against direct government involvement in business. He, however, did not see the issue clearly between government participation on the one hand and private initiative on the other. Quite typically, he chose the middle ground of advocating gentry participation in business, thus bringing in a class which was at once outside the government and yet closely related with the ruling circles. His ideas on private enterprise involving the gentry obviously grew out of his own gentry status and his experience in founding Dah Sun. Neither Dah Sun's original "private" nor its later "joint" status was a result of decisions made on doctrinal grounds. They evolved through practical necessity. Chang Chien always took the pragmatic view. In 1905, for instance, he urged the government to establish a precedent by extending official protection to Nan-t'ung industries, on the ground that government protection was essential to the country's industrial development.[179] Thus his advocacy of private enterprise was something considerably less than total commitment to the ideal in theory.

Similarly, he showed an affinity for the corporate structure in business organization, but not on doctrinal grounds. In two pieces of his writings, the *Reasoned Discussion on Reforms* and the "prospectus" for the T'ung Hai Land Reclamation Company,[180] he stressed the need for the formation of companies (*kung-ssu*).[181] These sources have led scholars to assert that he was an advocate of the corporate form.[182] Both of these sources, however, were written in 1901, the year when he began his land reclamation efforts. The context of these sources further shows conclusively that he was addressing himself specifically to the problem of forming a land reclamation company. Nowhere in any of this writings did he demonstrate an understanding of the concept of limited liability. As we have seen, Dah Sun was not organized initially as a limited liability company, and Chang Chien did not change Dah Sun's corporate structure until 1907, and then only at the suggestion of his long-time associate Cheng Hsiao-hsü, whose motives may have been to still the rising chorus of criticism against Chang Chien. Dah Sun's difficulties in the 1920s can be directly related to Chang Chien's own cavalier way with corporate funds. The conclusion that he never did fully grasp the basic difference between a partnership and a limited liability company seems inescapable.

What Chang Chien's various pronouncements on industrial activities does show is a strong feeling of paternalism on his part toward the workers of his enterprises. He regarded them as under his personal care. The detailed regulations of Dah Sun already alluded to above give ample evidence of this attitude. The working conditions of Dah Sun in the 1920s also reflect Chang Chien's concern for the welfare of his workers. Like most other Chinese cotton mills of the time, workers operated on twelve-hour shifts, but they had rest breaks at 6 A.M. and 6 P.M., and days off on the first, eighth, fifteenth, and the twenty-third of every lunar month.[183] Each worker had two weeks annual vacation, and up to two weeks off during the hottest part of the summer months.[184] These regulations were among the most humane in the entire Chinese cotton-textile industry at the time.

Finally, much has been made of Chang Chien's so-called cotton and iron policy, which he enunciated in 1913 while serving as the Minister of Agriculture and Commerce.[185] Actually this was merely a logical outgrowth of his concern for the raising of cotton to include the mining of essential metalic ores. For the latter he was willing to have the mining enterprises nationalized.[186] His policy was really nothing more than a practical program to ensure the uninterrupted supply of two types of basic resources: cotton for the consumer-goods textile industry and iron and other metals for basic heavy industry.

Taking Chang Chien's economic views as a whole, two things become readily apparent. First, he did not isolate his ideas on industrial efforts from his concern with the total economic development and growth of the country. He conceived of industry, commerce, agriculture, and conservation as interrelated facets of the whole economic picture. And to him China's economic development was in turn inextricably bound up with her educational and social advancement. Second, his economic ideas were nearly all reactions to specific needs and exigencies of the times. They were not meant to form a consistent and comprehensive program, systematically worked out. Typically Chang Chien arrived at his economic ideas from the specific to the general, applying working solutions to problems rather than advocating a doctrinal program of national economic development and then attempting to apply it to concrete cases.

Aside from examining Chang Chien's managerial duties and his economic ideas, we must view his role as an industrialist in yet another way. That is to conceive of him as a creative entrepreneur. The noted economist Joseph Schumpeter has conceptualized this kind of an entrepreneur as a type of daring and far-seeing individual who is primarily concerned with the establishment of new enterprises.[187] A further definiation conceives of this kind of an entrepreneur as "a decision-maker whose creative initiative draws all factors of productions together to initiate, maintain, and expand business enterprises."[188] Chang Chien seems to fit into this conception of an entrepreneur especially well. He served as the catalytic agent to bring together the various elements necessary for a productive enterprise: capital, raw material, technology, and management. He partook of the duties of day-to-day operations, but he also made decisions affecting the long-term growth and decline of enterprises, decisions which were outside routine management. Chang Chien's importance as an industrialist is precisely in his supplying the necessary vision, energy, and direction to existing factors of production to create enterprises where none had existed before.

We have already seen that as an entrepreneur Chang Chien had to overcome a number of formidable obstacles, the foremost of which was the lack of capital. Not being an official, he could not divert official funds to his various undertakings, as Chang Chih-tung and Li Hung-chang had done. In his appeal to the private investors, he was thwarted by their interest in investing their capital either in land or in ventures which promised a quick return. Traditionally land had always been regarded as the safest form of investment. Landowning also brought with it considerable social prestige. Those investors who dared to put their money into industrial enterprises had no institutional and social safeguards for their risk, in a kind of investment which, at best, can be expected to give a return only after a considerable length of time. Consequently Chang Chien was forced to turn to official subsidies of various kinds until he could convince private investors of Dah Sun's soundness.

As a creative entrepreneur Chang Chien successfully mobilized the advantages of his home district. Drawing upon his great personal prestige as a ranking scholar, with its attendant entree into the official world, he took Nan-t'ung's superior cotton, skilled crafts laborers, and ready market to establish Dah Sun as a going concern. What Nan-t'ung itself was not able to provide, its reasonable proximity to Shanghai made it possible for Chang Chien to draw upon the resources and services of that great commercial center. He also had the good fortune to have a group of devoted and able associates who helped him to carry through his ideas into reality.

In summary, Chang Chien's chief claim to distinction as an industrialist is in his establishing Dah Sun as one of the first predominantly private business ventures launched in China. Such enterprises as the China Merchant Steam Navigation Company (founded in 1885) and the K'ailan Mines were government-sponsored projects. As a matter of fact, early enterprises could hardly have gotten off the ground without official protection and support. Even Dah Sun required official aid in the form of the machinery turned over to the company as the government's share of investment. It is nevertheless true that Chang Chien had to blaze a new trail when he attempted to interest the limited number of people who had capital to invest to put it in Dah Sun. The difficulties he had during the time of the cotton mills' establishment give eloquent testimony to the prevailing business sentiments of the time. Ironically the other cotton mills which were being founded at about the same time hindered rather than aided Chang Chien's efforts by their cavalier treatment of their investors. Yet in spite of every obstacle and discouragement, in spite of false hopes and broken agreements, Chang Chien did not give up but pushed on to the successful founding of Dah Sun. This was his chief contribution as an industrialist. While Nan-t'ung was thus started on its way to be an important inland industrial center, he was able thereby to secure the financial backing which enabled him to go on to achievements in other fields of endeavor.

CHAPTER FOUR

Involvement in National Affairs

CHANG CHIEN's preoccupation with business matters did not exclude him altogether from involvement in national affairs. We have already seen how, relatively early in his life, his Korean experience had committed him deeply to speak out on national issues. In the years from 1898 to the early 1920s, he not only made known his views on a wide variety of important issues, but he became involved with several of the leading figures of the period: K'ang Yu-wei in 1898, Sun Yat-sen and Huang Hsing in 1911–12, and most importantly, Yüan Shih-k'ai in 1911–14. To be sure, he never occupied positions of real power. He accepted the position of cabinet minister twice, and then only for relatively brief durations. To the end of his life he, in the position of an uncommitted senior statesman, continued to dispense advice to one faction or another in the confused period of warlord rule in China. For all intents and purpose, however, we can consider his public career ended with the resignation of his last official post in 1915.

The Reform of 1898

In June, 1898, while still deeply involved with Dah Sun, he went north to Peking. Not since his triumph in the palace examination four years previously had he been back in the capital, and part of the reason for his going there at this time was to take the *san-kuan* examination required of Hanlin members.[1] In this examination, he failed to distinguish himself, passing with a very ordinary mark.[2] His presence in Peking, however, placed him in close touch with the events immediately preceding the "hundred days of reform."

One of the first things Chang Chien did upon reaching Peking was to call on his old benefactor, Weng T'ung-ho. Thereafter the two men met frequently, and held long, earnest conversations.[3] Chang Chien would call on Weng in the afternoon and stay until sundown, during which time there would be "nothing on which they did not talk," as Weng stated in his diary.[4] It seems fairly certain, therefore, that the name of K'ang Yu-wei figured prominently in the conversations.

By this time both Chang Chien and K'ang Yu-wei were considered to be among the more outstanding younger scholars of the day. The two men had first met in 1889, when both were in the capital for the metropolitan examination. Their relationship then had been quite cordial.[5] In 1888 K'ang had first made his advocacy of political reform known in a memorial, which failed to reach the Emperor because responsible officials disapproved of its radical tone. At this time K'ang had not yet become widely known. The event which catapulted him into prominence was the joint memorial of 1895, signed by some 1,300 candidates for the metropolitan examination in Peking. The memorial, a product of K'ang's efforts, called for the continuation of resistance against Japan in the Sino-Japanese War and the introduction of political reforms.[6] The government did not follow these suggestions, but through their presentation K'ang came to be recognized as the leading reformer of the time.

Six years previously, in 1889, the Empress Dowager Tz'u-hsi had relinquished the nominal power of the throne to the Kuang-hsü Emperor. The Empress Dowager continued to keep herself fully informed of all that went on, but the task of carrying on the day-to-day business of ruling the country fell on the shoulders of the Emperor. In 1895 this well-intentioned but inexperienced monarch was deeply perturbed by the outcome of the Sino-Japanese War. He was anxious to find some way to lead China out of the unfortunate position in which the country found herself. Most of the high officials at the Imperial Court, however, seemed totally devoid of effective ideas to cope with the situation.

A few officials at this time recognized K'ang to be a man of much promise. One of these officials was Weng T'ung-ho. As early as 1888, K'ang Yu-wei had sought to approach Weng, but without success.[7] It was not until the time of the submission of the joint petition, followed shortly after by the conclusion of the unfavorable peace treaty at Shimonoseki, that Weng came to regard K'ang with more favor. He forthwith sought out K'ang and absorbed much of the latter's ideas.[8] As a former imperial tutor, Weng had direct access to the Emperor. He became instrumental in drawing the Emperor's attention to some of K'ang's ideas.[9] For the time being, however, K'ang's talents were not put to use.

In March, 1898, Germany succeeded in gaining a ninety-nine year lease on Kiaochow Bay from China. In rapid succession Russia, France, and England extracted similar territorial concessions. China seemed on the verge of being partitioned by the powers. At this precise moment K'ang Yu-wei chose to send in another memorial, in which he tempted imperial anger by boldly stating that the end of the dynasty was inevitable unless reforms were undertaken immediately.[10] This time he found the Emperor sympathetic to his ideas. First a decree for responsible officials to meet with K'ang was issued. Then on June 16, the Emperor held a personal audience with K'ang. This signal honor granted to a relatively low-ranking official marked the beginning of several critical months, during which time the Emperor placed an extraordinary amount of confidence in K'ang.

This turn of events did not come as a total surprise to Chang Chien. He, of course, had been aware of K'ang's reputation as a reformer for several years previously. In 1895 Liang Ting-feng, a fellow provincial of K'ang's, had sent a telegram to Chang Chien inviting him to join the Ch'iang-hsüeh Hui, the Association for the Study of National Strengthening, organized by K'ang and headed by Chang Chih-tung. In spite of Chang Chien's favorable response to this bid, he did not become intimate with K'ang.[11] In fact Chang Chien developed a personal aversion to K'ang, disliking his vanity in particular. Soon after K'ang's sudden rise to a position of power, Chang Chien had occasion to call on K'ang. He found the reformer's residence thronged by a host of followers and servants, giving the place "an air comparable to that of an old and powerful official."[12] He ventured to advise K'ang against his proposed course of action. K'ang turned a deaf ear to this.

While K'ang's star was rising, his erstwhile patron Weng T'ung-ho found himself increasingly estranged from the Emperor.[13] On June 15, Weng was cashiered. Chang Chien urged Weng to leave the capital at once.[14] Weng left for his native town of Ch'ang-shu, Kiangsu, on July 1. Chang Chien left Tientsin for Nan-t'ung on July 25.[15] Thus both men left the scene at the height of the reform and were not involved with the failure of the movement brought about by the Empress Dowager's return to power.[16]

We have dwelt on these few months of Chang Chien's life in some detail because his reputation as a progressive and his presence in Peking coincident with the beginning of the reforms seem to suggest that he might have had some connection with the reforms.[17] That he was actually suspected of complicity at the time can be seen from what he wrote later:

> I was the last-named among the so-called "six followers of Weng T'ung-ho." Although I was not in the capital at the time of the reform, I was accused of being secretly in league with K'ang Yu-wei and Liang Ch'i-ch'ao. From the capital to Hupeh and Kiangsu, the rumors flew thick and fast.[18]

A more serious complication arises over the fact that Chang Chien's aversion toward K'ang Yu-wei seems to be strangely inconsistent with Weng T'ung-ho's alleged sponsorship of K'ang. In view of the intimate relationship between Chang Chien and Weng T'ung-ho, it would seem highly unlikely that the two could have held divergent views toward K'ang during the critical summer of 1898. To be sure, Weng later asserted that by 1898 he had had a change of heart concerning K'ang, and that he opposed rather than encouraged the Kuang-hsü Emperor's desire to use K'ang. Until recently scholars have generally dismissed this account as an unworthy attempt by Weng to avoid being implicated in the failure of the reform of 1898. In the last decade, however, new interpretations of the evidence have lent greater credence to Weng's own words.[19] It seems not altogether unreasonable to conclude that K'ang Yu-wei's failure in 1898 was to a considerable degree because of his failure to gain and retain the support of the "moderate" faction of reformers represented by Weng T'ung-ho and Chang Chien.[20]

The Boxer Uprising

The triumph of the reactionaries in 1898 led directly to the Boxer outbreak two years later. In view of fuller accounts elsewhere we need not go into the details of the uprising itself. It is worth noting, however, that the Imperial Court displayed a marked degree of vacillation throughout this entire affair. Decrees suppressing the Boxers were followed by counterdecrees protecting them. The attack on the legation quarters in Peking was never pushed home. Diplomatic channels were left open purposely to facilitate negotiations while Chinese troops were actively engaging the foreign troops in combat. To the outside world at the time the evidences seemed clear-cut that China was acting in bad faith. The truth of the matter was that the confusion of action was but a reflection of the clash within the Imperial Court among several factions holding divergent views.[21]

One faction which played a key role throughout the disturbance was composed of the southern officials, including Chang Chih-tung, Liu K'un-i, Yüan Shih-k'ai, Sheng Hsüan-huai, and Li Hung-chang.[22] This group opposed giving support to the Boxers. When the decree of June 20, declaring war on the foreign powers, reached the south, Governor-general Liu called on some of his trusted advisers for suggestions. Included in this group were T'ang Shou-ch'ien, Ho Ssu-k'un, Ch'en San-li, Shen Tseng-chih, and Chang Chien. These men, all scholars of repute and with considerable official experience among them, were unanimous in advocating the preservation of peace in the southern and central provinces at all cost.[23] Liu, after some hesitation, was won over to this point of view. He approached Chang Chih-tung and found the latter in substantial agreement on this subject. Meanwhile Sheng Hsüan-huai had been approached by Chao Feng-ch'ang, a close friend of Chang Chien and T'ang Shou-ch'ien. Sheng and Chao had reached the same decision independently.[24] The result was the two sets of agreements negotiated between the southern officials on the one hand and the foreign consuls in Shanghai on the other, in which the two groups agreed to maintain order in the Yangtze region and around Shanghai respectively without infringing upon each other's authority.[25] This effectively localized the disturbance to Chihli and Shansi, as provinces outside the direct jurisdiction of the southern officials, such as Szechwan, also steered clear of involvement in the disturbance.[26]

In subsequent actions the southern officials acted in general accord. They did not limit their efforts to preserving the peace in the central and southern provinces, but attempted to rescue the Imperial Court from what they regarded as a disastrous course of action. This took the form of sending memorials to the Court urging the abandonment of its pro-Boxer policy, continuation of the foreign debt payment, and advising the Chinese ministers abroad to maintain friendly relations with the powers at all costs.[27] In all these efforts the two governors-general Chang Chih-tung and Liu K'un-i played a leading part. Liu relied heavily on his group of advisors. Chang Chien was often called upon for advice. He was in Nan-t'ung when Li Hung-chang was still delaying in obeying the order for him to go north, and while the Imperial Court was deliberating the advisability of evacuating from Peking. He wrote Governor-general Liu to urge Li to hasten to the capital, adding that Liu should send a personal representative with Li. He also opposed the abandoning of Peking contemplated by the Court, on the ground that it would have a bad effect on national morale.[28] Li Hung-chang subsequently reached Tientsin in the latter part of September and went on to play a key role in reaching a settlement with the foreign powers. Before Li's arrival in Tientsin, the Imperial Court had fled from Peking on August 15, eventually reaching Sian in late October.[29] By this action the Court rejected the southern officials' suggestion to seek refuge in the Yangtze region.

A secondary factor which intensified the threat of disturbance in the Yangtze region was the existence of large roving bands of bandits. One of the largest was led by a certain Hsü Pao-shan. Chang Chien advised Governor-general Liu to grant Hsü a full pardon. He believed that removing Hsü's leadership from his band was the most effective method of neutralizing that particular danger. Liu also carried out this suggestion.[30]

Prior to the departure of the Imperial Court from Peking, Russia had moved troops into Manchuria in order to "pacify the rioters." After quickly overpowering some ineffectual resistance by the Chinese, Russian forces were in control of most of Manchuria by the beginning of September. This placed Russia in a strong bargaining position, by means of which she intended to extract heavy concessions from China. For this purpose, Russia, in the person of Count Witte, opened negotiations with the Chinese plenipotentiary Yang Ju in St. Petersburg in January, 1901. Basing his demands on a temporary agreement reached in November, 1900, by the opposing commanders, Witte presented a list of concessions in Manchuria to be agreed to by China. It called for the appointment of Russian advisers to key positions, Russian concurrence on all official appointments, and vital economic concession in railway and mining rights. In effect this would have guaranteed Russian domination of Manchuria. Neither the Imperial Court nor Yang Ju were willing to incur the onus of accepting these demands, and negotiations dragged on for several months.[31]

When details of the Russian demands reached China, opinions among the responsible officials were generally against their acceptance. The two Yangtze governors-general in particular were strongly against yielding to the Russians. Liu K'un-i once more called on the help of his advisers.[32] Among them Chang Chien again played a prominent role. He drafted two telegrams for Liu, one addressed to the responsible officials in Peking, and the other to the foreign powers directly. In the former he warned of the danger of alienating the other powers by submitting to Russia and urged the government to disclose details of the demand to the other powers. In the telegram to the foreign powers he pointed out the inadvisability of having the St. Petersburg negotiation taking precedence over the general negotiation at Peking. He further stressed the danger to all the powers concerned if China should disappear as a political entity.[33] These two telegrams were jointly dispatched by governors-general Liu and Chang. Their stand in this matter reinforced the strong pressures brought to bear on China by the other powers against giving in to Russia. The Imperial Court, after several months of vacillation, failed to give Yang Ju a clear-cut directive to sign the agreement. As a result of China's unexpected resistance and the unfavorable reaction of the other powers, Russia withdrew her demands. Russian troops, however, remained in Manchuria until her defeat at the hand of Japan in 1905.[34]

Efforts on Behalf of Constitutional Government

In March, 1901, while negotiations leading to a settlement of the Boxer uprising were still going on, Chang Chien published a small work entitled *Reasoned Discussion on Reforms*. This came as a result of the decree of January 29, in which the Empress Dowager, speaking in the name of the Emperor, called for detailed suggestions for reforms from officials throughout the country.[35] The comprehensiveness of the reform plan embodied in this work, however, suggests that most of the reforms had long been in the back of Chang Chien's mind. Altogether forty-two specific reforms were proposed: ten to be carried out by the Board of Civil Office, twelve by the Board of Revenue, eight by the Board of Rites, and four each by the boards of War, Punishment, and Public Works respectively. Not all of the suggested reforms were of equal weight, but among the more important ones were changes in the training and appointment of officials, establishment of a public education system, encouragement of private efforts in land reclamation, modernization of the armed forces, revision of the penal code, tax reforms, and establishment of deliberative assemblies to publicize reform measures.[36] The last were to be set up on both the national and local level. A national assembly or parliament was to be made up of members appointed by four or five ministers, themselves to be members of the assembly. Its function would be the planning of various stages of reforms to be carried out. At the same time local assemblies on the prefectural and the *hsien* level were to be established, with members elected from among the gentry. It would be the task of the local assemblies to educate the people to accept the various reform measures.[37]

Chang Chien's reform program probably influenced the thinking of governors-general Liu K'un-i and Chang Chih-tung, who jointly presented to the Throne three successive memorials in July of 1901, calling for a series of reforms, some of which paralleled Chang Chien's ideas.[38] The two officials, however, carefully couched their suggestions in such language so as to leave no doubt of their loyalty to the existing political structure of the Ch'ing dynasty. At that time Chang Chien himself did not recognize the need to change the basic political structure of the country. The reforms embodied in the *Reasoned Discussion on Reforms* would only graft some new branches of specific improvements onto the old tree of the existing governmental structure. Even his suggested national and local assemblies had only the most limited function of implementing the proposed reforms. He still clung to the view that successful reform needed only "men of ability" and the necessary funds.[39]

The idea that a constitution was a desirable thing in itself first came to him on his trip to Japan in 1903. Invited to attend the fifth Japanese industrial exhibition in Osaka, he took advantage of this opportunity to spend ten weeks in Japan, visiting thirty agricultural and industrial enterprises and thirty-five educational institutions.[40] He was much impressed by Japanese accomplishments. He reasoned that, if Japan, endowed with less natural advantages than China, could be so advanced in education and industry, she had to possess something which China did not. The obvious thing was her constitution.[41] Upon his return he took every opportunity to discuss constitutionalism with his friends. He carried on a correspondence with Shen Tseng-chih on this topic. In May of 1904 he was asked by governors-general Chang

Chih-tung and Wei Kuang-tao to draft a memorial requesting the adoption of a constitution by the Imperial Court. He fulfilled the task after consulting a number of his friends and revising the draft no less than seven times.[42] The submission of this memorial by governors-general Chang and Wei followed closely on the heels of similar moves made by governors Ting Cheng-to of Yünnan and Liu Shao-nien of Kweichow. Two months later Chang Chien completed the printing of *The Constitution of Japan.* His friend Chao Feng-ch'ang sent twelve copies of the book to Peking, some of which eventually got into the hands of the Empress Dowager herself.[43] Chang Chien followed this by sending copies of another book on the Japanese constitution to T'ieh-liang, the influential Manchu general then in charge of the Board of War, who was known to harbor some progressive ideas.[44] Chang Chien's single most outspoken act was the sending of a letter to Yüan Shih-k'ai, the governor-general of Chihli and one of the most powerful officials of the time. In this letter Chang Chien openly called on Yüan to take the initiative in constitutional reform:

> It is obvious that the dangers of 1894 and 1900 cannot be compared to those of today. Without fundamental changes in the body politic no amount of small improvements would prove beneficial. At this time when Japan and Russia have not reached a settlement in the Russo-Japanese War, it would be futile to attempt an appeasement policy. . . . Victory in the war will be the triumph of constitutionalism over autocracy. What nation today is completely autocratic? Can one autocratic state survive among all the constitutional nations? . . . In Japan, Ito, Itagaki and others have gained lasting fame by the introduction of constitutional government. Your talents are certainly not beneath those of the Japanese constitutionalists.[45]

The circumstances which permitted Chang Chien openly to advocate constitutionalism grew out of the disastrous consequences of the Boxer uprising. Saddled with an immense indemnity of 450 million taels, faced with the revolts of Sun Yat-sen and his followers, the Imperial Court sought at last for means to strengthen itself and to appease popular discontent. The reform movement, however, was not promoted by the Ch'ing government alone. The exiled remnants of the reform group of 1898, under the leadership of K'ang Yu-wei and Liang Ch'i-ch'ao, and members of the local gentry on the provincial level, were also active in the movement.

K'ang and Liang were still men with prices on their heads who had managed to find refuge in Japan. They therefore carried on their agitations entirely apart from the other two groups. Also, there was no degree of close cooperation between the Ch'ing government and the local gentry. About the only thing that the three had in common was their opposition to the revolutionaries.

The reformists under K'ang and Liang came into direct contact with the revolutionaries because they were both operating in Japan. When K'ang Yu-wei first arrived in Japan in late 1898, there was an attempt on the part of interested Japanese to promote an alliance between K'ang and Sun Yat-sen. The effort failed as much through disagreements between the two groups on basic issues as through the rise of personal antipathy between the two leaders.[46] Thereafter the reformists and the revolutionaries in Japan fought each other continuously for the allegiance of the overseas Chinese. This group was essential to the reformists and the revolutionaries alike because its members were the chief source of financial support for both. Consequently competition between the two groups was intense. Sometimes this took the form of roughhouse tactics, but primarily the two factions fought each other by means of Chinese-language newspapers. The central organ of the revolutionaries was the *Peoples Tribune* (*Min Pao*), published in Tokyo under the joint editorship of Chang Ping-lin, Hu Han-min, Wang Ching-wei, and Chu Chih-hsin. Opposed to it was the reformists' *New People Miscellany* (*Hsin-min Ts'ung-pao*) of Yokahama, edited by Liang Ch'i-ch'ao. Outside of Japan there were opposing newspapers in Hong Kong, Hawaii, San Francisco, Singapore, and Vancouver.[47]

The contents of those newspapers reveal quite clearly the stands taken by the two camps. Opposed to the revolutionaries' call for the immediate overthrow of the dynasty and the establishment of a republic, the reformists advocated the establishment of a constitutional monarch under the Kuang-hsü Emperor.

The essays of Liang Ch'i-ch'ao, written in classical style but with fresh vitality, had a great influence on the minds of the literate Chinese, particularly the younger group. His arguments received a hearing because the ideas embodied in them were fresh and seemed to have a particular pertinence for the contemporary situation. The Ch'ing government officials were not altogether blind to this. In Peking high officials like T'ieh-liang, Tuan-fang, and Hsü Shih-ch'ang were in favor of adopting a constitution.[48] Outside the country Sun Pao-ch'i, the ambassador to France, argued for such a step. These men persuaded the Empress Dowager to appoint a special mission in the summer of 1905. It was the mission's task to travel abroad for a study of various political systems.

The mission was originally composed of Duke Tsai-tse, Tuan-fang, Tai Hung-tz'u, Hsü Shih-ch'ang, and Shao-ying. As they were boarding the train leaving Peking on September 24, 1905, a young revolutionary named Wu Yueh attempted to kill them with a bomb. The bomb exploded prematurely, killing Wu Yueh and slightly wounding Tsai-tse and Shao-ying. As a result the departure was put off until December, at which time Hsü Shih-ch'ang and Shao-ying were replaced by Shang Ch'i-heng and Li Sheng-to.[49]

The mission split into two groups, Tsai-tse, Li, and Shang covered Japan, England, France, and Belgium, while Tai and Tuan-fang spent most of their time in the United States and the German Empire, with brief stopovers in Japan and eleven other European countries. The two groups were abroad from December of 1905 to August of 1906. Upon their return they were immediately received individually in a series of audiences. In addition, the members of the mission submitted a number of memorials separately and jointly. The joint memorial expressed the consensus of the members, requesting the reorganization of the government offices under a constitution.[50]

What kind of constitutional government did the members of the mission recommend? Basically it was to be modeled after those of Japan, Austria, and the German states of Prussia, Bavaria, and Saxony. The power of the emperor was to be strengthened rather than restricted. He would appoint a "responsible cabinet," whose duties were to recommend policies to the emperor in ruling the country and to absorb the blame of administrative failures. There would be a parliament which would reflect "the people's interests" with the power to approve budgets and impeach the cabinet. The members of the mission, however, were deliberately vague on the franchise upon which the parliament was to be based. Certainly they had no thought of making the parliament a truly representative body. In fact, they conceived of the constitutional system mainly in terms of increasing the administrative efficiency of the government. The participation of the people was to be allowed only in order to awaken their interests in the nation's needs, thereby leading to greater development of resources and a corresponding rise in tax revenue. Should the cabinet or the parliament exceed its prerogatives, the emperor could have it dismissed instantly. In short, the emperor would be ruling with the aid of the constitution, rather than under the constitution. None of the imperial prerogatives was to be curtailed in any way.[51]

The report of the constitutional mission caused no immediate action on the part of the government. In August, 1907, however, a decree came out changing the Political Investigation Bureau (K'ao-ch'a Cheng-chih Kuan) to the Bureau for Constitutional Planning (Hsien-cheng Pien-ch'a Kuan). The following month three officials were sent to Japan, England, and Germany respectively for follow-up studies of the constitutional system of these countries. At the same time the provinces were ordered to prepare for the opening of provincial assemblies, the rules and regulations of which were issued in July, 1908.[52]

Aside from the exiled reformists in Japan and the Ch'ing government itself, there was another group which was active in the promotion of constitutionalism. This group was composed of members of the local gentry in the provinces.[53] The most influential segment of this group was active in Kiangsu under the leadership of Chang Chien, Cheng Hsiao-hsü, and T'ang Shou-ch'ien. The three men were all ranking scholars. T'ang was a native of Chekiang, and held the *Chin-shih* degree.[54] Cheng, a Fukienese, was a *Chü-jen* of 1882 who had served as an official in Anhwei and Kwangtung prior to his retirement to Shanghai in 1906.[55] T'ang, Cheng, and Chang Chien were the chief organizers of the Association to Prepare for the Establishment of Constitutional Government (Yü-pei Li-hsien Kung-hui) in 1906. This association was active in the three adjoining provinces of Kiangsu, Chekiang, and Fukien and included many outstanding dignitaries among its membership.[56] Organizations similar in nature to the Association to Prepare for the Establishment of Constitutional Government sprang up in Hunan, Hupeh, and Kwangtung.

From the very start of the association Chang Chien took a moderate, practical stand. While his colleagues were arguing over the relative speed with which the constitutional movement should be pushed, he was willing to let the ultimate initiative come from the government. For private individuals, he believed, industry, education, and local self-government should be the primary concern.[57] This view, however, did not prevent him from exerting his influence whenever he deemed it would do the most good, as his letter to T'ieh-liang in 1906, supporting the latter's pro-constitution sympathies, amply demonstrated.[58]

Meanwhile the various steps undertaken by the government toward the eventual promulgation of a constitution had attracted a certain degree of popular response. In 1907 Liang Ch'i-ch'ao and several of his colleagues founded in Tokyo the Political Information Club (Cheng-wen She) for the express purpose of advocating the establishment of a constitution. Members of this organization who were students in Japan were active in promoting this cause after their return to China. Liang, however, was still *persona non grata* with the Ch'ing government, which in December, 1907, issued an order prohibiting students from participating in political activities. When members of the Political Information Club persisted in their efforts, a few key leaders were arrested in July, 1908, and the organization in China ordered dissolved.[59]

The government was more circumspect in dealing with the provincial gentry. Many of them were, after all, men of considerable prestige. They were no less outspoken, however, about their advocacy of constitutionalism. The same month that the Political Information Club was ordered suppressed, Cheng Hsiao-hsü was the leading spirit in sending in a joint petition asking for the establishment of a national assembly. Acting in the name of the Association to Prepare for the Establishment of Constitutional Government, Cheng and his colleagues contacted the Constitutional Government Association (Hsien-cheng Kung-hui) in Hunan, the Constitutional Government Preparation Association (Hsien-cheng Ch'ou-pei Hui) in Hupeh, and the Self-governing Association (Tzu-chih Hui) in Kwangtung, as well as outstanding constitutionalists in Hunan, Chihli, Shantung, Szechwan, and Kweichow. Delegates representing these associations were sent to Peking in August, 1908. They submitted a petition calling for the institution of a national assembly within the shortest possible time. This move met with some unexpected support from among the officials. Faced with this manifestation of popular will, the government made public on August 27, 1908, a draft outline which had been drawn up by the Bureau for Constitutional Planning. This outline, modeled after the Japanese constitution, reflected the ideas of the constitutional mission of 1905–06. It was far short of the expectation of the petitioners. This gesture by the government was further vitiated by the announcement that a preparatory period of nine years was to pass before the establishment of the constitution.[60]

The death of the Kuang-hsü Emperor and the Empress Dowager Tz'u-hsi within a day of each other on November 14 and November 15, 1908, seemed at the time the end of an era. The enthronement of the infant Hsüan-t'ung Emperor and the appointment of his father, Prince Ch'un, as regent were generally regarded hopefully by the adherents of constitutionalism. Their expectation seemed to be justified with the actual establishment of provincial assemblies in October of 1909.

In the establishment of the Kiangsu Provincial Assembly Chang Chien played a leading role.[61] Because a representative meeting of any kind was totally unprecedented, much preparatory work had to be done. One immediate problem was the fact that there was no suitable place for holding such a meeting in Nanking, the provincial capital. One had to be constructed. In March, 1909, Chang Chien went to Nanking and chose an elevated spot northeast of the famous Drum Tower for the location of the assembly building. Meanwhile he dispatched a person to Japan to obtain plans of the National Diet Building in Tokyo. Actual construction of the provincial assembly building began in May.[62] While work was going on some 230 delegates gathered in Nanking for a preliminary conference. Chang Chien was elected chairman by a vote of 196. Under his guidance the financial aspect of the coming assembly was thrashed out.[63] He tended to his duties despite a lessening of his usual vigor. From May on he suffered from loss of sleep due to organic difficulties. He was finally cured in July through the treatment of a Chinese physician.[64]

The Kiangsu Provincial Assembly began its first session on September 16, 1909. Ninety-five delegates met in the impressive new Assembly Building. Chang Chien was elected chairman, getting fifty-one of the ninety-five votes cast.[65] The subsequent actions of the Kiangsu Provincial Assembly and assemblies of other provinces showed that, if the Ch'ing government had expected the various provincial assemblies to confine their activities only to local affairs, it could not have been more mistaken.

Upon his election as chairman of the Kiangsu Provincial Assembly, Chang Chien telegraphed the provincial assemblies of fifteen other provinces, requesting that they join Kiangsu in asking the government for the establishment of a parliament without delay.[66] To back up his appeal he sent three men to circulate among the provinces and to elicit positive reactions from them. Their efforts were successful, as representatives from all sixteen provinces met at the Association to Prepare for the Establishment of Constitutional Government headquarters in Shanghai in December, 1909, to form a new organization, the Association of Comrades to Petition for a Parliament (Kuo-hui Ch'in-yüan T'ung-chih Hui). Members of this organization vowed to remain together until the day the Parliament began its first session. Until then, the decision was made to adjourn in Shanghai and meet in Peking two months later.[67]

Without Chang Chien, who remained in Shanghai, the ACPP reconvened in February, 1910. Two immediate steps were undertaken. One was the submission of a joint petition; the other was the effort to raise support among the various high officials for the project. These efforts had to be abandoned temporarily when the government issued a restraining order forbidding the continuation of such activities.[68] Three months later, however, the Delegation to Petition for a Parliament (Kuo-hui Ch'in-yüan Tai-piao T'uan) was set up under Sun Hung-i to remain in Peking while others returned to their own provinces to agitate for further action. The result was the submission of a number of separate petitions. The government once again refused to consider the requests.[69]

Matters remained in this impasse until October, 1910, when the National Assembly, the establishment of which had been promised by the government at the time when it released the constitutional outline the previous year, was convened. Thereupon the Delegation to Petition for a Parliament sent its petition to this body, which, however, was really an advisory council with little actual power. At the same time various governors-general and governors also found it advisable to urge some kind of action. Thus the government received recommendations for the immediate establishment of Parliament and a responsible cabinet from both the National Assembly and the provincial officials. In early November the government announced the shortening of the preparatory period from nine to five years, setting the date for the opening of Parliament in 1913, and promising that a cabinet would be formed prior to the opening of Parliament. The decree also ordered all further activities to petition the government to cease at once.[70]

The issuance of the November decree split the constitutionalists into two camps. The one that represented the Association to

Prepare for the Establishment of Constitutional Government believed that its limited objective had been reached and that no reasonable purpose could be served by further agitation. This view was sharply disputed by representatives of other provinces. Men like T'ang Hua-lung of Hupeh and T'an Yen-k'ai of Hunan persisted in agitating for the immediate opening of Parliament. In December, 1910, the government cracked down hard on the dissatisfied constitutionalists. Some were ordered to return to their home provinces, and one man, Wen Shih-ling of Tientsin, was sent in exile to Sinkiang. These measures broke the back of the constitutionalists' movement for the immediate opening of Parliament.[71]

True to its promise, the government set up a cabinet in April, 1911. If, however, the constitutionalists had hoped to see a truly representative cabinet, they were greatly disappointed. Of the thirteen posts on the cabinet, nine were held by Manchus, revealing the basic distrust held by the Throne toward the Chinese officials. Five of the Manchus were members of the imperial house, thus providing the basis for the cabinet being nicknamed the "royal cabinet." This move by the government pleased few. The constitutionalists began to doubt the government's sincerity, while the revolutionaries received fresh support for their argument that the Ch'ing government was incapable of genuine reform.

For Chang Chien the makeup of the cabinet came as a distinct disappointment. Some two months after the organization of the cabinet he submitted a petition to that body. In it he urged the cabinet to take three actions: (1) to formulate and announce an over-all policy; (2) to establish direct coordination between the cabinet and the various government agencies; and (3) to open its sessions to the public and to call in experts for consultation. He laid particular stress on the last point as an indispensable step toward securing public support for the cabinet.[72] There appeared to be no response to this petition.

The Year 1911

The year 1911 turned out to be a fateful one for Chang Chien. Both by accident and by design he was thrown into the midst of events; and although the key events revolved around such men as Li Yuan-hung, Sun Yat-sen, Huang Hsing, and Yüan Shih-k'ai,

Chang Chien was never far from the scene of action. He was in Peking when the decision to nationalize the railroad in Szechwan was made. He was in Wu-ch'ang the night when the outbreak occurred. And he was in the Lower Yangtze region during the uncertain days of the brief period when that section of the country was the scene of the establishment of the first provisional government of the infant republic. Throughout this time Chang Chien represented that large segment of the people which were neither involved directly in the revolutionary activities nor had a vested interest in the continued survival of the Ch'ing dynasty. He had been a leading advocate of constitutionalism up to 1911. When he supported the revolutionary cause after the initial outbreak, he was acting the part of a typical member of the local gentry of the country, who switched from constitutionalism to republicanism as a means of saving China.

In May of 1911 Chang Chien was selected by the chambers of commerce of Shanghai, Tientsin, Canton, and Hankow to go to Peking in order to obtain government permission for the founding of a joint Chinese-American bank, and a joint shipping line. This scheme came as a result of the visit of an American delegation to the Southern Industrial Exposition (Nan-yang Ch'üan-yeh Hui) of 1910 in Nanking,[73] in which delegation the American financier Robert Dollar was a prominent member. Through Dollar, Chang Chien had met with the group of American businessmen and worked out the details for a joint Chinese-American bank with a total capital of five million yuan (about 3.5 million taels), to be established with the American half of the capital. At the same time a steamship line was also to be set up on a share-and-share-alike basis, starting with a new 18,000-ton ship ordered by Dollar.[74] Chang Chien made ready to travel to Peking by way of Hankow. On his way from Hankow to Peking he paused on June 7 at Changteh, where Yüan Shih-k'ai had been living in retirement ever since his dismissal in 1908. The two men had not seen each other for twenty-eight years. On this occasion Chang Chien talked about one of his pet projects, the Huai River Conservancy Scheme.[75] The next day he reached Peking, arriving a day earlier than the original schedule in order to avoid the elaborate welcome which various organizations had planned for him.[76] He chose to stay at the office building of the Mongolian Industrial Company, which had been the residence of Weng T'ung-ho a dozen or so years back.

On June 11 he received word through Prince Ch'ing that the Regent, Prince Ch'un, the father of the infant Hsüan-t'ung Emperor, wished to see him. Chang Chien accordingly first paid a visit to Duke Tsai-tse, the Minister of Finance, on which occasion he requested that it be made clear that he was not seeking an official appointment.[77] The actual audience with the Regent took place on the evening of the thirteenth. After granting him the privilege of being seated, the Regent opened the interview by saying, "You have not been to the capital for over a decade, during which time the peril to the nation has certainly increased." To this Chang Chien replied, "It has been fourteen years since I left the capital. As for the state of affairs confronting the nation today, the Former Emperor began political reforms in 1898. Then came 1900 and the imperial trip to the west. Those were all days when the Former Emperor encountered grave danger. Today the world knows China has adopted a constitution; the world respects our people. This is all due to the efforts of the Former Emperor.[78] The Regent was gratified by this reply. Chang Chien went on to indicate his efforts in the field of industry, education, and local government, and requested permission to offer a few suggestions concerning national affairs. The Regent told him to speak freely. Thereupon Chang Chien outlined three critical periods of external relations and three vital domestic issues. In China's international position he saw danger in that very year (1911) and in 1913 and 1915. The agreement with Russia concerning the Ili Valley in Sinkiang was due to expire before the year was out. He feared that Russia might seek this occasion to press for further advantages. Two years hence the Anglo-Japanese Alliance was due to expire. He urged that China should exert all efforts in preventing the renewal of this partnership. Finally in 1915 the Panama Canal was scheduled to be completed. He warned of the danger of Japan trying to seek some decisive advantage in China before the power of the United States in the Pacific was increased thereby. Within the country itself Chang Chien urged, in the first place, the speedy establishment of the constitutional system of government, in order to be able to relieve the ravages of floods and other natural disasters without reliance on foreign nations. Secondly he pressed for active government support in the industrial growth of the country, as the sole means of redressing the highly unfavorable balance of trade. Lastly he referred to his own mission to Peking this time and said that, although friendly relationship with the United States was desirable, China must rely on herself in the long run by introducing responsible ministry and a modern system of government. These points were well taken by the Regent, who asked him to discuss them in detail with Duke Tsai-tse. Chang Chien then went on to talk about precautionary steps to be taken in the nationalization of the railroad in Szechwan, and other topics. The audience lasted an hour and a half.[79]

Immediately afterward Chang Chien paid a visit to Prince Ch'ing, on which occasion he discussed the importance of Manchuria and urged the Prince to give strong support to a request for twenty million taels by Governor-general Chao Er-sun toward the development of Manchuria. He went on to talk about the country as a whole: the sufferings of the people, the danger of the revolutionary movement, etc., and ended with the hope that Prince Ch'ing would live up to the duties of his exalted position. Prince Ch'ing was so moved by the plight of the country that he burst into tears. In his personal record Chang Chien commented that this showed the Prince to be "not unduly confused and stupid," as he was reputed to be.[80]

Within a few days Chang Chien had fulfilled his original mission, obtaining the necessary approval from Duke Tsai-tse for the establishment of the joint bank and joint steamship line. The revolution which broke out later in the year cut short the scheme, and it never materialized.

While he was in the capital the Minister of Education, T'ang Ching-Ch'ung, appointed him to the chairmanship of the forthcoming National Education Conference to be held at the end of July. As this would keep him in the capital longer than he had intended to stay, he tried to decline the appointment, but without success. He thereupon proposed to wait for the opening of the conference by putting the intervening time to the best possible use, by making a tour of Manchuria.[81]

Prior to his departure for Manchuria an interesting episode occurred which was to have some bearing on the revolution that broke out four months later. Duke Tsai-tse summoned both Chang Chien and Sheng Hsüan-huai to discuss the proposed nationalization of the railroad in Szechwan. Sheng had discovered that certain members of the Szechwan gentry had managed to obtain over three million taels from people of the province on the pretext that it would be used to finance the planned railroad.[82] The question of the moment was, in view of the fact that the government planned to take over the railroad, how much should the investors be compensated. Sheng wanted to pay off only a fraction of the sum. Chang Chien argued for full reimbursement.[83] As events turned out, Sheng Hsüan-huai had his way. The unrest in Szechwan caused by the government's decision to take over the railroad contributed to the successful outcome of the outbreak at Wu-ch'ang on October 10.

On June 29, Chang Chien, accompanied by Chiang Tao-ming, Meng Seng, and several other close associates, arrived at Mukden, where he visited the Manchu palace museum to view the rare objects on display. On July 2 he consulted with Governor-general Chao Er-sun on the twenty million taels requested by Chao. The following day he visited the local agricultural station. On the fourth he traveled by way of the South Manchuria and the Chinese Eastern railways from Ch'ang-ch'un to Harbin. He noted the obvious Japanization of Ch'ang-ch'un and the equally apparent Russification of Harbin, and that in neither of the two places was the Chinese section on a par with the foreign zones as far as neatness and cleanliness were concerned. On the eighth he arrived at Chichihar and stayed at the residence of Governor Chou Shu-mo of Heilungkiang. The following day he had a chance to visit a Russian-operated lower primary school in nearby K'un-k'un-ch'i, before returning to Harbin. On the way he noticed immense stretches of uncultivated land along the right of way. On July 11 he left for Ch'ang-ch'un, continuing on to Mukden the next day. South of Mukden, because the Liao River had flooded the railroad tracks, his party had to detour by way of Ying-k'ou. By inquiring into the source of the Liao River, Chang Chien first conceived of the possibility of connecting the Liao with the Sungari River. He arrived in Peking on the fourteenth. The Education Conference opened three days later.[84]

This trip to Manchuria was more than just an excursion for Chang Chien. Although he had traveled extensively in China he had never been in Manchuria before. Out of this trip he received a deeper impression of the penetration of Japanese and Russian influence into that part of China. More concretely, the germs of the reclamation scheme and the Liao-Sungari Canal project were planted in his mind. Later he was to attempt the implementation of these schemes during his term of office as the Minister of Agriculture and Commerce.[85]

Less than two months after he had returned to Nan-t'ung from the north, Chang Chien went to Wu-ch'ang to help draw up the operating regulations of the Ta Wei Cotton Mill.[86] He arrived on October 4. On the evening of the ninth two revolutionaries were arrested by the authorities. The city gates were closed immediately while the authorities sought to round up other revolutionaries. At ten o'clock on the morning of the tenth the gates were finally opened. Chang Chien promptly went across the river to Hankow. That evening he boarded ship for his return trip to Nan-t'ung.[87] When he boarded the ship at eight o'clock, he could see across the river the burning of an engineering corps camp just outside Wu-ch'ang. The river was too wide at this point for him to hear any distinct sounds, but seven miles downstream he could still see the horizon bright with the reflected glow of the conflagration.[88]

On the evening of the eleventh the boat arrived at Anking, the capital of Anhwei Province. Next morning Chang Chien went ashore to call on Governor Chu Chia-pao to discuss the Huai River Conservancy Scheme. It was then that he learned that Wu-ch'ang had fallen to the revolutionaries on the previous evening.[89] Anking was then in a most precarious position, as there was a shortage of ready funds for emergencies, and the new-style troops stationed there were rife with revolutionary sentiment and could not be relied upon. Under the circumstances Chang Chien gave up any hope of pursuing the subject of controlling the Huai and left Anking that very evening. The following night his boat tied up together with a later arrival, from the passengers of which Chang Chien got the details of the events of the ninth and tenth in Wu-ch'ang.[90]

He reached Nanking on October 14 and went directly to T'ieh-liang, who was the commanding general of the region at the time. He urged the Manchu general to send troops at once to Hupeh and to memorialize the government for the immediate establishment of a constitutional government.[91] T'ieh-liang evaded the issue by asking Chang Chien to refer the matter to Chang Jen-chün, the governor-general of Liang-Kiang. This Chang Chien did on the following day. Governor-general Chang, however, not only treated the proposal to urge the establishment of constitutional government with great contempt, but refused even to entertain the notion of sending troops to the aid of the authorities in Hupeh. He turned a deaf ear to Chang Chien's argument that, should the revolutionary forces come downstream to Anking, that city was as good as lost and Nanking would be in grave peril.[92]

Chang Jen-chün's action did not deter Chang Chien from making all efforts to press for the establishment of constitutional government. He went on the sixteenth to Soochow, where Ch'en Te-ch'üan, the governor of Kiangsu, backed his proposal and asked him to draft a memorial to be sent to the Imperial Court. That evening he and two of his fellow constitutionalists, Lei Feng and Yang T'ing-tung, worked jointly until midnight before the memorial was done.[93] It was sent to Peking in the name of Governor Ch'en and Governor Sun Pao-ch'i of Shantung. In this memorial Chang Chien argued that the latest disturbance in Hupeh was but a symptom of unrest and that even its successful suppression would not be a permanent solution to the ills of the country. He urged that the "royal cabinet" be dissolved and a genuinely responsible ministry of the most able officials be substituted at once. The ultimate step, he went on to say, must be the promulgation of the constitution.[94] He backed this up five days later by sending a telegram to the cabinet in the name of the Kiangsu Provincial Assembly, asking for the beginnings of a constitutional government by the establishment of Parliament.[95]

Meanwhile in Nanking, Governor-general Chang continued in his obstinate ways. People arriving in Nanking from the Wu-han cities were full of praise for the orderliness of the revolutionary troops. Consequently rumors flew thick and fast. Governor-general Chang, in attempting to forestall any disaffection on the part of the new-styled army stationed in Nanking, ordered the troops to withdraw outside the city walls. He further aggravated the situation by issuing only five rounds of ammunition per man to the troops.[96] When Chang Chien heard this, he went at once to his friend Fan Tseng-hsiang, who was serving under Governor-general Chang at the time. Because of Fan's intercession, the governor-general ordered another ten rounds to be doled out to each soldier.[97] This episode revealed how the usefulness of the new-styled army as a fighting force was effectively destroyed by the inept administration of Chang Jen-chün.

Staying in Nan-t'ung during the latter part of October and the first days of November, Chang Chien noted the spread of revolutionary fervor throughout the country. On November 4 revolutionists in Shanghai, Soochow, and Hangchow declared the independence of Kiangsu and Chekiang. Governor Ch'en Te-ch'üan was pressured into becoming the new military governor of Kiangsu, while T'ang Shou-ch'ien was made the military governor of Chekiang.[98] As for the unfortunate Chang Jen-chün, faced with the critical test, he could only plead incapacity and laid down the power of his office without a murmur.[99]

Up to this moment Chang Chien had not gone beyond the point of urging the government to adopt the constitution at once. Events in early November, however, apparently convinced him of the hopelessness of efforts to shore up the tottering Manchu regime. He forthwith abandoned the constitutionalists' cause, which he had championed for nearly a decade, and threw his support behind the revolutionary movement.

Upon hearing of the rapidly deteriorating situation in Nanking, he immediately dispatched a letter to T'ieh-liang in an attempt to head off any bloodshed which might arise between the revolutionary forces and the loyal troops under the Manchu general. In the letter he appealed to T'ieh-liang's reform sentiments by tracing the chief cause of popular discontent to the failure of the government to give real meaning to its decision for the establishment of a constitutional government. He urged the Manchu general to take the long-range view by cooperating with the new forces in order to preserve Chinese-Manchu harmony.[100]

He next turned to the problem of what the Mongols in Inner and Outer Mongolia would do if their traditional relationship with the Manchu government was broken. To forestall any separatist tendencies on the part of the Mongols he and T'ang Shou-ch'ien, Hsiung Hsi-ling, and Chao Feng-ch'ang sent jointly a telegram to Kalgan, urging the Mongols of Inner and Outer Mongolia to support the republican forces in China. Their effort bore fruit when the Mongols declared their willingness, for the moment, to be on the side of the republicans.[101]

The desperate Ch'ing government at this time turned to the only man who could cope with the situation, Yüan Shih-k'ai. After shrewdly delaying and maneuvering until he wrung from the Regent virtually unlimited power, Yüan consented to come back into power and organized an interim cabinet on November 16.[102] Chang Chien was appointed the Minister of Agriculture, Industry, and Commerce in this cabinet and concurrently the Pacification Commissioner for the Southeast. These posts Chang Chien firmly declined to accept.[103] This was Yüan Shih-k'ai's first attempt to enlist Chang Chien's support, but by no means the last.

On his side Chang Chien sent a series of telegrams and letters to Yüan. He was concerned with Yüan's true sympathies, and wished to win him over to the republican point of view. He now indicated his definite break with the constitutionalists. Citing Japan as an example of a small, homogeneous nation to which the constitutional monarchical form of government was best suited, he stated that a republican form of government was preferable for China because of her vast size and diverse peoples. To achieve this end he suggested the voluntary abdication of the emperor.[104] He was concerned lest revolutionary fervor turn into excesses against the ruling house and thereby touch off racial strife between the Manchus and the Chinese.

At this time Hu Han-min, a leading revolutionary, sought out Chang Chien to draft an abdication decree. Chang Chien turned the draft over to Hu, who, after obtaining T'ang Shao-i's approval in the matter, sent it to Yüan Shih-k'ai. Subsequently this draft was published as the cabinet's decree, signifying the willingness of the Throne to abdicate.[105]

Throughout these few eventful months the military governors of both Kiangsu and Chekiang, Ch'en Te-ch'üan and T'ang Shou-ch'ien, called on Chang Chien frequently for advice. The three having been close associates for some time previous to the events of 1911, Ch'en and T'ang freely wrote of their difficulties to Chang Chien.[106]

On December 15 Ch'en, T'ang, and Ch'en Ch'i-mei, another leading revolutionary, arrived in Nanking to organize a provisional national government. There they were faced with an immediate problem. Nanking was in a state of unrest at the time, caused by the presence of revolutionary troops from outside Kiangsu. These troops would not leave the city until they were paid. The republicans could count on only one ready source of revenue: the salt tax of Liang-Huai region. Chang Chien was thereby appointed the salt commissioner of Liang-Huai. In this position he borrowed 200,000 yuan (about 140,000 taels) from the various local chambers of commerce, pledging the salt revenue of Liang-Huai as securities. With this fund he succeeded in paying off the troops, facilitating their departure from Nanking.[107]

The year 1912 was the first year of the republic. Sun Yat-sen had returned from abroad in the last days of December and immediately became the rallying point of the revolutionary cause. He was nearly unanimously elected as the president of the provisional government. The cabinet he organized on January 3 included Huang Hsing as Minister of War, Ch'en Te-ch'üan as Minister of Interior, and T'ang Shou-ch'ien as Minister of Communications.[108] Chang Chien was tapped for the post of Minister of Industries, which he held until the provisional government was dissolved three months later. During this brief period he came into close contact with Huang Hsing, Ch'en Ch'i-mei, and two other leading revolutionaries, Chang Ping-lin and Wang Ching-wei. He, of course, kept up his contact with Ch'en Te-ch'üan and T'ang Shou-ch'ien.

When the cabinet was first formed, Chang Chien was originally slated for the post of Minister of Finance, but he declined, advising the government that even with the revenue from Huai salt and the custom receipts from Shanghai, the government would run into an annual deficit of eighty million taels. He proposed that Sun Yat-sen negotiate a foreign loan of fifty to a hundred million taels until the various provinces could supply the government's financial needs.[109] Chang Chien's subsequent appointment to be the Minister of Industries, however, did not allow him to steer clear of the problem of government finance altogether. For the immediate operating expenses, there were those in the government who wanted to go to the local chambers of commerce again to borrow another 500,000 yuan (about 350,000 taels). Chang Chien opposed this move, arguing that the government should not be placed in a position of excessive indebtedness to these associations. Instead he pledged himself to raise the 500,000 yuan and made good on the pledge.[110] Of the amount, 300,000 yuan was obtained on a loan without security from the Mitsui Bank in Shanghai, solely on the past good relations between the bank and the Dah Sun Mills.[111] On February 7 Chang Chien was in Shanghai and heard that the sum he managed to raise was not sufficient and that Sun and Huang had decided to raise further funds by reorganizing the Han-yeh-p'ing Iron and Coal Company into a joint Sino-Japanese corporation. He jumped to the conclusion that Sheng Hsüan-huai must have been behind the scheme, and wrote at once to Sun and Huang opposing the move. The letter setting forth his reasons clearly showed his distrust of both Sheng and Japan.

Recently, I received a letter from Hupeh, asking about rumors that Han-yeh-p'ing is to be jointly operated with the Japanese. I myself have heard that Sheng Hsüan-Huai proposes to use that company to secure loans, and further lending sums thereby to the government. We know that the Kiangsu railroad affair was defeated but recently. Yet now the news is abroad that 30 million yuan is to be raised, half Chinese and half Japanese, with 5 million to be lent to the government. You two gentlemen must know the details of this matter. That's why I am sending this post haste, intending to offer my humble opinion.

I happen to know the history of Han-yeh-p'ing especially well. In a word, of all the commercial enterprises, iron mills in particular should not be made joint ventures with foreigners. Even if this is done, it should not be done with the Japanese. They have patiently and earnestly plotted our ruin for many years, but have not succeeded. The reason is that within their three islands there is not one iron mine, a source of eternal regret to the Japanese. In contrast China's riches in coal and iron exceeds that of any other country. I have said on occasions that the day our iron industry is fully developed will mark the day when Japan will be bested by China. This is no exaggeration. In recent years, the Japanese have exhausted every means to gain control of T'ung-kuan-shan, Ta-yeh, and Peng-ch'ih-hu, without success. Now Sheng Hsüan-huai, because the industries of China's interior have been taken over by the republican army, and knowing that the army is in financial straits, is up to his usual unscrupulous tricks. If our government does not take due notice of this and falls for his wiles, it is bound to suffer great harm in its national defense and diplomacy. The republican government has recently been established. It must look after the people with the best policy at its command. How could it forfeit the boundless riches of the future for mere millions of borrowed funds, and thereby become the laughing stock of the world. The foreign-language newspapers of Shanghai are already frequently critical toward the government. I hope you will hold the long-range view and not be led astray by the counsel of rascals, concentrating on some small immediate advantage. Sheng Hsüan-huai has his limited abilities, but he has no grasp of the over-all situation and has no thought for the good of the nation whatsoever. Even in the case of the nationalization of railroads, an intrinsically sound move, he chose to use arbitrary methods, leading to nation-wide opposition, and thereby causing the downfall of the Manchus. . . . In a word, Sheng has brought Han-yeh-p'ing to its present stage of growth through the efforts of some ten years. The republican government should aid in its growth, and not because Sheng has been its manager, allow him to ruin it now. Even if it were Sheng's private estate, the government should still protect it for the general good. As for joint operation with the Japanese, *this must not be done.*[112]

As an indication of his sincerity he begged to be relieved of his post. Both Sun and Hu Han-min tried to dissuade him from the step. His mind, however, was made up, and he would not change his decision. The inauguration of Yüan Shih-k'ai on March 10, 1912, effectively solved this problem, as the Nanking provisional cabinet was thereby ended.

Interest in Politics

In late December, 1911, Chang Ping-lin, Ch'en Te-ch'üan, Chao Feng-ch'ang, and Chang Chien met to discuss the possibility of organizing a new political party as a counterpoise to Sun Yat-sen's T'ung-meng Hui. Ch'en and Chao, of course, were long-time associates of Chang Chien's in his Association to Prepare for the Establishment of Constitutional Government. Chang Ping-lin had been an independent revolutionary who had suffered imprisonment for his activities in Shanghai. After his release he went to Japan and cast his lot with the T'ung-meng Hui. At that time all revolutionary factions buried their differences and worked for the common cause of overthrowing the Ch'ing government. Now that the primary goal had been achieved, the original differences began to reappear. Chang Ping-lin headed what was called the Kuang-fu Hui faction, which opposed the T'ung-meng Hui radicals by advocating a moderate course of action.[113]

On January 3, Chang Ping-lin reorganized his Kuang-fu Hui into the Chinese Republic Association (Chung-hua Min-kuo Lien-ho Hui), whose membership reputedly grew to over 20,000.[114] Shortly afterward the Chinese Republic Association was combined with the adherents of the Association to Prepare for the Establishment of Constitutional Government to form the Union Party (T'ung-i Tang). Its platform called for establishment of a responsible cabinet, sound fiscal practice, development of industry, concern for people's livelihood, and advocacy of international peace. Chang Chien, Chang Ping-lin, Ch'en Te-ch'üan, Hsiung Hsi-ling, T'ang Shou-ch'ien, T'ang Shao-i, T'ang Hua-lung, and Chao Feng-ch'ang were among its more prominent members.[115]

Because of the Union Party's anti-T'ung-meng Hui nature, it naturally gravitated toward Yüan Shih-k'ai. Thus in the matter of opening of the Parliament and the choice of a capital between Nanking and Peking, the Union Party supported Yüan's preferences.[116] A heavy representation of former officials, such as Ch'en Te-ch'üan, Hsiung Hsi-ling, and T'ang Shao-i, within its membership also guaranteed its generally conservative outlook.

Aside from the T'ung-meng Hui and the Union Party, there was the United Republican Party (T'ung-i Kung-ho Tang). In addition there were a host of lesser parties: the People's Society (Min She), centering around Li Yüan-hung, the hero of Wu-ch'ang; the Nationalist Union Association (Kuo-min Hsieh-chin Hui); the Republican Reconstruction Discussion Association (Kung-ho Chien-she T'ao-lun Hui), supporting Liang Ch'i-ch'ao. There were also such splinter parties as the Nationalist Party (Kuo-min Tang, not to be confused with the Kuomintang of later vintage); the Republican Public Association (Min-kuo Kung-hui); the United Progressive Association (Kung-chin Hui); the Republican Union Party (Kung-ho T'ung-i Tang); and the Socialist Party. These parties were organized around competing personalities and did not maintain their identity for long or pursue any consistent policy. Most of them soon went out of existence or merged with one another to form more party labels.[117]

After the shifting of the political center from Nanking to Peking, the polarization between government and opposition parties became more definite. Upon Yüan Shih-k'ai's urgings the Union Party and the People's Society took the lead to join with the Nationalist Party, the Nationalist Union Association, and the Republican Public Association to form the Republican Party (Kung-ho Tang). It was formally launched on May 9, 1912. It stood for national unity, national progress, and international peace. Li Yüan-hung was chosen as the Director General. Chang Chien, Chang Ping-lin, Ch'en Te-ch'üan, and T'ang Hua-lung were among the leading members. Soon afterward Chang Ping-lin broke away to revive the Union Party once more.[118]

The consolidation of the opposition came about in August, 1912, with the transformation of the T'ung-meng Hui into the Kuomintang. Into this new party went the United Republican Party, the United Progressive Association, and several other lesser parties.[119]

Nearly all the remaining parties consolidated to form the Democratic Party (Min-chu Tang), under the nominal leadership of Liang Ch'i-ch'ao. This political organization proposed to act as the swing group between the two bigger parties.[120]

Chang Chien never looked with favor upon interparty struggle as a necessary adjunct of a republican government. In a letter to T'ang Hua-lung after the establishment of the Republican Party of 1912, he indicated his willingness to leave Kiangsu to go to Peking if his presence would help bring about harmony among the parties. He promised to contact the leaders of the other parties and urged members of his own party to desist from attacking the government.[121] Largely due to the advice of Chao Feng-ch'ang, Chang Chien did not venture northward until September, when he heeded Yüan Shih-k'ai's call to discuss the salt problem.[122] He stayed barely a month in Peking.

On March 20, 1913, Sung Chiao-jen, one of the leading figures in the Kuomintang, was assassinated at the railroad station in Shanghai. Suspicion at the time, and a later investigation conducted by Ch'en Te-ch'üan, implicated Yüan Shih-k'ai.[123] This event brought to a head the latent hostility harbored by most of the Kuomintang leaders toward Yüan, and caused the open break between the northern and southern factions, which Chang Chien had hoped to avoid. In vain he pleaded with Chao Feng-ch'ang, Huang Hsing, and Wang Ching-wei to put the interests of the nation above those of the party. In vain he counseled moderation.[124] He had to stand helplessly by as his native province Kiangsu declared independence from Yüan and suffered the inevitable consequences at the hands of Chang Hsün and others of Yüan's better-organized forces during the summer of 1913.

The last significant political shift of that year found the three anti-Kuomintang parties, the Republican Party, the Union Party, and the Democratic Party, combine into the Progressive Party (Chin-pu Tang) on May 29. This again was done at the bidding of Yüan Shih-k'ai.[125] For the third time Chang Chien's name was among the leaders of a political party. As it turned out, the new party enjoyed only a brief period of power, coinciding with the premiership of Hsiung Hsi-ling. Not long afterward the political picture became further blurred, as the more radical elements of the Kuomintang were driven from Peking upon their support of the abortive revolt in the south. The Kuomintang moderates came over to join the Progressive Party. Yüan Shih-k'ai soon grew powerful enough to dispense with the support of a government party.[126]

Precisely how active was Chang Chien as a politician? All evidences point to the fact that, although his name appeared prominently among the leaders of the pro-Yüan Shih-k'ai and anti-T'ung-meng Hui parties, he took very little active part in the successive transformation of the parties. At the time of the formation of the Union Party, Chang Ping-lin sought him out because he had been a key figure in the constitutionalist's camp in the prerepublic days. His active support of the Union Party helped ensure a strong element of the constitutionalist sentiment on the side of the Union Party and its successors. When the Union Party joined with the others to form the Republican Party in Peking, Chang Chien was not present at its inauguration. He, However, clearly regarded himself as a member of this new political group and maintained contact with other prominent members. Still his absence from Peking during 1912, and his interest in salt affairs and Huai river projects,[127] disengaged him from the developing political situation. As a result, by 1913, he had grown out of touch with political maneuvers. He had so little to do with the formation of the Progressive Party that he did not even deign to note the event in his personal record. His subsequent official career came more as a result of his association with Yüan Shih-k'ai than of his political activities.

Minister of Agriculture and Commerce

Since the time of Yüan Shih-k'ai's restoration to a position of power in late 1911, Chang Chien had been in frequent communication with Yüan. His refusal to serve on the final prerepublican cabinet did not end Yüan's attempt to have Chang Chien on his side. Soon after Yüan became the provisional president in early 1912, he telegraphed Chang Chien to request him to go north and assume some public office. Again Chang Chien begged off, citing as the reason his recent resignation as Minister of Industries in the Nanking government. He did not close the door to all appointments, however, as he intimated in a letter, personally delivered by his friend Liu Hou-sheng to Yüan, that he would be willing to serve in some capacity which would give him power to introduce salt reforms, carry out the Huai River project, or encourage the growth of cotton.[128] For the time being Yüan did not choose to follow up these hints. This did not prevent Chang Chien from offering advice to Yüan on the latter's choices for cabinet posts. For the cabinet of T'ang Shao-i, organized in March, 1912, Chang Chien expressly recommended Tuan Ch'i-jui for the post of Minister of War, Hsiung Hsi-ling for Minister of Finance, and Chou Hsüeh-hsi for Minister of Industries. Yüan followed his advice on Tuan and Hsiung. The appointment of Tuan was to be expected, since he had long been a loyal subordinate of Yüan's. Hsiung's appointment however, was more in the nature of a political concession on Yüan's part. That Hsiung and not some other prominent member of the opposition parties was picked for the post must be attributed in part to Chang Chien's recommendation.[129]

In July, 1913, Chang Chien did Hsiung a greater service. Yüan was then dissatisfied with the cabinet of Chao Pin-chün, who had followed T'ang Shao-i and Lu Cheng-hsiang to the premiership. Yüan would have preferred Hsü Shih-ch'ang, one of his closest associates, as the new premier. Knowing that the selection of Hsü would encounter difficulties in receiving the approval of the Parliament, he offered Chang Chien the premiership. Once more Chang Chien declined the offer, and strongly suggested that Hsiung Hsi-ling be considered instead.[130] Yüan submitted the name of Hsiung to the Parliament primarily as a political manuever. To his surprise the moderate faction in the Kuomintang combined with solid Progressive Party support to get Hsiung approved.[131]

The cabinet organized by Hsiung Hsi-ling included, among others, Tuan Ch'i-jui as Minister of War, Sun Pao-ch'i as Foreign Minister, and Liang Ch'i-ch'ao as Minister of Justice. Because Hsiung had expressed the desire to organize a cabinet composed of "first-rate men with first-rate experiences" his cabinet soon acquired the name of the "first-rate Cabinet."[132]

Yüan now pressed Chang Chien to accept the post of Minister of Agriculture and Commerce. Hsiung also urged Chang Chien to join his cabinet. Having refused Yüan's offer a number of times, Chang Chien found it difficult to decline once again. It was at this time also that General Chang Hsün's troops were committing a series of outrages in Nanking, which they had occupied when the revolting Kuomintang forces were driven out. Chang Chien protested this incident to Yüan in the strongest terms. Yüan promised to dispatch Chang Hsün's troops elsewhere. Thus having been placed under Yüan's obligation for a number of reasons, Chang Chien consented to take up the portfolio of agriculture and commerce.[133] When his appointment was eventually submitted in September, 1913, to the Parliament for ratification along with the rest of the slate, he had the honor of receiving the largest number of ratifying votes in the brief history of the Chinese Republic, 598 out of 619 cast altogether.[134]

Chang Chien's term of office as the Minister of Agriculture and Commerce from October 21, 1913, to December, 1915, was characterized by a number of useful projects. That many of them did not become permanent must be evaluated against the conditions of the time. A newly established republic, led by a president singularly bent on building up his own personal power, with a parliament torn by petty political bickerings, can hardly offer the stable political background necessary for long-term projects. In any case, it is certain that Chang Chien stepped into the cabinet post with the resolve to achieve certain definite objects. He indicated this in the first published statement upon his appointment, in which he enumerated the four basic steps which needed to be taken by the government: (1) to set up the necessary legal framework by providing forestry regulations, corporation laws, bankruptcy laws, etc.; (2) to stabilize the fiscal system of the country; (3) to put the tax system into order; and (4) to offer encouragement to private enterprise in all fields.[135]

Before he set his sights to achieve any of these aims, however, he first reorganized the ministry under him. Technically he was the concurrent head of both the Ministry of Agriculture and Forestry and the Ministry of Labor and Commerce. These two ministries had been set up in place of the single Ministry of Industries by Yüan Shih-k'ai as a temporary political expedient. Chang Chien received Yüan's support in recombining the two into the single Ministry of Agriculture and Commerce. By this move he reduced the personnel by half and eliminated much unnecessary duplication in administration.[136]

Starting in December, 1913, when he initiated, and the Parliament approved, the promulgation of the Labor and Commercial Profit Law, he had a hand in the passage of seven basic commercial laws within a period of three months, from August to October, 1914. The more important among them were the Regulations for the Registration of Commercial Enterprise and Corporations, the

Corporations Establishment Law, the Chamber of Commerce Act, and the Hunting Law, all except the last having to do with industrial or commercial enterprises.[137] These laws provided the framework under the republic for the growth of private business, although it must be said that mere promulgation of these laws did not signify that they went into actual effect throughout the country.

Chang Chien next turned to the encouragement of agricultural and livestock production. He announced the awarding of prize money to farmers and herders for outstanding achievements in crop cultivation and animal husbandry. He followed this by establishing experimental stations for the improvement of cotton, sugar cane, forest products, and domestic animals. Other projects which he sponsored included the legalization of land reclamation efforts by private enterprise and the Manchurian reclamation projects.

One of Chang Chien's most cherished projects was the standardization of all weights and measures in the country. He was certainly not the first in the country who felt that the multiple system of weights and measures then existing was a hindrance to the nation's growth in production and trade. His effort was not without precedent. The former Ministry of Agriculture, Labor, and Commerce in the Ch'ing dynasty had originally initiated the effort to set up a standard system of measurement for length, capacity, and weight. Now in 1914 Chang Chien proposed to revive the project and carry it out to a successful conclusion. He went about it in two ways. On the one hand he dispatched men abroad to study the measures used in the other countries; on the other he established a standard measurements bureau, which made official measuring devices for use throughout the country. This project, laudable though it was, suffered the same fate that befell so many of Chang Chien's other efforts, namely, his personal interest was not enough alone to cause a permanent change, and when he left his position, the project died.[138]

When Hsiung Hsi-ling resigned his premiership under political pressure in February of 1914, Liang Ch'i-ch'ao and another minister resigned with him. Chang Chien was approached on this matter. He replied that he took up his post as a political free agent, intent only upon the achieving of certain aims. He therefore felt no obligation to follow Hsiung's lead.[139] He stayed on in the same position in the cabinet of Sun Pao-ch'i. His responsibilities as the concurrent Director General of Water Conservancy, however, kept him away from the ministry through a good part of 1914. Indeed, he personally was more concerned with water conservancy work than with his ministerial responsibilities.[140] Early in 1915 he attempted to resign his ministership so that he might concentrate on water conservancy projects. His resignation was not allowed.

At this time Yüan Shih-k'ai first betrayed unmistakable signs of his intention to revive the monarchy, with himself as the new emperor. For months his critics had accused him of harboring such designs, but he had denied it categorically. In July, 1915, the formation of the Ch'ou-an Hui by Yen Fu and five others, all known for their monarchical pro-Yüan sentiments, finally brought the matter into the open.[141] Chang Chien at once attempted to dissuade Yüan from his course of action. Once more, as was the case in the summer of 1898 when he tried to dissuade K'ang Yu-wei from the latter's course of action, his words fell on deaf ears.[142]

In late September Chang Chien submitted his resignation for both the ministry and the water conservancy directorship. This was again not allowed by Yüan. By this time Chang Chien had already left the capital and had returned to Nan-t'ung. He therefore sat tight and waited until December, when he again submitted his resignation. This was accepted on December 28, 1915.[143]

In the last analysis we are forced to conclude that, in spite of all his involvement in national affairs, he was of surprisingly little influence on the key events of his time. Compared to such men as Yüan Shih-k'ai and Sun Yat-sen, or even to such as Liang Ch'i-ch'ao and Li Yüan-hung, he had far less to do with the outcome of what was one of the crucial periods in the history of modern China. His role was a subsidiary one at best.

The reform of 1898 was centered around K'ang Yu-wei. Chang Chien disassociated himself from K'ang because he disliked K'ang as a person and disagreed with his program. In the Boxer uprising Chang Chien was only one of several advisers of Governor-general Liu K'un-i, who in turn was only cooperating with the efforts of Sheng Hsüan-huai and Governor-general Chang Chih-tung. Chang Chien's advocacy of constitutionalism was certainly more important than his part in either of the two events of 1898 and 1900, yet his outspoken criticisms and proposals, along with the efforts of other constitutionalists, only prompted the Court to go through the motions of setting up a constitutional government. As events were to prove, the entire movement for a constitutional government became so much wasted effort when the revolution broke out in 1911.

It might be argued that the role of Chang Chien in setting up the Kiangsu Provincial Assembly contributed to the success of the revolution. This would be true if the provincial assemblies were active agencies in the overthrow of the Ch'ing regime. No evidence, however, exists to support such a contention. The members of the provincial assemblies were almost all leading gentry members. They had little real sympathy for the revolutionaries and made no systematic effort to pursue a common cause with them. That most of the provincial assemblies declared their provinces independent of the Court after October 10, 1911, must be regarded as a sign of the weakness of Ch'ing central power in a time of crisis rather than as evidence that the provincial assemblies were centers of revolutionary activities.

Finally, although Chang Chien occupied cabinet posts in both the provisional government and under Yüan Shih-k'ai, he did not at any time possess real political power. His term of office as the Minister of Industries in 1912 lasted only the three months' duration of the short-lived provisional government in Nanking. His appointment came primarily as a result of his great prestige in Kiangsu. His later term of office as Minister of Agriculture and Commerce in Peking also bore very little actual results. The post itself was a minor one in the cabinet and Chang Chien made it plain that he had no intentions of using it as a springboard to greater political prominence. It must not be overlooked also that he was then already over sixty years of age.

Inasmuch as Chang Chien seemed perpetually to be just off the stage where the key events were being enacted, it is apparent that he was seldom directly in touch with national political events, and then only for short periods of time. In this sense he may be said to have suffered from a degree of provincialism. Yet this is precisely where he had the advantage over the other leading persons of his time. By shunning a straight political career he avoided the plight of such men as Yüan Shih-k'ai and Li Yüan-hung. Chang Chien was to go on to achieve far more concrete results in the fields of industry, education, and conservation by confining his activities largely to the local level.

CHAPTER FIVE

Chang Chien and Educational Reforms

CHANG CHIEN'S career as an educator has attracted less attention than has his career as an industrialist. Yet he himself always emphasized the fact that education stood foremost in his mind. Writing in 1912 on the tenth anniversary of the founding of the Nan-t'ung Normal School, he set forth clearly the factors which led him to the field of education.

From the time of China's utter defeat in 1894 and the lowering of her national prestige at the signing of the treaty of Shimonoseki in 1895, the Chinese intelligentsia have come to realize the necessity of universal education. Yet universal education must rely on the training of teachers, therefore I began to see the necessity for establishing normal schools. The establishment of a normal school requires not an inconsiderable sum of money. The normal schools of other countries are rightfully supported on the national or local levels. In China at the time the examination system had yet to be abolished; the people remained unenlightened. On the one hand, the nation merely announced its intentions without making concrete plans, on the other, each locality preserved its original public funds with no thought of contributing them to a normal school system. Thinking through to the root of the problem, I had no recourse except to enter the business world. However, I had been a poor scholar all my life. Where would I find the necessary capital? Fortunately Nan-t'ung had long been famous internationally as a region where fine cotton is grown. When the opportunity presented itself for someone to establish a spinning factory in Nan-t'ung, I accepted the task. By arduous labor and rigid standards I managed to build up public confidence in the venture. In forty-four months the enterprise had its start, two years passed by without it foundering, and two more years later it began to show a profit. From the day of its inception, I had accumulated my share of the salary, which, with accrued interest, amounted to some 20,000 taels. With the encouragement of two or three of my comrades, this sum was used to establish a normal school. . . . Then came the division of the school into practice courses, preparatory courses, and regular courses. The graduates of the practice and preparatory courses became teachers for the lower primary schools which came into being, while the regular courses provided teachers for the higher primary schools. Thereafter technical courses, courses on surveying, and the agricultural school were added one by one.[1]

Thus Chang Chien stated that it was patriotism which turned him to the career he followed, and that for him business served as means to attain the end of education. His business turned out so well that in later years he devoted less and less of his time and energies to it, delegating much of its control to his brother Chang Ch'a and several other associates. Education, however, remained one of his chief concerns to the end of his life.

Before we examine Chang Chien's career as an educator in detail, it may be well to trace the development of modern education in China, so that his achievements can be seen in perspective.

Early Developments in Modern Education

For close to two thousand years China had a gradually developing system of education based on the Confucian classics and formalized by the civil service examination system. This educational system became the foundation of Chinese society and culture, and was widely copied by neighboring peoples like the Koreans and the Japanese. When European scholars first learned about it from the reports of the Jesuit missionaries in the seventeenth century, it seemed to some of them to be the perfect system, leading to a government of philosophers. The basic validity of this Confucian-based educational system was not seriously challenged by the Chinese educated class until the nineteenth century, when repeated political and military disasters led some to attribute China's weakness to the formal structure of her educational system. Even then few questioned the basic tenet that ethical teaching must be the foundation of all education. This was to be expected, since such outstanding Chinese leaders in the nineteenth century as Lin Tse-hsü, Tseng Kuo-fan, Li Hung-chang, and Chang Chih-tung, men generally regarded as representing the more progressive element among Chinese officialdom, were themselves products of the traditional education system. Little by little some Chinese came to recognize that the system itself was inadequate to cope with China's problems. And it was through their efforts that reforms were eventually initiated in education. Necessarily, each step had to be painfully slow, since it must be made in the face of centuries-old inertia and the conservatism of the bulk of the Chinese educated class. It was not until a new generation had come along in the twentieth century, free from the influence of single-minded concentration on Confucian classics and the decade-long preparation for advancement through the examination system, that the change could be thought of as permanent.

Into the coming of modern education went several separate strands, namely, the revision in the thinking of the Chinese about the need to introduce an alien institution, the creation of a modern educational administration, the establishment of new-model schools, the sending of students abroad, and the contributions made by the foreign missionaries. As might be surmised, these steps, which seem so logically to grow out of one another, were taken more or less haphazardly. This was due not so much to the lack of over-all plans, several of which received more than passing attention, but rather to the existence of the conservative opposition already alluded to, which made it impossible for the more enlightened minority among the Chinese to carry out the reforms logically. It must also be remembered that educational reform was but one among many types of reforms proposed at the time. It had to move slowly by necessity.

After China's second defeat at the hands of the "foreign barbarians," an institution called the T'ung-wen Kuan was created in 1862.[2] Prince Kung and Wen-hsiang, who were chiefly responsible for its establishment, conceived of it as a foreign-language school for the training of competent clerks to staff the newly created agency for the handling of "barbarian affairs," the Tsungli Yamen. From the humble beginning of this institution, however, can be traced the development of a number of new-type schools alien to the traditional scheme of Chinese education. The T'ung-wen Kuan was joined in the two succeeding years by the founding of the Kuang-fang-yen Kuan in Shanghai and the T'ung-wen Kuan of Canton, both for the express purpose of foreign-language training. Later the Kiangnan Arsenal and the Foochow Shipyard both had attached schools for translators. In 1863 the T'ung-wen Kuan added courses in French and Russian to the original English course. In 1866 it further broadened its scope by adding instruction in mathematics, chemistry, science, international law, and astronomy. This trend, however, proceeded no further until the Reform of 1898, when the T'ung-wen Kuan became the model for an institution of higher education, the Ching-shih Ta-hsüeh-t'ang (generally referred to by foreigners as the Imperial University). The T'ung-wen Kuan continued to exist side by side with this new institution until 1902, when it was merged with it.[3]

While these institutions were being established, there arose a separate movement for the training of Chinese students abroad. Its prime mover was Yung Wing, the first Chinese graduate of an American university. He succeeded in persuading Tseng Kuo-fan and Li Hung-chang to endorse his scheme for sending thirty students to the United States each year under the supervision of a Chinese scholar. The first group of youths went abroad in 1872.[4] Although the scheme collapsed after only four groups of students had been sent, other students, notably the graduates of the school attached to the Foochow Shipyard, were sent abroad from time to time from 1879 on.[5] After Shimonoseki the government again allowed students to go abroad. The largest contingent of students went to Japan, but European nations as well as the United States also received substantial numbers of students. The influence of these "returned students" eventually far exceeded their actual number. They were responsible for the continued growth of modern education, as well as other political and social reforms.

The establishment of modern schools and the sending of students abroad, however, represented no direct threat to the basic system of traditional education itself. At the time when the T'ung-wen Kuan was set up and when the first group of Chinese students went abroad, most Chinese officials regarded these as steps designed solely for the acquisition of foreign tongues and foreign skills. When these steps seemed likely to have wider implications, they were reluctant to lend their continued support. The battle between traditional and modern education at first ran strongly in favor of the former. Even Tseng Kuo-fan and Li Hung-chang, who were chiefly responsible for establishing new schools and sending students abroad, were highly antagonistic to the idea of tampering with the institutions of classical learning and civil service examinations.[6] As late as 1898, Chang Chih-tung enjoyed a good deal of support for his proposal to give central emphasis to Chinese learning, as embodied in his famous *Ch'üan-hsüeh P'ien*. But events in the last decade of the nineteenth century, starting with the defeat by Japan and culminating with the Boxer uprising, made drastic changes inevitable. In 1903 a three-men commission composed of Chang Po-hsi, Jung-ch'ing, and Chang Chih-tung recommended the establishment of a national system of modern schools and the gradual abolition of the examination system. Two years later Chang Chih-tung and Yüan Shih-k'ai were responsible for the outright abolition of the examination system, a step which removed a major obstacle to the successful erection of a modern educational system.[7]

There remained the task of creating a national educational administration. For, following the example set by Japan, the Chinese Government wanted to centralize the development of modern education. The decade following the Sino-Japanese War had seen the appearance of a number of schools which were largely the result of individual efforts. This, however, was regarded as undesirable. Instead, a complete system of schools and educational policies was mapped out. It included an educational administration which would be headed on the national level by a minister holding "cabinet" rank. Directly under him would be officials in charge of the educational affairs of the capital (Peking). This central body would also have supervision over regional educational administrations to be organized on substantially the same line as the national administration. For the school system, the proponents of the scheme envisaged a ten-year primary school, a three-year middle school, a three-year preparatory school, and topped by a three-year college.[8] These details were changed several times even before the system left the blueprint stage, but the concept of a centralized, standardized scheme of education remained essentially unchanged. Time schedules were drawn up giving a year-by-year plan of how the establishment of each part of this administration and school system was to be carried out.[9]

An account of the gradual development of modern education in China must necessarily mention the efforts of foreign missionaries in establishing a number of schools. As early as 1839 a school dedicated to the memory of Robert Morrison, the first Protestant missionary to come to China, was opened in Macao. It was this school that Yung Wing attended. A decade or so later, both

Catholic and Protestant schools were operating in Shanghai. Until 1877, however, the openings of these schools were only isolated individual efforts. That year the formation of a school and textbook committee at the General Conference of Protestant Missionaries in China heralded the beginning of a period of organized efforts.[10]

The contribution of Protestant missionary education to the development of modern education in China was twofold. Missionaries were in the vanguard of those who early agitated for a national educational system, and missionary institutions served as models of new-style schools. Beginning in 1899 the missionary-backed Educational Association of China took on the task of drawing up a national education scheme and attempted to influence the Ch'ing government to recognize the need for such a scheme. The missionaries were confident that they would be called on to play key roles once the scheme was approved. At the same time missionary schools taught English and science while serving as a breeding ground for a new crop of Chinese teachers trained in modern methods of teaching.[11]

The fond hopes of leaders in education among the Protestant missionaries were not destined to be realized at first. When the government decided on educational reforms in 1903 it turned to Japan instead for its model of a national system of education. A distinction between government and missionary school was drawn, so that in effect students in the missionary schools were discriminated against as products of schools without official approval.[12] Not until after the Revolution of 1911 did missionary education become a part of the mainstream of Chinese education.[13]

Thus we can see that at the time when Chang Chien assumed the role of an educator in 1902, some changes in the Chinese education system had been made, but the process had hardly begun. The abolition of the examination system and the creation of an education administration were substantial advances, and they materially aided Chang Chien's efforts. His achievements, however, were on a totally different level, and it is to these we now turn.

The Establishment of a School System

The disastrous consequences of the Boxer uprising of 1900 finally forced the Empress Dowager and her conservative advisers to institute reforms. Officials both at the Court and in the provinces were ordered to submit memorials on the ways and means of bringing about reform. Among the officials, the two governors-general, Chang Chih-tung and Liu K'un-i, came to the forefront with their famous joint memorials of 1901, stipulating a number of specific reforms.[14] That same year, as a step toward the introduction of modern education into his own provinces, Governor-general Liu asked Chang Chien to draw up the curriculum for primary and secondary schools. Chang Chien took this opportunity to urge upon Liu the necessity of opening normal schools in order to provide the trained teachers needed for the various primary and secondary schools envisaged. Liu was at first agreeable to this suggestion, but was later dissuaded by some of his subordinates, who, like many other officials of the time, argued that the traditional education system of China was far superior to those of other nations.[15] Thwarted in his bid to see a public-supported normal school established, Chang Chien fell back on his own resources and proceeded to work for the establishment of a normal school in Nan-t'ung. This school was initially financed by his unused salary from Dah Sun, accumulated over the years to the amount of 20,000 taels, together with 10,000 taels contributed by his close friend Shen Hsieh-chün and others.[16] His petition to Governor-general Liu for such a school was duly approved in 1902, and in June of that year a local temple, the Ch'ien-fo Ssu, was taken over for the purpose of converting it into a schoolhouse. The temple had outlived its usefulness for some time. Its single resident monk was relocated in another temple with little difficulty.[17] The grounds were enlarged to the extent of six acres, and additional rooms were constructed so that up to three hundred students could be accommodated in the temple. First classes began in May, 1903.[18]

The Nan-t'ung Normal School was the first independent institution of its kind in China. Prior to its establishment there existed only a department for teachers' training at the Nan-yang School established by Sheng Hsüan-huai in 1897.[19] Nan-t'ung Normal School later became integrated into the provincial normal school system of Kiangsu when the province took over half of the financial burdens of the school.[20]

Chang Chien's wife proved to be the motivating force behind the founding of a normal school for girls. She and the wife of Chang Ch'a, Chang Chien's brother, convinced their husbands that such a school was needed.[21] Plans were first laid in 1905. The following year a private residence was purchased to be converted into school quarters. Delays, however, prevented the holding of the first class until 1909. Additional land and buildings were provided in 1910 and again in 1920, and an attached primary school was opened.[22] The founding of this school for the training of women teachers was another first in China, and many of the students came from parts of Kiangsu other than Nan-t'ung and its immediate environs.

The establishment of these normal schools provided trained teachers, without which no system of primary schools could exist. The next step was the primary school system itself. As was his custom Chang Chien worked out the scheme in detail. His first comprehensive plan in 1906 called for a network of 400 lower primary schools for Nan-t'ung, which had an estimated area of 10,000 square li (about 1,000 square miles).[23] This would provide one school for every twenty-five square li. One rainy day in 1910 Chang Chien was traveling, and the condition of the roads and the difficulty of making progress caused him to reflect how nearly impossible it would be for a child of less than ten years of age to have to travel up to ten li a day just to go to and from school. The plan was thereupon revised, raising the number of schools from 400 to 600, so that each school would serve an area of only sixteen square li. Five hundred of the primary schools would be three-year schools with eighty students each, while the remaining one hundred would each have four grades and 120 students. This would produce an estimated number of 16,500 lower primary graduates a year, of which some 10 percent were expected to continue on into higher primary school. To provide for this number adequately, eighteen schools on the higher primary level were thought to be necessary, ten regular and eight vocational, the latter further specified as five agricultural, two industrial, and one commercial schools. Each of these would be a four-year school with ninety students.[24]

To finance this system of schools, Chang Chien proposed a kind of local school tax levied on the landowners. The total cost of constructing the 600 lower primary and eighteen higher primary schools was estimated at 290,000 yuan (about 207,000 taels). This was to be covered by a levy of six fen (about U.S. $0.03 at the time) on each of the estimated five million mow (about 757,000 acres) of cultivated land in Nan-t'ung. In 1910, when this plan was drawn up by Chang Chien, seventy lower primary schools had already been established by various gentry members of Nan-t'ung under Chang Chien's leadership. The remaining 530 schools were to be in existence by the end of 1914.[25] Unfortunately this carefully worked-out scheme of financing the schools was never put into effect. Instead, the schools continued to be supported by individual contributions. Chang Chien's plan is significant nevertheless because it provided a blueprint for a locally supported school system.

With support for the school system coming only from private sources, Chang Chien's goal of universal education for Nan-t'ung never reached the level he envisaged. Still, the number of lower primary schools grew impressively during his lifetime. From seventy such schools in 1910, the figure rose to 357 by 1926.[26] One of the chief reasons Nan-t'ung came to be known as a model district was its extensive school system, which provided a concrete illustration of what conceivably could have become the pattern of universal education for all of China.

It should not be assumed, however, that all of Chang Chien's projects in the field of education followed a set plan and schedule. While he was busy establishing the normal school and planning for the primary schools, he founded an apprentice school for the children of his workmen, and a sericulture and silk-weaving training school for the women of his district. These and other projects, including the aforementioned normal schools and several of the earliest primary schools, were all financed out of Chang Chien's own share of the profits of the Dah Sun Cotton Mill. These exhausted his available funds, so that when the need for a middle school arose in 1906, Chang Chien was unable to finance it privately. Consequently he appealed to the provincial government to permit the establishment of a consolidated middle school at Nan-t'ung to serve the needs of the four adjoining communities of Nan-t'ung, Hai-men, Ju-kao, and T'ai-hsing. These communities were to pay for the construction of the school in the following proportions: five tenths from Nan-t'ung, two tenths each from Ju-kao and T'ai-hsing, and one tenth from Hai-men. He further proposed that the provincial authorities allocate annually one tenth of the amount in excess of 40,000 taels collected on a certain local cloth tax to be the operating fund of the school.[27] This Nan-t'ung Five-district Middle School opened its doors in June, 1908.[28] After 1911 the provincial government assumed complete control of the school, and its name was changed to Kiangsu Provincial Middle School No. 7.[29]

Before the consolidated middle school had gotten past the planning stage, the first step toward what eventually was to become Nan-t'ung University was laid in 1906. In that year courses on improved methods of farming were added to the curriculum of the normal school. Three years later courses in sericulture were added. In 1910 these courses received independent existence as the Combined Agricultural School. After the republic came into being, it was reorganized into the Combined Class-A and Class-B Agricultural School. In 1912 Chang Chien founded a textile school and a medical school. The textile school was another pioneering venture, as there were only two schools of its kind in the country at the time.[30] Located near Dah Sun in T'ang-chia-cha, the school provided its students with the benefit of actual experience in one of the most successful cotton mills in the country. Many graduates of the school were later prominent in China's cotton-textile industry. The medical school had separate departments for Chinese and Western medicine. In 1915 the textile school acquired the status of a college. A year later the agricultural school gained similar status, followed by the medical school in 1918.[31] The logical next step would be to combine the three colleges into a university, and in 1920 the three did indeed join to form Nan-t'ung University.[32] As endowment for the university Chang Chien bought for 500,000 yuan (about 350,000 taels) a substantial tract of land from the Hua Ch'eng Land Reclamation Company, one of many such enterprises founded along the coast of northern Kiangsu as a result of Chang Chien's influence.[33] He became the first head of Nan-t'ung University, to be followed after his death in 1926 by his son, Chang Hsiao-jo.[34]

In the field of adult vocational education, mention has already been made of the Sericulture Training School. In 1919 Chang Chien opened a school for Chinese musicians as a part of his project to support in Nan-t'ung two repertory theaters giving regular performances of Chinese opera. Though periodically closed whenever the theaters were forced to suspend operations, the school lasted until 1925.[35] Continued efforts on his part to better the means of livelihood of the girls in his area prompted him to add courses in embroidery and hairnet-making to the sericulture course already in being.[36] The embroidery classes began as a part of the girls' normal school curriculum in 1914. The famous embroiderer, Yü Shen Shou, was persuaded by Chang Chien to come to Nan-t'ung to take charge of the course. Two years later the course was detached from the normal school and made into a separate training school. It flourished until Mrs. Yü's death in 1921. Chang Chien devoted a great deal of personal interest to the Embroidery School, and it was generally regarded as one of his pet projects.[37]

Even taking into account the fact that not all of the primary schools were directly financed by Chang Chien, the school system of Nan-t'ung must still be considered one of the largest privately controlled systems in the country. Except for the middle school, Chang Chien had complete control of all Nan-t'ung schools until 1926. The higher educational authorities in the province generally deferred to him out of regard for his great prestige and his influence as head of the Provincial Education Association. His position in Nan-t'ung can be seen in his handling of the local manifestations of the students' unrest prevalent throughout much of China during the years of 1919 through 1925.

In 1919 the two local schools most affected by the wave of student agitation were the textile school and the Provincial Middle School, with the normal school affected to some extent. Chang Chien promptly suspended the textile school, but since the middle school was beyond his control, he wrote to the Provincial Education Bureau urging it to act promptly.[38] The bureau first agreed to replace the principal of the middle school with another man, then reversed its decision. Meanwhile the principal yielded to student pressure and promised to grant salary increases to the teachers and greater freedom to the students. These concessions came as students clashed with the local police, causing minor damages. Chang Chien immediately wired the bureau, strongly berating it for its indecisive action and almost insisting that the bureau go through with the removal of the principal. The bureau apparently complied, and things quieted down temporarily.[39] During the following year a group of students bicycled into an athletic field reserved for the use of girl students. When they were ordered off the field, the group, now increased to several hundred strong, invaded the premise of the primary school attached to the girls' normal school. Although no damages were incurred, Chang Chien ordered the prompt dismissal of the ring leaders.[40]

Student agitation, however, was by no means over. In his New Year's Day Speech to the assembled students of Nan-t'ung in 1923, Chang Chien found it necessary to appeal to their sense of fair play and patriotism and to remind them that quiet and solitude were essential to study and that they should be prepared to undergo hardships.[41] These well-meaning words apparently were not altogether effective, for two years later he announced the policy of expelling all students engaged in political agitation and of lengthening class hours and course preparations.[42] These episodes show us how thoroughly the schools of Nan-t'ung were under Chang Chien's control. His lack of complete success in keeping the students in line merely points up the latent strength among the new generation of politically aroused students.

Chang Chien's desire to foster the growth of Nan-t'ung's schools remained unabated throughout his life. He was past seventy years of age and in semiretirement in 1924 when news reached him of the decision of the United States to return the remainder of the Boxer Indemnity Fund to China for educational purposes. To Chang Chien this represented a chance to put Nan-t'ung University on a sound financial basis. He applied to the American Government for 20 to 30 percent of the fund, amounting to about five million yuan (about 3.6 million taels), to be used to purchase half a million mow of land (about 76,000 acres), which would serve as the endowed land of Nan-t'ung University. After development this land would provide enough income to make enlargements and improvements of the various schools in the university possible. He cited the following reasons why Nan-t'ung should be favored over other localities: (1) freedom from government and official interference; (2) record of prior achievements; (3) the practicality of the project; (4) Nan-t'ung's superior location in regard to transportation and communication; and (5) the special contributions which could be made by the agriculture school and the textile school.[43] Even though Chang Chien was unsuccessful in this venture, it amply demonstrated his lifelong concern for education in his own district.

Descriptions of Nan-t'ung Schools

What were the Nan-t'ung schools like? How did they compare with similar schools elsewhere in Kiangsu and in China? Details of Nan-t'ung schools are not readily available, but by piecing together information contained in Chang Chien's own writings and those in accounts of visitors to Nan-t'ung, some idea of the schools can be gained. The following are details on three of the schools as they were up to 1917.

Nan-t'ung Normal School.[44] Situated south of Nan-t'ung city, this school was originally modeled after Japanese normal schools in administration and procedure. It had an administrative and teaching staff of thirty, while its enrollment after the first few years fluctuated between 200 and 285. The students ranged from sixteen to thirty years of age. The school was divided into six grades: four regular grades, one preparatory grade, and one practicing grade. All the students, some of whom came from as far as Kansu, Yünnan, and Kweichou, lived in the dormitories. Tuition and room were free, while the students originally paid for the meals supplied by the school. This rule was later changed and students were given facilities to prepare their own meals. The physical plant consisted of several buildings with a total of 400 rooms, including dormitory and classrooms, and three athletic fields. The annual expenditure, including the expenditure of the attached primary school, exceeded 30,000 yuan (about 21,000 taels), one third of which was provided by Kiangsu Province.[45] From its inception in 1903 to 1917, the school graduated 556 students, averaging just under fifty per year. For the first two years of the school's existence the graduates were granted a unique subsidy of ten to thirty yuan monthly, in order to attract worthy students away from the traditional studies in preparation for the examination system. This practice was stopped when the examination system was abolished.[46]

Girls' Normal School.[47] Located in Nan-t'ung city, this was a smaller counterpart of the normal school for men. An administration and teaching staff of twenty members served the needs of seventy students, divided into four grades. The students ranged in age from sixteen to twenty-four, with about half of them boarding in the school. Tuition was free. The school had 200 rooms and two athletic fields. The annual expenditure was around 6,000 yuan (about 4,300 taels), with Nan-t'ung providing two thirds of this amount.

Primary schools.[48] As there were more than 300 primary schools in Nan-t'ung by 1917, a great deal of variation existed among them as to the number of students, the physical facilities, etc. The oldest and best primary school was the one attached to the normal school. It had a staff of eleven teachers and had 233 students, divided into six classes. The students varied in ages from seven to twenty, and were almost equally divided between boarding and day students. The school had sixty-six classrooms, but its dormitory facilities for many years consisted of converted houses and temples. Its expenditure was included in that of the normal school.

These descriptions do not indicate how the educational facilities in Nan-t'ung compared with those of other cities in Kiangsu and with those of the rest of the country. How far had modern education advanced in China by the time the Ch'ing dynasty was replaced by the republic? Both quantitatively and qualitatively speaking, where did the Nan-t'ung schools stand in relation to the over-all picture?

Without dwelling over the oft-repeated statement that statistics in China are most uneven in coverage and not always reliable, especially for the years prior to the 1930s, we need only to note that, fortunately for the quarter century under our consideration (1902–26), some records do exist. Especially detailed are the statistics on the over-all state of Chinese education compiled by the Ministry of Education in Peking from 1912 to 1917. As this period covers the crucial years immediately after the overthrow of the monarchy and falls nearly in the middle of the quarter century we are interested in, it will serve as a basis for answers to the questions we have raised.

Table 2 shows the number of schools from mid-1912 to mid-1917.

Taking these five years as a whole, some indication of the nature and trend of educational progress in China can be seen. First of all, it is apparent that the schools were largely public-supported, with the privately supported schools amounting to considerably less than one third of the total number of any of the six classifications of schools listed. Secondly, these five years followed a generally rising trend in the number of schools, as might be expected, but there was a noticeable decline after 1914, with the normal schools reaching their peak earlier in 1913–14. This over-all drop might reasonably be attributed to the increase of domestic political instability after 1914. Thirdly, the figures show that the differences in the number of schools among the various levels were quite great, the low number of agricultural and industrial schools being

Table 2

NUMBER OF SCHOOLS IN CHINA AND KIANGSU[49]

Type of Schools	*Location — Kind*		*Years* 1912–13[a]	1913–14	1914–15	1915–16	1916–17
Lower Primary	China:	Private	22,660	29,425	33,840	35,156	33,701
		Total[b]	78,679	98,782	111,143	118,952	111,908
	Kiangsu:	Private	848	801	820	843	883
		Total	4,740	4,968	5,378	5,845	6,169
Higher Primary	China:	Private	1,727	1,904	2,232	1,897	1,614
		Total	6,554	7,363	8,623	7,862	6,442
	Kiangsu:	Private	143	128	147	126	131
		Total	467	433	446	458	455
Middle	China:	Private	54	46	64	59	51
		Total	373	406	452	444	350
	Kiangsu:	Private	13	6	9	11	11
		Total	25	19	19	23	24
Normal	China:	Private	22	44	21	13	9
		Total	253	314	231	211	195
	Kiangsu:	Private	3	3	2	2	2
		Total	19	25	21	19	18
Agricultural	China:	Private	3	5	4	2	2
		Total	39	42	41	42	41
	Kiangsu:	Private	1	2	1	1	1
		Total	6	7	6	6	6
Technical	China:	Private	3	3	3	6	2
		Total	22	20	22	30	21
	Kiangsu:	Private	1	1	—	—	—
		Total	3	3	2	2	2

[a]The school years from August of the first year to July of the following year.
[b]The total figures include three classifications of schools: government (nationally supported), official (locally supported), and private.

especially noticeable. As for a comparison of the figures of China as a whole to those of Kiangsu Province, their ratio shows a fairly close correlation. The one exception is found in the growth of lower primary schools, where Kiangsu continued in 1915–16, while the rest of the country declined. These points aside, the most important fact which these figures reveal is that quantitatively

China as a whole had made noticeable progress in the growth of modern education by 1912 and generally continued to do so through 1917. The progress of Nan-t'ung must be taken in conjunction with that of the rest of China for it to be properly judged.

For a comparison of Nan-t'ung with other localities in Kiangsu, the following nine localities have been chosen: Nanking, Shanghai, Soochow, Wusih, K'un-shan, Hai-men, Ju-kao, Ch'ung-ming, and T'ai-hsing. Nanking, Shanghai, Soochow, and Wusih were and are leading centers south of the Yangtze River. They are contrasted with Nan-t'ung and the four localities around Nan-t'ung: Hai-men, Ju-kao, Ch'ung-ming, and T'ai-hsing. K'un-shan, located between Shanghai and Soochow, is included as contrast to T'ai-hsing, smallest of the five localities north of the Yangtze River.

Table 3 gives the figures of schools for the ten Kiangsu localities.

This breakdown does not deviate markedly from the national picture in the year-to-year growth and decline or in the marked drop in number of schools as we go from the lowest schools to the higher ones. The figures do suggest two points. First, the five localities on the north bank of Yangtze (including Ch'ung-ming) had a generally more noticeable rate of increase than that of those localities south of the Yangtze, especially in the lower primary schools. Secondly, even as Nan-t'ung came to rank about on a par with Wusih and Shanghai by 1917, both Hai-men and Ch'ung-ming had progressed to a point not far behind Soochow's position. The significance of this lies in the fact that both in population and natural resources none of the north-bank localities can be compared with Soochow and Shanghai.

Qualitative differences between Nan-t'ung schools and those of other cities in Kiangsu and elsewhere are even more difficult to establish conclusively. In the absence of complete information we can only mention a few things as suggestive. In the matter of staff members, number of classes, number of classrooms, hours of study, teaching method, and yearly expenditure, Nan-t'ung Normal School was comparable with other normal schools established prior to 1908 in Kiangsu, Chekiang, Hunan, and Fukien. The one outstanding feature of the school in Nan-t'ung was its library of 2,200 Chinese and Western-language books, with which other normal schools, having collections ranging from 1,420 books down to a low of 50 books, could not begin to compare. As the first

Table 3

TOTAL NUMBER OF SCHOOLS IN SELECTED KIANGSU LOCALITIES[50]

Localities	*Lower Primary*				*Higher Primary*			
	1913–14	1914–15	1915–16	1916–17	1913–14	1914–15	1915–16	1916–17
Nanking	82	83	99	98	7	11	9	9
Shanghai[a]	193	195	181	206	36	53	45	44
Soochow	203	299[b]	217	213	21	23	22	20
Wusih	225	226	238	266	22	21	19	18
K'un-shan	85	93	100	108	4	5	5	5
NAN-T'UNG	195	239	263	271	10	13	14	13
Hai-men	143	164	172	180	6	8	7	8
Ju-kao	118	129	147	164	14	12	11	11
Ch'ung-ming	146	156	156	180	10	14	15	14
T'ai-hsing	62	90	105	108	5	7	7	6

Localities	*Middle*				*Normal*			
	1913–14	1914–15	1915–16	1916–17	1913–14	1914–15	1915–16	1916–17
Nanking	...	...	...	1	1	...	...	...
Shanghai[a]	5	5	5	6	1	...	1	1
Soochow	...	...	...	...	1	...	...	...
Wusih	2	2	2	1	3	1	1	1
K'un-shan	...	...	...	...	1	...	...	...
NAN-T'UNG	...	...	...	...	2	1[c]	1	1
Hai-men	...	1	1	1	1	...	...	...
Ju-kao	1	...	...	...	3	2	2	1
Ch'ung-ming	...	...	1	1	3	...	...	...
T'ai-hsing	...	...	...	...	1	...	...	...

[a]It is not clear whether these figures include schools in the foreign concessions or not. The latter possibility seems more likely.

[b]This may have been a typographical error, as the number seems excessive, compared to those of the previous and the succeeding years.

[c]There seems to be a discrepancy here. Records show clearly that both normal schools in Nan-t'ung were in existence by 1914, and continued to operate thereafter.

normal school in China, it had graduated 556 students by 1917. This figure was topped only by Hunan Provincial Normal School No. 1, which graduated 741, and Fukien Provincial Normal School No. 1 with 660. Likewise, Nan-t'ung Girls' Normal School compared favorably with the girls'normal schools of Kiangsu, Chekiang, and Hunan in staff members, classes, classrooms, and teaching methods, but its total number of graduates by 1917 was only seventeen, far below Kiangsu Girls' Normal School No. 1 with fifty-two. Its annual expenditure of 5,940 yuan (about 4,240 taels) was dwarfed by the 33,000 yuan and 29,000 yuan spent by Kiangsu Girls' Normal School No. 1 and Chekiang Provincial Girls' Normal School respectively. Comparing the primary school attached to the Nan-t'ung Normal School with similar primary schools attached to normal schools in other provinces, figures on staff members, number of graduates, number of classrooms, and teaching methods were nearly the same. To Nan-t'ung's credit was its library of 1,900 books, but it had only seven classes to the others' ten to thirteen. All of its students put in a minimum of twenty-nine hours of classwork, as compared to the twenty-three hours minimum required from the youngest classes of the primary schools attached to the Chekiang Normal School No. 1 and Kwangtung Normal School No. 2.[51]

It seems clear that by the time of the republican era Nan-t'ung's schools no longer stood out as noticeably different, either quantitatively or qualitatively, from those of the rest of the country. Nan-t'ung's high reputation was based on the fact that its normal schools, agriculture schools, textile school, and its system of primary schools, had all broken new ground when they were first established. The first three types of schools remained prime examples in their own fields. Another striking fact was that the whole system remained under the over-all control of one individual. Compared to the province of Kiangsu as a whole, Chang Chien's achievements can best be appreciated when we are reminded that it was quite an achievement for the relatively backward areas north of the Yangtze River just to keep pace with the more prosperous centers such as Shanghai, Soochow, and Wusih.

Educational Activities Outside Nan-t'ung

Chang Chien showed himself no less concerned with educational matters outside his own district. In general, however, he enjoyed much less success outside Nan-t'ung. Among his efforts was the plan of a complete school system, which he drew up for Yang-chou, Kiangsu, in 1906.[52] This plan provided for the establishment of primary, middle, and normal schools. That same year he organized the Merchant Marine School of Woosung.[53] In 1907, together with two colleagues, he completed the establishment of another school at Woosung. This was the Chung-kuo Kung-hsüeh, created for the express purpose of providing continued instruction for a score of students forced by circumstances to return from Japan.[54] Then in 1909, while he was in Nanking for the opening session of the Kiangsu Provincial Assembly, he accepted the position of the director of the Kiang-ning Combined Commercial School.[55] In 1914 he converted the then unused Provincial Assembly Hall in Nanking into the temporary quarters of the School of Hydraulic Engineering, which he had established. This school remained one of his close concerns until it was merged with the National Southeastern University and others to form the National Central University in 1927.[56]

These concrete achievements in Kiangsu contrasted sharply with the barrenness of his role as an educator on the national level, where he had no official status and could only rely on his prestige as an individual scholar and educator. His first attempt to advise the government in educational affairs actually preceded his active educational career on the local level. In the lengthy document entitled *Reasoned Discussion on Reforms*, which he submitted in 1901, he made the following suggestions on education:

1. Establishment of a public education system, starting with primary education and then proceeding upwards.
2. Changing the examination system to conform to the new education system.
3. Introduction of the teaching of drawing and cartography in primary schools.
4. Establishment of provincial translation bureaus.
5. Creation of a national ministry of education.
6. Rewarding graduates of the new system by granting them the traditional titles along with their prestige and privileges.[57]

These suggestions probably had some influence upon the thinking of Liu K'un-i, who, together with Yüan Shih-k'ai, was instrumental in the eventual abolition of the civil service examination system in 1905. The connection between Chang Chien's petition of 1913 advocating the creation of a national library and a national museum, with the later founding of national libraries and museums in China, is more difficult to establish.[58]

Within Kiangsu his influence was more substantial. His advice was sought and his ideas were listened to. Certain measures which he proposed to Governor-general Chou Fu in 1906, including the creation of a provincial educational association and the conversion of the space occupied by the examination stalls in Nanking into a market place, were carried out.[59] In 1907, at the request of Tuan-fang, the new governor-general of Liang-Kiang, he drew up in detail a plan for the establishment of a university to be called Nan-yang Ta-hsüeh (University of the South).[60] This institution failed to materialize, but the fact that he was asked to provide a plan for it indicated his high reputation among the educators of Kiangsu. The most important role that he assumed in the educational affairs of Kiangsu, however, was his position in the Provincial Educational Association.

The growth of provincial societies for the promotion of modern education was a by-product of the abolition of the examination system and the reorganization of the educational administration, both of which took place in 1905. The Kiangsu Educational Society (Chiang-su Hsüeh-hui) was founded on Chang Chien's advice in 1906 and the members chose him as its first president. The following year the province was divided into two educational districts, each of which had its own commissioner of education, one in Nanking and one in Soochow. The educational society similarly divided into two branches, with Chang Chien staying on as the head of the Nanking branch. In 1909 this arbitrary division of the society was abolished, with the resultant change of its location to Shanghai and its name to the Central Educational Association of Kiangsu (Chiang-su Chiao-yü Tsung-hui). Once again Chang Chien was chosen to be the president. He resigned in 1911, stating his belief that a two-year term was enough for an officer and suggesting that someone in the Soochow educational district should be chosen for the position.[61] In 1913 the organization, now known as the Kiangsu Provincial Educational Association

(Chiang-su-sheng Chiao-yü-hui), once more elected him president. Thereafter he was reelected regularly for a number of years. While the association was located in Nanking and Shanghai prior to 1911, he played an active role in it, even though he was not able to attend all its meetings. Important matters were referred to him for decisions, while an executive officer carried on the daily duties of the association.[62] From 1913 on, however, his presidency became purely honorary, and there is no record of his ever having been present at any of the meetings. The actual leadership in the association passed into the hands of Huang Yen-p'ei and Shen En-fu, two educators who began their active careers under him.

Other honors which were bestowed upon Chang Chien in tribute to his achievements in education included his election in 1905 to the board of trustees of Aurora College (Chen-tan, a French Catholic school which became a university in 1917), his holding of a similar position with Futan University (an outgrowth of Aurora University), his election to the chairmanship of the board of trustees of the National Southeastern University, and the honorary presidency of the First Far Eastern Athletic Meet, held in Manila in 1921.[63] Generally speaking, he played a limited role in the affairs of these institutions.

Ideas on Education

In the course of tracing Chang Chien's career as an educator, we have already touched upon some of his ideas. Among these are his belief in the primacy of teacher training, his belief in the importance of primary education over other forms of education, and his advocacy of vocational training. It now remains for us to examine further these and some of his other ideas on education.

Chang Chien was an advocate of universal education. We have seen his concern for setting up his primary school system in such a way that all the school-age children within a given area would have an opportunity to attend school. He preferred the system to be a voluntary one, but recognized that there would be areas where a voluntary system would not be workable. In such cases, he was not opposed to a compulsory system.[64] In line with his belief that education was the fundamental prerequisite to a new and revitalized China, he regarded universal education as the basis for both local self-government and a constitutional system of government on the national level.[65] He attributed the rapid advancement of the West and of Japan to their systems of universal education.[66]

Chang Chien emphasized utility in education and advocated the teaching of science and technology. He cautioned his students on numerous occasions against retreating into ivory towers. He emphasized the utilitarian aspect of modern education, saying that knowledge was to be applied rather than pursued for its own sake. Students should keep abreast of the latest developments at home and abroad so that they could take stock of the larger situation and preserve a proper balance between learning and living.[67] He had no doubt that the pursuit of science and mastery of technology would lead to enormous benefits.[68] He believed that the traditional Chinese tendency to shun exactitude had to be overcome and be replaced by a proper regard for scientific precision.[69]

Against these evidences of a progressive outlook should be balanced certain of his more traditional beliefs. On a number of occasions he spoke up in favor of Chinese classical writing as an indispensable component of the school curriculum. At the outset of his efforts to establish Nan-t'ung Normal School he defended classical writing against those who wanted it de-emphasized, extolling its clarity and exactness.[70] In 1907 he added a special section to the curriculum of the middle school for the mastery of classical Chinese, especially as a tool of communication.[71] Ten years later he was to reiterate his belief, saying at an interview, "Chinese must be the basis of any curriculum. A school which does not emphasize the study of Chinese has no hope of achieving a balanced curriculum, even if its science courses are adequate."[72] On this point he never wavered.

Even more fundamental than his belief in the importance of classical Chinese, however, was his firm conviction that the essence of Confucian teachings must be the moving spirit of all Chinese education. One of his earliest writings on education was an essay entitled "On the Propriety of Having School Regulations Follow Confucian Precepts," in which he ingeniously traced the origin of the modern school system to one section of the *Li Chi*.

> Chinese school regulations should follow the Chou classics. In the *Li Chi*, "Weng Wang Shih Tzu" and "Wang Chih" both discuss in detail national education and the art of teaching.... The conclusions of "Hsüeh Chi" are suitable for the training of teachers in normal

schools. As for universal education and the ages at which different subjects can be taught, we should be familiar with that part of "Hsüeh Chi" which states: "At six, teach them numbers, directions, and names. At seven, boys and girls should not sit and eat at the same table. At eight, begin to teach them to defer to elders when entering and leaving a house or when approaching a table at mealtime. At nine, teach them arithmetics. At ten, send them out to live away from home and learn bookkeeping . . . and proper etiquette. At thirteen, let them study poetry and music. . . . At twenty, when they become adults, let them begin the study of *Li Chi*."

The "Hsüeh Chi" says "a *shu* [village school] is found among families." The *shu* of twenty-five families was therefore equivalent to the elementary school of a *lü* [village of twenty-five families]. Children between the ages of six to nine generally attented a *shu*. The text of "Hsüeh Chi" further states that ten-year-old girls did not attend school, by which we know that up to nine years of age they still did so. If a *shu* is a school which taught the children of twenty-five families, was it not comparable to the modern lower primary school?

It ["Hsüeh Chi"] says "a *hsiang* [a higher school] is found in a *tang* [village of five hundred families]." The students of a *hsiang* were from ten to thirteen years of age, including those boys who advanced from a *lü* elementary school. The *hsiang* would be equivalent to the modern higher primary school.

It says "a *hsü* [a still higher school] is found in a *chou* [territory of 2,500 families]." Those attending a *hsü* were from thirteen to nineteen years of age, including the graduates of a *hsiang*. Thus a *hsü* would be equivalent to the modern middle and higher schools.

It says further that "a *hsüeh* [the most advanced school] is found in a country." This would be the kind of school attended by students of twenty years of age and older. Its emphasis on serving the offspring of princes, nobles, and officials, as well as the best products of the *hsü*, makes it comparable to the *Ching-shih Ta-hsüeh* [Imperial University] of today."[73]

Chang Chien went on in the same essay to argue that such essential components of the modern curriculum as mathematics, geography, and biology were no more than elaborations of what Confucius called numbers (*shu*), directions (*fang*), and names (*ming*). He concluded by exclaiming, "How can the talents of the youths of today be considered superior to those of the seventy-two [of

Confucius' top disciples], and the teaching method of a primary school teacher superior to that of Confucius himself?"[74] This was written in 1903. Fifteen years later he was to promote a society called the Association for Honoring Confucius, which advocated restoring the teaching of Confucian classics in primary schools.[75]

As a direct result of his Confucian training, he strenuously opposed coeducation above the primary schools. Although he was the first Chinese to open a girls' normal school and to establish various vocational training schools for girls, he thought it " 'inconvenient' that boys and girls should be educated together after the age of ten years."[76] The benefits of coeducation seemed to him illusory. He argued that the segregation of sexes should not be regarded as relegating woman to a lower status.[77] Later as chairman of the board of trustees of the National Southeastern University, he could not be dissuaded from his opposition to the efforts of P. W. Kuo, the president of the university, to introduce coeducation into that institution. The scheme was eventually carried out over his opposition.[78]

Finally, we should note his belief in the importance of maintaining rigid discipline in the teacher-student relationship. In this respect he was fond of the practice of backing up his classical quotations by mentioning the stand taken by Western thinkers such as Pythagoras, Carlyle, Burke, and William James against lax discipline.[79] Another of his favorite devices was to compare a school with an army.

> An army cannot relax responsibility. A school cannot relax responsibility. This is the custom of all the republics in the world today. If an army relaxes responsibility, then it cannot be led by a general. If a school relaxes responsibility, then it cannot be taught by a teacher. An army unled would meet certain defeat. A school without teaching is bound to collapse. The ills of a nation start nowhere else. The "Hsüeh Chi" states: "Among the ways of conducting a school, the most difficult is in achieving strict discipline." Strict discipline leads to the proper method [of dealing with other problems], and this in turn causes people to respect education. Nowadays in the schools of Europe and America, aside from teaching and administration, training and obedience are still stressed. The educators of the world have admitted the impossibility of following a policy of "no-control" in education. That school discipline must be

strict is recognized both here and abroad. Without it there can be no teaching, no education.[80]

The conviction that discipline is all-important in education was a central theme of Chang Chien's ideas. He had on more than one occasion expressed this view. On May 4, 1919, students in Peking demonstrated against China's signing of the Versailles Treaty because of the provision turning former German concessions in Shantung over to Japan. The government made a half-hearted attempt to suppress the movement, whereupon it spread to other classes and became nationwide. This turn of events prompted Chang Chien to write an open letter entitled "Warning to the Students of the Entire Nation" in 1919, in which he reiterated the necessity for discipline in schools and called upon the students to divert their energies to more useful channels than political agitation.[81]

Taking Chang Chien's ideas as a whole, it must be admitted that most of them cannot properly be called *educational* ideas. They are rather his ideas and beliefs as they applied to education.

Chang Chien as an Educator

Because of his own regard for the importance of education, and his repeated assertions that China was to be saved mainly by reforming her educational system, we have dwelt at some length on the career and the ideas of Chang Chien as an educator. Now we must pose the question: What kind of educator was he, and how did his educational efforts affect China as a whole?

Chang Chien's qualification as an educator lay chiefly in his thorough classical training. In addition he was at one time or another in charge of three old-style academies: the Hsüan-ch'ing Academy of Kan-yü, Kiangsu, in 1888; the Yin-chou Academy of Ch'ung-ming in 1893; and the Wen-cheng Academy of Nanking in 1895. Until 1901 he remained in charge of the Wen-cheng Academy, where English and mathematics were taught along with Chinese classics. In this academy he took an active role in administration and teaching. Several of his students later became his associates and were instrumental in helping him to carry out some of his numerous projects.[82] However, he had almost no contact with modern education of the Western type, the sole exception being his 1903 trip to Japan, where he visited primary schools, middle schools, normal and vocational schools, as well as many factories and workshops. He was especially impressed with Japanese school administration. We have already noted how he modeled the Nan-t'ung Normal School closely after normal schools in Japan.[83]

As an educator Chang Chien differed from men like Chang Po-hsi, who set up a complete system of school administration with the government centralizing all controls, and Sheng Hsüan-huai, who was responsible for the founding of schools on the college level. These men worked from the top down, while Chang Chien, always following the practical course, established a normal school in order to supply teachers for the primary schools, and set up vocational schools to teach new trades. His plan for a network of primary schools was the prototype of a system toward the establishment of universal education and compulsory education.

Although Chang Chien's accomplishments were largely confined to the area centering on Nan-t'ung, they were of more than local significance. He, as one of the leading scholars in Kiangsu, was highly respected as an educator, and his ideas on education never failed to receive a hearing. His work with vocational schools, for example, served as a model for the entire country. In the vocational education movement throughout the 1920s and 1930s, Huang Yen-p'ei, one of Chang Chien's associates in provincial educational affairs, played a leading role.

Chang Chien's interest in education extended throughout the period of 1902 to 1926. The Revolution of 1911 marked no noticeable break in his career as an educator. In the meantime an entire new generation of educators, men like Ts'ai Yüan-p'ei, Hu Shih, Chang Po-ling, and others, came upon the scene. These men were Western-trained, schooled in the philosophies and methodologies of Europe and America, and full of new ideas which they were eager to put into practice. These men eventually took over the burden of completing the task of weaning Chinese education away from its traditional mold. Chang Chien, however, deserves a place among the ranks of the handful of men who marked the way for the growth of modern education in China. In his own time he was as great a departure from the conventional as any of his successors.

CHAPTER SIX

Land Reclamation and Salt Reform

IN CHANG CHIEN'S mind land reclamation and salt reform originated as interrelated projects. Salt reform started out as no more than his efforts to cope with a specific problem which confronted the salters *(yen-hu)*, those inhabitants of the salt-producing coastal areas who for uncounted generations had been restricted by nature and law to the production of salt as their livelihood. At the same time the conversion of these same salt-producing areas into cultivated land would support many more people than they were capable of as salt fields. Although he initiated land reclamation before salt reform, he was fully aware of the close yet divergent relationship between the two.

The incompatability of land reclamation and salt production is comparable to the opposition of ice and hot coal. Salt production requires salinity in the soil; land reclamation requires the lack of salinity. Salt production calls for the growth of reeds to be used for fuel; land reclamation means replacing reeds with crops. Salt production must have the constant inflow of tides, precisely what land reclamation can not abide. Since this is so, why have salt production and land reclamation always gone hand in hand up to the very present? It is because land reclamation is a gradual process, while salt production cannot be eliminated all at once.

Land bordering the sea where tides do not penetrate will have salt-free soil. Land bordering the sea where tides occasionally penetrate will have abundant growth of reeds. However, those places where tides penetrate repeatedly will need the protection of dykes and the planting of grass to dispel salinity. Only on salt-free and grass-covered land can land reclamation be undertaken. That is why land reclamation is a gradual process.

As for salt production, we must consider the livelihood of the salters, as well as the investment of the merchants. On land belonging to the commercial salt producers, the removal of stoves and kettles must take their set values into account and abide by legal procedures. And if land reclamation should fail, we must still rely on salt production. That is why salt production can not be eliminated all at once.[1]

Here Chang Chien was referring to the situation in Huai-nan, that section of the Kiangsu seacoast south of the former outlet of the Huai River, which includes part of Nan-t'ung district. For centuries the stretch of uncultivated land along the seacoast had been given over to the production of salt. Due to natural factors, however, salt production by the traditional method had become increasingly unprofitable in Huai-nan. As a result the salters were in dire straits. One solution to their dilemma would be the introduction of improved methods of producing salt, which would require new techniques and large sums of money for capitalization, both beyond the capabilities of individual salters. The conversion of salt fields into cultivated land, on the other hand, would be a partial solution to the problem. As a matter of fact, some salters had turned to cultivation of a portion of the land as a secondary source of income. This was, however, an illegal activity. Decrees issued in the time of the T'ung-chih Emperor, designed to protect the source of salt, strictly forbade the conversion of salt fields into cultivated land. By the end of the nineteenth century, however, human necessities were again proving to be more powerful than legal restrictions.

To Chang Chien land reclamation did not merely represent a partial solution to the salters' problem. He foresaw the unlimited potentialities which lay in the eventual conversion of the whole vast region of Huai-nan into arable land. A whole new area would then be opened to provide livelihood for many more people than the comparatively small number of salters then found in the area. The expected influx of farmers from nearby districts in Kiangsu would relieve directly the overcrowded conditions in Nan-t'ung, Hai-men, Ju-kao, and districts to the north. The new land would also increase substantially Kiangsu's total agricultural production, especially cotton.[2]

Chang Chien had been aware of the abundant possibilities of land reclamation, especially as it applied to Nan-t'ung, as early as 1895. At that time the Sino-Japanese War was going badly for China. To guard against the possibility of Japanese efforts to extend the area of conflict to the Yangtze region, Governor-general Chang Chih-tung asked him to raise and train a local defense corps for Nan-t'ung. The war ended not long after this project had begun and it was terminated forthwith. During the short duration of the project, however, the local defense corp had held a number of drill sessions in the open coastal areas straddling the boundary line between Nan-t'ung and Hai-men. It was then that the realization of just how much land was uncultivated first struck Chang Chien. For although he had lived nearly all his life in Nan-t'ung, he had had little opportunity to become acquainted with the comparatively sparsely populated coastal areas, lying some three days' distance on foot from the city of Nan-t'ung.[3]

For the time being, however, he was not in a position to do anything about this discovery. Until late in 1899 he was totally occupied with the task of establishing the Dah Sun Cotton Mill. By 1900 he had succeeded in putting Dah Sun on a relatively stable basis. He turned his attention at once to the land reclamation problem.

The seacoast of Nan-t'ung was typical of the Huai-nan region. The land there was geologically new, created in the most recent millenium from the accumulation of alluvial soil deposited by the Yangtze and the Yellow rivers. During this time a gradual recession of the level of the sea had contributed to the process by converting a wide strip of the shallow off-shore floor of the sea into dry land. This land, however, was still very much under the influence of tidal fluctuations. Numerous shallow streams bisected the coastal area, allowing the sea water to flow in and out with the changes of the tide. The soil had a porous structure, particularly suited to the growth of cotton. Its high degree of salinity, however, permitted only the growth of reeds, which were used by the salters as fuel in the boiling of brine.[4] Years later Chang Chien was to recall the scene presented by the Kiangsu coast prior to the introduction of land reclamation in these words:

> I stood on an isolated dyke and looked toward the southeast. It was a time when the strong northeast wind was at its height, and the tide was striking against the base of the dyke. There was water wherever I looked. The spray of the waves came up against the dyke here and there, causing an uneven erosion of the soil. In the worst places the farmers had tried to check it with logs.

The land inside the dyke was only partially cultivated, with cabbages interspersed with reeds. I toured the seashore in a cart at a time when the tide was low and the wind had died down. I saw flocks of wild geese flying by and crying overhead. Deers and rabbits darted out suddenly in front of my cart. Throughout the entire day I did not meet a single soul. Yet on summer nights the lights of people out catching land crabs were as numerous as stars in the sky.[5]

This area traditionally had been the salters' domain. Without removing the high salinity of the soil the land was not in a condition to be cultivated. What Chang Chien proposed to do was to form a company, so that steps to turn the land into productive fields could be undertaken. He envisioned the construction of a series of dykes and sluice gates, which would keep the seawater out and provide proper drainage for the acrerage. The fields were to be planted first with reeds and salt-resistant grass similar to the type growing wild in the area. Then in the course of a few years, the exclusion of seawater and the growth of reeds and grasses would reduce salinity in the soil to the point that cotton and wheat could be grown.[6]

Establishment of T'ung Hai

From the outset Chang Chien had the staunch support of Governor-general Liu K'un-i. Under Governor-general Liu's guidance he drafted a memorial to the Court in 1900, requesting permission to develop the land along the seacoast of Nan-t'ung and Hai-men. This was submitted in the name of Governor-general Liu and received imperial approval.[7] Then Chang Chien persuaded the governor-general to assign three young graduates of the provincial military academy at Nanking to the task of surveying the coastal areas of Nan-t'ung and Hai-men to determine their exact extent. The survey was completed by January, 1901.[8] The data obtained provided Chang Chien with the needed information to draw up a set of company regulations. He worked painstakingly on this document, revising the original draft seven times before he was satisfied.[9] The name of the company was to be T'ung Hai K'en-mu Kung-ssu, the Nan-t'ung Hai-men Reclamation Company. It was to cover an area of 120,000 mow (approximately 18,000 acres), divided into seven sections, laid out in an irregular shallow arc along the coastal area of Nan-t'ung and Hai-men. It was the aim of the company to foster crop cultivation by individual tenant farmers on reclaimed land. The initial capital was set at 220,000 taels, all to be solicited from private investors.[10] For fund raising Chang Chien had the able help of two of his close friends, T'ang Shou-ch'ien and Cheng Hsiao-hsü, among others. With their help and contributions he managed to raise 140,000 taels by August of 1901.[11] The comparative ease with which the amount was raised, in sharp contrast to the difficulties he encountered in soliciting funds for Dah Sun, was no doubt due primarily to the fact that investment of land traditionally had been regarded as the soundest form of investment. However, his success in establishing Dah Sun did no harm to his reputation as an entrepreneur.[12]

The backing of Governor-general Liu proved to be a real blessing. For what Chang Chien and others had regarded as "wasteland" turned out to be completely owned. Nearly every section of the land was under someone's title. The system of ownership along the salt-producing coast of Kiangsu was complex. Generally there were two types of ownerships. Under one, the salt merchant owned everything; the land, the stoves for boiling salt, and the reeds, so that the salters who worked for him were merely hired laborers. Under the other type of ownership, the salter owned the land and the stoves, but the merchant held an exclusive franchise for the production of salt in a given area.[13] It is the second type which caused T'ung Hai the most trouble, as both the displaced salter and the merchant had to be compensated. Naturally when the news was circulated that T'ung Hai wanted to buy a certain piece of land, its price would rise immediately. Not infrequently a stretch of unoccupied land with perhaps a single salt stove long out of use would be represented by its owner as a most valuable piece of property, with a flourishing salt business. A further complication arose out of the fact that two sections of land which Chang Chien wished to acquire for T'ung Hai belonged to two army garrisons. The effort to acquire all the needed land encountered innumerable delays. Only through the support of Governor-general Liu and the active aid of Li Fan-chih and Chang Yün-t'i, two members of the gentry of Hai-men, could the task make any headway. By late 1901 most of the needed land had been acquired and construction of dykes began.[14] The complex business of gaining titles to all the necessary land was not completely resolved until nine years later.

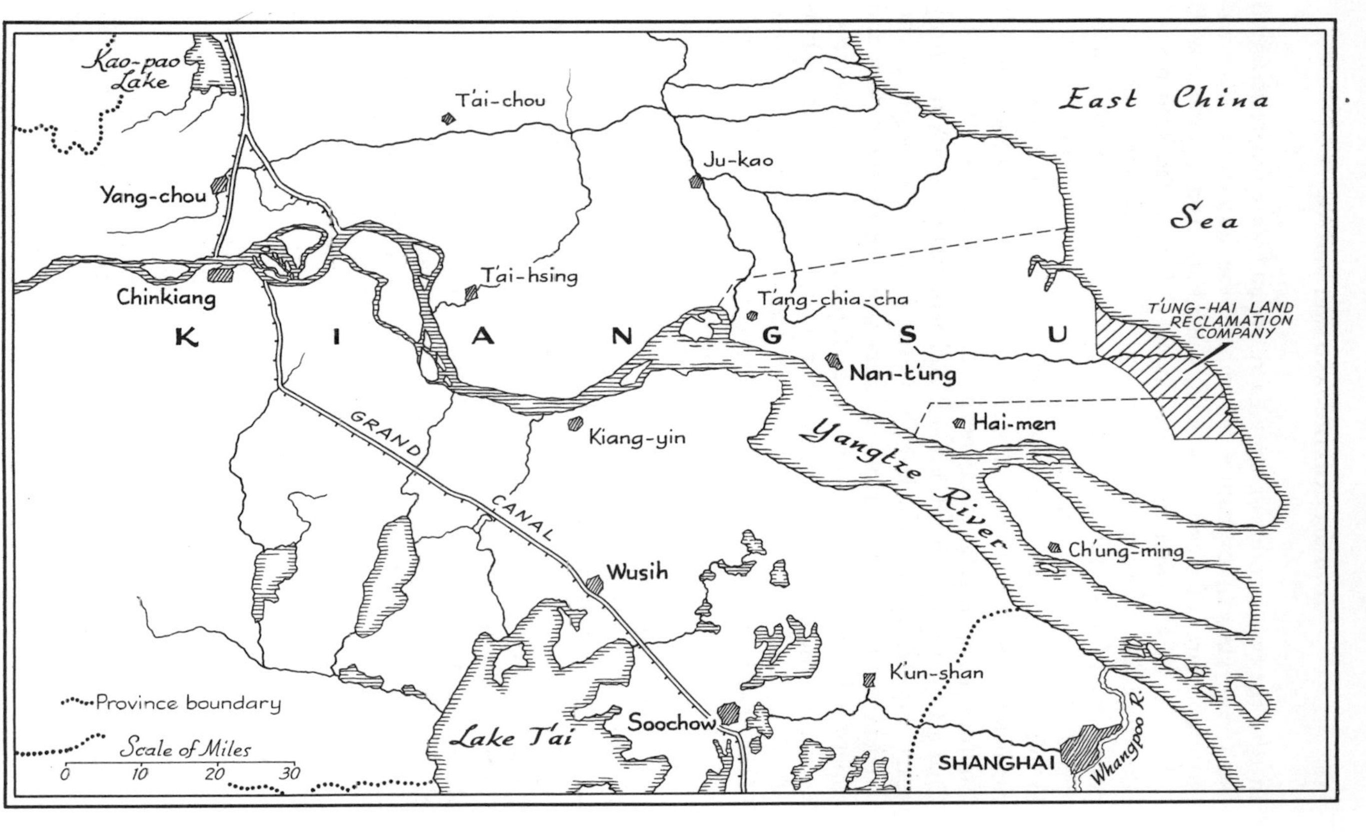

Map One Nan-t'ung and Lower Kiangsu

In 1910 the two sections of army garrison land were finally acquired by T'ung Hai, in exchange for which the authorities received fifty-two shares of company stocks, valued at 4,500 taels in total.[15]

Because of his other interests, Chang Chien needed someone to take over the active management of T'ung Hai. He found the perfect man for the job in the person of Chiang Tao-ming. Chiang was a former student of Chang Chien's at Wen-cheng Academy in Nanking and was later one of the three military-academy graduates who undertook the task of surveying the coastal areas.[16] Youthful in appearance and energetic by nature, he was to remain Chang Chien's right-hand man in land reclamation work for many years. He headed a small but dedicated group of managers, who lived in the field, directed the laborers working on the dykes, and supervised the settling of the tenant farmers, all at a pittance of what they could have earned in other lines of work.[17] The success of T'ung Hai was due in no small part to their efforts. Chang Chien was fully aware of the devoted contributions of these men and paid them proper tribute in his report to the stockholders of T'ung Hai in 1922.[18]

It was fortunate that the field managers were a hardy and resourceful group. When work began at the end of 1901, conditions were highly unfavorable. There were no roads or navigable waterways leading to the fields or among the various sections of reclaimed land. The necessary food and drinking water had to be supplied from outside the immediate area. The only available housing for the skeleton crew of field managers was the local temple of the sea god. This was converted into their temporary headquarters.[19] In spite of these operational difficulties, work on the dykes and fields proceeded as planned. Within three months two of the seven sections had been drained and provided with earthwork dykes on their seaward sides. In the spring of 1902 two more sections were ready. At the height of building activities, upwards of 7,000 laborers worked on the projects.[20] Chang Chien himself drew up the regulations governing the relationships between T'ung Hai and its tenants. The first tenant occupied his plot in late 1902.[21]

Just as the first phase of the establishment of T'ung Hai was reaching completion, calamity struck. On September 1, 1902, at the height of the typhoon season, severe winds battered at the newly completed dykes, breaking them in fifty places and causing the collapse of a total of 1,200 yards of dykes. The damages would have been even more extensive had not the field managers and laborers stayed on their jobs throughout the emergency and made on-the-spot repairs wherever possible.[22] Despite this discouraging setback, the work of the company did not stop. By the spring of 1903 most of the damages had been made good, and work on improving the remaining portion of the company land was resumed. In 1903 also, the building of an entire village, aptly called Hai-fu-chen (Village-recovered-from-the-sea), was started.[23] In 1904 the shallow stream forming the northern boundary of the company was deepened and widened. This served the dual purpose of providing adequate drainage and irrigation for adjacent fields, while at the same time providing a side outlet to the sea for a portion of the waters of the Huai River system.[24]

Almost three years to the day after the typhoon of 1902, another and more severe typhoon bore down on the Kiangsu coast. This one lasted five days. Cheng Chien has left a vivid account of this second onslaught on the property of T'ung Hai and its sister enterprise, T'ung Jen T'ai Salt Company:

On August 25, 1905, I went to Shanghai in response to wired instructions of the provincial commerce bureau to facilitate the flow of accumulated goods there. On the night of September 1, the wind rose sharply and tides became menacing. The water reached a depth of three feet at many spots along the roads of the foreign settlement. By noon of the second, the tide had risen still further, until evening time, when the wind gradually abated. I thought of T'ung Hai and T'ung Jen T'ai, and the heavy damage they must have sustained. On the third I sent a courier across the Yangtze River to inquire into the situation. On the fifth letters reporting the general damages of the respective companies reached me. I proceeded to cross the river on the seventh, arriving at Ch'uan-hung Harbor in Hai-men. Because of the damages inflicted on the roads and bridges within two miles of the harbor, I took a smaller boat and went downstream to San-ho Outlet. A warehouse of the Dah Sun Branch Mill was located there. Water had left a mark on the walls of the warehouse three feet high. The bottom parts of the boxes stored in the warehouse were completely soaked. Upon further inquiry, I discovered that not a single dyke escaped heavy damage along the entire coast. . . . I discovered that within an area of some twenty miles by six miles, houses were flattened everywhere; only a few which were located on higher grounds escaped destruction. Nine out of ten persons lost their lives. The newly harvested maize and kaoliang were thoroughly soaked and spoiled. The fresh water streams had all become salty. Consequently a number of persons lost their lives after the typhoon because of the lack of drinking water. The bodies of dead men and carcasses of animals were everywhere. Within an area of 130 square miles the stench was unbearable, bringing all traffic to a standstill. This was the situation I found in the northern section of Ch'ung-ming and the eastern section of Hai-men.[25]

He then went on to describe the losses sustained by T'ung Jen T'ai and T'ung Hai. For the latter he enumerated the damages to the dykes section by section, showing the exact location and the extent of each collapse, ranging from damage of 10 percent to total loss.

Among the field managers some were forced to make temporary rafts or swim in the middle of the night, others mounted tables throughout the night, losing all their clothes and possessions, but none lost his life. Three of the ablest foremen, however, were drowned. A most grievous loss! . . . It is known that high tide occurs on the third and the eighteenth of each lunar month. . . . The typhoon of 1902 fortunately occurred before the first. Consequently the force of the tide was not comparable to the force of the wind. At that time T'ung Hai alone took the brunt of the assault. The fields protected by the main dykes were not affected, and the people remained in safety. This time, according to the forecast of the weather station at Ziccawei, the typhoon came from the Philippines, and its center remained for some time just off the coast of Kiangsu. The coastal areas of Shanghai, Nan-huai, Ch'uan-sha, Ch'ung-ming, Hai-men, and Nan-t'ung were situated squarely in the zone of the fiercest winds. Coupled with the high tide, the storm was the worst in some eighty or ninety years. . . . The wind started in the evenings, and the tide came up in the night. That's why the people could not make preparations to meet the threat. . . . Among the oldest inhabitants of the area it was said that even the great storm of 1848 did not match the severity of this year's typhoon.[26]

The damage caused by this second typhoon was so extensive that appeals for more funds had to be resorted to. Of the original capital of 220,000 taels, all had been subscribed. Now Chang Chien asked for an additional 80,000 taels to round out the capital at 300,000 taels. In addition, he appealed to the provincial Agriculture and Commerce Bureau for funds, to make up the estimated 120,000 taels needed for thorough repair of the whole system of dykes and fields.[27] The appeal went unanswered, and from the investors he received somewhat less than half of the 80,000 taels he asked for. As a result he had to proceed with the repair job on a piecemeal basis, depending on the additional capital received and the rent from the increasing number of tenant farmers recruited by the company.[28] One thing he never had to worry about was the supply of labor. Three thousand men responded to his call for workers in the spring of 1906. The following year saw the complete repair of all damages, and in 1908 some of the earthwork dykes were replaced by new stone dykes.[29]

The typhoons of 1902 and 1905 were costly setbacks, but they were calamities which were beyond human control. More infuriating to Chang Chien was the overt and covert opposition from people who were against T'ung Hai. These were largely the salt merchants and the salt officials. Among the latter, one in particular, Chao Pin-yen, the salt commissioner of Liang-Huai, proved to be his personal nemesis. Commissioner Chao opposed every one of his measures to make the reclamation company a success.[30] The commissioner's motivation is not difficult to conjecture. He reflected the general hostility among salt merchants and salt officials for reformers and entrepreneurs of Chang Chien's kind, who represented a genuine threat to the traditional and profitable salt business.

The opposition which Chang Chien encountered throughout the years when he was attempting to build up T'ung Hai culminated in a six-point indictment which Commissioner Chao lodged against him in 1908. The indictment boiled down to two major points: (1) that the taxes on various types of reclaimed land were inequitable and the tax payments improper; and (2) that land reclamation was destroying the salt business.[31] Chang Chien fought back by appealing directly to the Salt Bureau of the Board of Revenue in Peking, refuting each of the six indictments point by point, setting forth in detail the taxes as they applied to the reclaimed land and the guarantees to salt producers included in the original policies and regulations of the company. The indictment against Chang Chien was dismissed, but the salt merchants and officials salvaged a partial victory in the ruling of the Salt Bureau that no other land reclamation company was to be formed in Kiangsu.[32]

Spread of Land Reclamation in Kiangsu

This stipulation lasted only as long as the dynasty. With the fall of the Ch'ing dynasty, Chang Chien and Chang Ch'a realized the opportunity to expand their land reclamation activities was at hand. Shortly after Chang Chien was appointed the Minister of Agriculture and Commerce, the two went ahead in 1914 and organized a second company, Ta Yu Chin, on land immediately adjacent to T'ung Hai. Since Chang Chien was away in the north the greater part of that year, Chang Ch'a was responsible for handling the details of its establishment. Ta Yu Chin covered an area twice as large as T'ung Hai, but the cost of establishing the former was comparable to that of the latter, since it benefitted from the experience gained in establishing T'ung Hai.

The founding of Ta Yu Chin was the signal which touched off the establishment of a whole rash of land reclamation companies. No less than forty companies were started between 1916 and 1930.[33] Together they covered the greater portion of the coastal area from the boundary of Ta Yu Chin northward to the outlet of the Kuan River, encompassing a territory of some 3,800 square miles and stretching over a coastal strip of nearly 200 miles.[34] Not all of these land reclamation companies were founded as a direct result of the efforts of Chang Chien and Chang Ch'a, but many of the companies were established by them and their associates, and all of them were influenced by the work of the Chang brothers. Due to this division between those that were directly established by the Chang brothers and their associates and those that were established by others, the land reclamation companies came to be known as the Nan-t'ung group and the non-Nan-t'ung group respectively.[35] The former included sixteen companies. Aside from T'ung Hai and Ta Yu Chin, of these sixteen Chang Chien was personally connected with four others.[36] Chang Ch'a was instrumental in the founding of seven land reclamation companies, including the largest of them all, Ta Feng.[37]

Without exception the founders of the companies experienced the same kind of difficulties that plagued Chang Chien in his initial attempt with T'ung Hai. When approached by the companies for their land, both salt merchants and the salters pursued the policy of asking for all that the traffic would bear. The price of individual stove sites jumped from 1,000 yuan (about 700 taels) to 3,000 yuan after 1918.[38] The companies also found it necessary to assume salters' debts to salt merchants on land they acquired from the salters. Nor were the latter honest in their dealings. All too frequently individual salters would pit the offer of one company against that of another in order to derive maximum profit from land that could no longer support them. Consequently the initial cost of establishing the land reclamation companies was abnormally high.[39]

Partly to combat this and partly to facilitate the operations of the Nan-t'ung group of land reclamation companies, Chang Chien called the stockholders of the Nan-t'ung group companies to their first annual meeting in 1922. At that time it was decided to centralize the direction of all the companies represented by the creation of a Reclamation Office. Chang Chien was chosen its first director.[40] Three years later this agency was merged with the Textile Office, a similar agency which supervised the operations of Dah Sun and its affiliated cotton mills, to form the Head Office of Nan-t'ung Industries.[41]

Land reclamation companies of both the Nan-t'ung and the non-Nan-t'ung groups were all modeled after T'ung Hai in organization and operations. Each company had to undergo the costly and difficult initial process of making the land suitable for cultivation. This involved the construction of various types of dykes to keep the seawater out, the dredging of ditches for irrigation and drainage purposes, and the erection of sluice gates to control the influx and outflow of water.[42] The first few years the company generally operated at a loss, since the land had to be made productive by the addition of animal and vegetable manure. In organization the land was divided into "fields," further divided into "sections," which were in turn divided into "units." Each unit averaged twenty-five mow (about four acres) and was generally alloted to one household of tenant farmers.[43] At the time a tenant contracted to cultivate a unit he paid a deposit, which was refundable in case he vacated his land, but a smaller process fee, which he had to pay along with the deposit, was not refundable. In addition to this small risk, tenants must also build their own dwellings and provide their own tools, seeds, and fertilizers. These measures restricted tenants of the land reclamation companies to those who were serious in their endeavors and had the minimum amount of capital to make the attempt.[44]

In actual cultivation the tenant farmers had a free hand. Two crops were generally grown during the year, a main crop of cotton in the fall and a secondary crop in the spring, generally wheat or beans.[45] For each mow of secondary crop planted the companies collected a minimum of ten fen (a tenth of a yuan). The primary interest of the companies, however, was in cotton. At harvest time 40 percent of the yield went to the company.[46] This arrangement sometimes led to friction between the land reclamation companies and their tenants, as some tenants attempted to evade giving the companies as large a return as they had expected by concentrating on the secondary crops to the neglect of the main crop.[47]

The reclamation of land on the entire coast of Kiangsu had been one of Chang Chien's earliest projects. He had envisaged the success of the scheme in terms of providing livelihood for upwards of a million people.[48] Yet by 1933, seven years after his death, the reclaimed land was supporting only 200,000 people, with most of the companies having gone out of operation before the 1930s.[49] The reason for this general failure was threefold. First of all, a series of natural disasters struck the area successively in 1921, 1922, 1924, 1926, which increased difficulties of the land reclamation companies manyfold and drove a number of them to ruin.[50] Secondly, a number of the companies were speculative ventures, whose promoters merely wished to preempt suitable sites for resale at a profit. Their lands remained unimproved when the natural disasters made their gambles a failure.[51] Finally, the financial structure of the land reclamation companies was not sound. Most of them were undercapitalized and would have had a difficult time of it even without the natural disasters. In the end only T'ung Hai and Ta Yu Chin, because of their stronger financial basis, showed a profit in their operations.[52]

Chang Chien's efforts for land reclamation extended beyond his accomplishments in Kiangsu. During his term of office as Minister of Agriculture and Commerce in 1913–15, he attempted to convert many of his own ideas into national policy. Land reclamation was included in his general plans for the promotion of improvement in agriculture. In 1914 he proposed to Premier Hsiung Hsi-ling and the Ministry of Finance that the wastelands of the Huai region be the first area designated for reclamation work. Later in the same year he drew up the Provisional Regulations for Land Reclamation, in which the procedures of land reclamation by private organizations and individuals were regularized. This was passed by the Parliament and duly promulgated in July of 1914.[53]

Another project of his term of office as Minister of Agriculture and Commerce was his plan for land reclamation and colonization of Manchuria. He had become aware of the opportunity for agricultural expansion in that part of the country on his three-month tour of Manchuria in the summer of 1911. He proposed entering into extensive land reclamation projects there, thus providing livelihood for hundreds of thousands of farmers who would migrate into Manchuria.[54] Unfortunately he was not destined to remain in office long enough to give his plans a fair trial.

The Need for Salt Reform

As has been indicated, Chang Chien's efforts in land reclamation grew out of the decline of the Huai-nan region in salt production. But land reclamation was not, and never could be, a direct solution to the problem of profitable salt production. The situation called for a more positive approach, the introduction of improved methods of salt production. This was the starting step by which Chang Chien became involved in salt reform. For he found it impossible to introduce new methods of producing salt without disturbing the *status quo* of the entire structure of the salt business. From his dealings with the salt officials and other salt merchants he came to realize the extreme injustice of the entire salt system, in which a few privileged merchants amassed huge fortunes at the expense of both the producers (the salters) and the consumers (which, of course, included everyone in the country). Therefore Chang Chien's interest and efforts in salt reform should be traced on two levels. First, his efforts to improve the method of salt production in Huai-nan, and second, his efforts to revise the national structure of the salt system, including the production, transportation, sale, regulation, and taxation of salt.

The immediate situation which turned Chang Chien's interest to the salt problem was the deterioration of the natural conditions in the Huai-nan district under which the unique, traditional, salt-producing method of this area had flourished. In contrast to other coastal salt-producing areas, where the sun-dry method was in general use, salt was obtained in the Huai-nan district by means of the ash-brine method. This was done because the humid climate of the district made the adoption of the standard sun-dry method impractical.[55] The ash-brine method was ingenious. Ashes from reeds burned as fuel were spread over certain designated fields, which had been made smooth and flat several years previously. With the aid of moisture in the atmosphere, the salt content in the soil was transferred to the absorbent ashes, forming salt crystals around ash particles. The crystals were gathered and dissolved in water to form brine. The brine then was boiled in huge kettles until the pure salt crystals were separated from the impurities. The reeds used to boil the brine provided more ashes to repeat the process all over again.[56]

Even though the ash-brine method was more expensive than the sun-dry method, it had been particularly suited to the Huai-nan district. Conditions, however, had changed to the extent that even the ash-brine method was becoming impractical. Nature herself was responsible for this development. The sea fronting the Huai-nan district had been slowly receding eastward in the course of several centuries, thereby creating new land. As the distance between the sea and the original salt fields increased, the latter's salt content decreased, until many of them became useless for further salt production.

Establishment of T'ung Jen T'ai

The opportunity for Chang Chien to assume an active role in coping with the salt problem of Huai-nan presented itself while he was touring in Japan in 1903. Hsü Hsien-min and Lo Shu-yün, two of his fellow townsmen, founded a salt company at Lü-ssu on the coast of Nan-t'ung district near the Hai-man line. Chang Chien was informed of this development in Japan. He forthwith changed his itinerary and spent six days in the Japanese salt-producing districts, learning the Japanese method of making salt. Upon his return in August, Messrs. Hsü and Lo made him the director of the newly organized T'ung Jen T'ai Salt Company.[57]

With an initial capital of 100,000 taels, largely raised by the original backers, Chang Chien began his direction of the company by taking several important steps. He changed the status of the salters under company control from individual producers to regularly hired laborers. This meant steady employment for the salter and greater efficiency for the company. He made a survey of the existing reed fields and stove sites. Those which were too widely scattered were abandoned in favor of the more conveniently located fields and sites.[58] These preliminary measures ate up nearly half of the initial capital, and in order to introduce improved methods for the production of salt, Chang Chien had to appeal for further capital in 1904. He proposed to the original backers that an additional 120,000 taels be raised.[59] This met with a response of only 40,000 taels, but he managed to raise 50,000 taels from various moneylenders and 40,000 taels more from official sources.[60]

With these additional funds he introduced the Japanese boiling method. Eighteen acres of land were acquired by the salt company from T'ung Hai for this purpose. In two years' time some 40,000 taels were expended for this experiment. The venture resulted in the successful production of a superior type of refined salt, one which was good enough to receive a medal at the International Exposition at Milan, Italy, in 1906, but it proved to be commercially unprofitable.[61] The failure was not due to any lack of effort on Chang Chien's part. He had sent several workmen to Japan to learn the process at firsthand and had employed three Japanese supervisors directly on the project.[62]

Following this failure Chang Chien tried successively the Chekiang method and the Huai-pei sun-dry method, with no more success than his initial attempt. Salt produced by the Chekiang method turned out to be unattractive because the atmospheric conditions of the Huai-nan district gave it a dark gray color. The Huai-pei method was too costly because drying fields in the porous soil of the Huai-nan district had to be lined with brick or concrete. It was only when he tried the Sung-kiang movable-tray method that a limited measure of success was achieved.[63] By this method the resourceful salters of the Sung-kiang district had gotten around the unfavorable climatic conditions for the practice of sun-drying salt by drying the brine in wooden trays, which could be placed under shelters in inclement weather. Naturally the initial cost was high, because in addition to building the shelters, the drying trays had to be specially made for maximum efficiency. Some 13,000 of them were ordered from Ningpo.[64] The cost of introducing the Sung-kiang method came to nearly 35,000 taels.[65]

Chang Chien's difficulties with his salt venture extended beyond his search for an improved method of producing salt. The typhoon of 1905, so devastating to his land reclamation project, was equally destructive to his salt enterprise. Upwards of 70 percent of the salt-field dykes was destroyed, all accumulated salt and reed ashes were lost, and all of the shelters sustained varying degrees of damage. Ten salters lost their lives in the catastrophe.[66] The material losses were eventually made good, but at a cost which further strained the limited financial resources of the enterprise.

Difficulties from another source came from the salt officials. Chao Pin-yen, the salt commissioner of the Liang-Huai district, proved to be as hostile toward Chang Chien's salt project as toward his land reclamation schemes. Commissioner Chao was adament in maintaining the position that salt produced by T'ung Jen T'ai not only would get no special considerations, it would not even enjoy some of the advantages allowed the regular Huai-nan and Huai-pei salt. During 1905 Chang Chien successively requested that the improved salt be permitted a higher selling price, that the company be permitted to open its own retail outlet, and that T'ung Jen T'ai salt be sent to parts of Kiangsi during a period of salt shortage there. These requests were all ignored or turned down by Commissioner Chao.[67] In the following years he further disallowed requests for sample sale of improved salt at reduced prices in Hupeh and for the sale in Kiangsi of salt produced by the movable-pan method. Because of the system of government salt supervision existing at the time, Commissioner Chao held the power of discretion in matters dealing with salt throughout the provinces of Kiangsu, Anhwei, Kiangsi, Hunan, and Hupeh. Consequently his opposition to Chang Chien was formidable. Finally in 1907 Chang Chien took the case directly to the Salt Bureau at Peking, which after an investigation allowed most of his requests.[68] This did not, however, mark the end of opposition against him. In fact, the continued opposition of salt officials and salt merchants was one of the primary reasons which prompted Chang Chien to turn his attention to the salt problem on the national level.

The National Salt System

The salt administration of the Ch'ing dynasty was an outgrowth of of the state-monopoly system which had existed with short interruptions since Han times. The system, however, had undergone a series of changes during these 2,000 years. The great T'ang official Liu Yen changed what had been a total state monopoly, under which the state operated the entire salt business, from production, transportation, to sales, into a system which might be termed "turnover monopoly." Under this system the production, transportation, and sales of salt were undertaken by private producers and merchants, the government retaining only the right to purchase all salt produced, thereby requiring the merchants to repurchase the salt from the government. In this manner Liu Yen guaranteed to the government a set profit, while at the same time abolishing the large and unwieldly body of officials that had grown up around the salt administration. The power of regulation was concentrated in the hands of a few high officials, eliminating all opportunities for corruption by petty functionaries. The number of supervisory offices was reduced, covering the ten chief producing areas. Salt production in all other areas was prohibited. At the same time thousands of salt storage houses were constructed throughout the country, so that the government could control the practices of the salt merchants, and ensure a steady supply of salt to all parts of the country.[69]

Liu Yen's system was further modified by Fan Hsiang in A.D. 1048, during the reign of Emperor Jen-tsung of Sung. Fan Hsiang introduced the "salt voucher," by means of which merchants would pay cash for vouchers, which would in turn permit them to obtain the stipulated amount of salt for transportation and sale. This system prevailed with no major changes until A.D. 1617, when it was replaced by the "enfranchised merchant monopoly" system. Under it the state retained the salt monopoly in theory, but the actual conduct of the salt business fell into the hands of a relatively small group of favored merchants. Each of these merchants, in exchange for a set sum which he agreed to turn over to the government every year, retained the exclusive right to conduct the distribution and sale of salt in certain designated areas. During the revolt of Wu San-kuei (1674–81), when the government relied heavily on ready cash, the "enfranchised merchant monopoly" system became thoroughly entrenched.[70] In time an elaborate system of division of spoils grew up around the salt business. The "enfranchised merchants," descendants of the originally designated merchants who received the franchises through inheritance, no longer handled the business personally but rented out their franchises to the "field merchants." The latter, having exclusive rights to purchase all the salt produced in certain areas, in turn permitted the "transport merchants" to handle the transportation and distribution. The result was the growth of a powerful group of salt merchants who made most of the profits in the successive stages of the salt business, with the government receiving only a small part of the total profit.[71] The various levels of salt officials who were theoretically in control of the situation came to be identified completely with the interests of the salt merchants. The post of a regional salt commissioner was a much sought-after position, since it offered the incumbent many chances to enrich himself during his term of office. Because of this, few salt officials were allowed to retain office for long.[72] Therefore, even if an official wished to pit his reforming zeal against the evils of the system, he would not have time to consolidate his efforts into permanent improvements.

The "enfranchised merchant monopoly" system flourished throughout Ch'ing times with one notable exception. In the 1830s T'ao Shu, the governor-general of Liang-Kiang, who was the first governor-general to hold the post of regional salt commissioner concurrently, instituted the "salt ticket" system in the area under his jurisdiction. Under this system any merchant could engage in the salt business by paying the tax on the salt tickets, each of which allowed him to buy a set amount of salt. Although this system proved its worth by bringing in more revenue than the existing system had done, its practice did not extend beyond the Liang-Huai district. Eventually the "ticket merchants" became so entrenched that they were virtually indistinguishable from the "enfranchised merchants" elsewhere.[73]

Liang-Huai district, in which the "salt ticket" system prevailed, was but one among eleven salt distribution districts in the country. The other ten were: (1) Ch'ang-lu, covering Chihli; (2) Feng-t'ien, including nearly all of Manchuria; (3) Shantung; (4) Ho-tung, covering Shansi; (5) Fukien; (6) Liang-Che, covering Chekiang and southern Kiangsu; (7) Szechwan; (8) Liang-Kwang, the regional term for Kwangtung and Kwangsi; (9) Yünnan; and (10) Shen-Kan, equivalent to Shensi and Kansu. Each of these districts took its name from the producing area whence the salt originated. In several cases, however, their area of distribution took in other territories in addition to the producing areas. The example of Feng-t'ien district, including Manchuria, has already been mentioned. In addition, Shantung district included a large part of Honan, and Szechwan district covered Kweichow province as well.

The largest of all the salt districts was Liang-Huai, which included most of Kiangsu, Anhwei, Kiangsi, Hunan, and Hupeh. These provinces became a part of Liang-Huai because salt produced in the two coastal areas of Huai-nan and Huai-pei could be transported up the Yangtze river system to the provinces faster and cheaper than salt produced elsewhere. By Ch'ing times these economic considerations had been given legal backing; each of the salt distribution districts was made a self-sufficient unit, in which the circulation of salt produced outside the district was prohibited.[74]

Efforts Toward Reform of the Salt System

This was the situation which confronted Chang Chien when he became actively engaged in salt manufacturing. In 1904, one year after his taking over the directorship of T'ung Jen T'ai, he published an essay with the resounding title, "On Changing the Salt Policy in Order to Guard the Nation, Aid the People, Transform the Smugglers, and Pacify the Bandits." In it he advocated a return to the system of Liu Yen, citing a list of sixteen expected benefits, headed by higher revenue and the eradication of salt smuggling. He followed this closely reasoned essay with another which dealt with the more practical aspects of the salt problem, blaming the low production of salt and the prevalence of smuggling on the existing setup of the salt fields and advocating the use of Japanese boiling kettles, as well as the use of steamships for salt transportation.[75] These initial efforts on his part, devoid of results though they were, served to place him solidly in the camp of the salt reformers.

It is pertinent to introduce at this point the account of Ching Pen-po (the better-known name of Ching Hsüeh-ch'ien) of his meeting with Chang Chien about this time. Ching later became the leading salt reformer of his day. In 1903, however, he was merely a minor official in Chekiang. He became familiar with the plight of the fishermen of the Ningpo and Wen-t'ai area. On their fortnightly trips out to sea the fishermen faced the unhappy choice of either having their catch limited by not carrying a sufficient amount of salt for curing the fish or taking the chance that they might have to dump all the excess salt. The salt dumping was forced upon them by the salt merchants, who had induced the Liang-Che salt commissioner to rule that any salt found unused eight days after purchase was to be regarded as smuggled salt. This seemed so unjust to Ching that he became the fishermen's spokesman.[76]

Just at that time Governor-general Chang Chih-tung, concerned by the appearance of Italian fishing vessels off the coast of China, organized a seven-province fishing company to boost the fishing industry. He chose Chang Chien to head the company. Ching Pen-po went to Nan-t'ung and laid the case of the Chekiang fishermen in front of Chang Chien, who assured him that the problem would be solved once the Chekiang branch of the fishing company was founded.[77] Unfortunately the projected fishing company was never organized. Through this incident, however, Ching recognized in Chang Chien a sincere advocate of salt reform. The association between the two men was to last for many years.

Ching Pen-po's meeting with Chang Chien also gave him the chance to learn of Chang Chien's decision to shelve his salt reform efforts for the time being. Chang Chien's outspoken advocacy of the "turnover monopoly" system had caused the Board of Revenue to take action. He had offered to form a company to underwrite any losses which the new system might incur. The board asked Governor-general Chang Chih-tung for advice. Governor-general Chang merely endorsed the opinion of his secretary, Ho Feng-shih, agreeing with Chang Chien in principle but asking the latter to guarantee the total salt revenue for an entire year while the scheme was being tested. As the sum came to about seven million taels, Chang Chien had to back down.[78] Yet the salt merchants were not satisfied with this maneuver. They induced the Board of Revenue to consult the senior salt commissioner, Yen An-lan, on the matter. After lengthy procrastination Yen came out against the proposal on the ground that the proposed salt company might be a front for foreign capitalists! This convinced Chang Chien of the hopelessness of the situation. He told Ching Pen-po that the existing political situation was certain to be drastically altered within a decade and that salt reforms would have a better chance of success under the new form of government.[79]

Here we must assume that Chang Chien was alluding to the establishment of constitutional government, because Ching Peng-po's account remains uncorroborated. Nowhere in Chang Chien's own writings does he mention his meeting with Ching and the subsequent details, except the fact that he was chosen to head the abortive fishing company.

The establishment of the provincial assemblies in 1909 and the announcement by the Imperial Court that a parliament would be set up spurred Chang Chien to renewed efforts on behalf of salt reform. In 1910 he drafted a tentative program for the Central Legislative Council, in which he called attention to the importance of salt tax as a source of revenue, denounced the existing salt system, and reaffirmed his belief in the efficacy of Liu Yen's system.[80]

In 1911 the Ch'ing government, recognizing the need to centralize salt control, made a belated attempt to rectify the situation by the creation of the concurrent post of Minister of Finance and the Minister of Salt.[81] Before anything came of this move the dynasty was overthrown.

In the uncertain early days of the republic, the different salt districts operated largely on their own. The provisional government at Nanking, faced with a shortage of funds, sought to tap the salt revenue of the Liang-Huai region. Chang Chien was asked to assume the post of salt commissioner of that region. Before he would take the post, however, he laid down the condition that the Kiang-nan district, which traditionally had been included in the Liang-Che region, be placed under his supervision. He therefore had the effective control of salt production in all of Kiangsu. He held the post for one year, during which time he had a chance to try out his ideas, including a modified form of the "turnover monopoly" system. He resigned in October of 1912, and with his resignation the Kiang-nan district was again placed under the Liang-Che region.[82]

Before he resigned from the post of Liang-Huai Salt Commissioner, Chang Chien felt that the time was propitious for him to make known his salt reform policy. He gathered together all his ideas into a comprehensive *Plan for the Reform of the National Salt Policy*. This document began with an unequivocal statement.

> The salt policy of China perpetuates the policy of a thousand and some hundred years ago; and because it remains unchanged, it is complex, contradictory, and difficult to understand. Today, in attempting to reform it, our aim is to abolish completely all the old, outmoded regulations, because they are not worthy of systematic study.[83]

After briefly setting forth the existing salt policy, he outlined the eight points of his reform program:

1. To concentrate all aspects of the salt business under government control, in order to achieve standardization throughout the country.
2. To increase revenue from salt without raising the taxes.
3. To provide salt at reasonable prices throughout the country.
4. To eliminate all illegal salt by means of effective control in producing areas, thereby removing the necessity for cumbersome control agencies in the rest of the country.
5. To abolish the system of salt distribution districts, without affecting the livelihood of the salters and the salt merchants.
6. To differentiate salt prices in conformity with quality, the difference in the cost of production to be adjusted by differential tax rates.
7. To find means to reduce production cost, thereby cutting salt prices.
8. To equalize the supply and demand of salt.[84]

For the realization of the above goals, Chang Chien advocated the eventual establishment of complete government monopoly. He drew up what might be termed the "private-production, government-transfer, merchant-transportation, private-distribution" scheme. This was to be in full operation after six years. Under such a scheme the production of salt would be left in the hands of individual salters, under general government supervision. All the salt produced must be sold to the government. It would then resell the salt to salt companies, the profit of this transaction replacing the salt tax. The salt companies would make their profits by transporting the salt to various parts of the country and reselling the salt to privately operated salt shops. Salt transportation companies would not be allowed to operate retail outlets themselves. Although the actual transportation of salt would be conducted by the privately organized salt companies, the government would retain a heavy controlling hand. It would designate the eligible companies, require them to post heavy securities for the privilege of transporting salt, and allow them to purchase from any government agencies, but restrict their operations to specific areas. In addition, the government itself was to transport salt to those outlying areas where the excessive transportation cost would discourage private companies from supplying these areas.[85] In spite of all these conditions, Chang Chien fully expected the profits made in the transportation of salt to be sufficiently high to attract private companies into the salt business. As a further inducement, government subsidy was to be made available to companies that needed help initially.[86]

The securities deposited by the companies with the government were to be used for three purposes: to recompence the owners of certain of the less economical salt-producing areas which would be shut down; to build storage facilities for salt; and to make the necessary improvements on harbors, boats, and other adjuncts of salt transportation.[87] The total cost of all these activities was estimated at 38,500,000 yuan (27,500,000 taels), of which 35,000,000 yuan were to be realized from the securities deposited by the companies.[88]

To facilitate the financial transactions involved in this scheme, Chang Chien suggested the establishment of a salt bank with a capitalization of 20,000,000 yuan (about 14,000,000 taels). This bank would be wholly independent from other government banks and concerned solely with the financial aspect of the salt business.[89]

The significance of Chang Chien's proposed plan of salt reform lies in the fact that by arguing for the government monopoly scheme he abandoned the "turnover monopoly" scheme which he had espoused for a decade. To be sure, the actual transportation of salt was to be undertaken by merchants under both schemes, but in contrast to an absolutely free hand which the merchants would enjoy under the "turnover monopoly" system, the "government monopoly" scheme sought to place them under effective government supervision. In a letter to Premier Hsiung Hsi-ling in 1913, Chang Chien freely admitted this switch, giving as his reason the confused state of salt affairs at the time, which required a period of readjustment. He believed that this would be most effectively done under the "government monopoly" scheme, but he specifically reserved the right to return to advocating the "turnover monopoly" system at a later date.[90] He asserted virtually the same thing in answer to William J. Calhoun, the American minister in Peking, to whom Chang Chien had sent his plan for comment. Calhoun was sympathetic toward the scheme, but stated his personal preference for a single-tax system.[91] Chang Chien admitted that this was also his eventual goal, but defended his plan on the basis that it would have the greatest immediate effect in coping with the entrenched interests of the salt merchants.[92]

From this we might deduce that Chang Chien adopted the "government monopoly" system as a matter of tactics. On this point Ching Pen-po's account again offers some revealing information. In 1912, according to Ching, Yüan Shih-k'ai was putting pressure on Chang Chien to go to Peking by promising to discuss the entire salt situation. Chang Chien wired Ching to meet him in Shanghai. There Chang Chien stated that, since the active salt reformers were but a mere handful compared to the number of powerful salt merchants, they ought not to weaken their position further by offering conflicting reform schemes. Ching concurred, but went on to state that if the two of them were to come to a common course of action, they should devote themselves completely to this task in the next few day to the exclusion of all other business. Chang Chien agreed to this. The evening following this conversation Ching received word to come to the Shanghai office of the Dah Sun Company. There he found the lights of the building turned off and the gates locked. It turned out that Chang Chien had instructed the gatekeeper to inform all callers that Chang had returned to Nan-t'ung, in order to remain uninterrupted with Ching. In the darkened building the two men, accompanied by a few trusted colleagues, thrashed out their differences in three hours. Ching prevailed upon Chang Chien to accept the necessity of adopting the "government monopoly" scheme. The basic outline of the salt reform plan was drawn up at this meeting.[93] This incident seems entirely plausible, but again we have no corroborating evidence from Chang Chien himself.

Upon the publication of the salt reform plan, the salt merchants at once organized opposition to the proposal. The opposition took two forms. On the one hand the merchants exerted pressure on the responsible government officials, especially those in the Ministry of Finance and in the Salt Bureau within the ministry. On the other hand they attempted to discredit Chang Chien. For this purpose a pamphlet entitled *Detailed Refutation of Chang Chien's Salt Reform Plan* was published by an organization calling itself National Salt Business Federation (T'ung-kuo Yen-yeh Lien-ho I-hui). This pamphlet enumerated fifty-five specific objections to Chang Chien's proposals. Several of these objections struck at the basic assumptions of the plan. Chang Chien's belief that smuggling would cease under an equitable system of salt transportation was disputed. The scheme for the government to purchase all the salt produced was seen as leading to the possibility of overproduction. Chang Chien's assertion that improved methods of salt production would lead to cheaper prices was challenged. The pamphlet further attacked his motives and ability, seizing upon the stipulation that the commercial use of salt was to be exempt from certain regulations as evidence that he was favoring his private interests. It took exception to his statement that "the old regulations are not worthy of systematic study" and disputed his figures on the country's population and salt production. Moreover the pamphlet, in the name of "republican ideals," protested the elimination of the "field merchants," who were engaged in the business of buying salt from the salters and selling to "transport merchants." It also asserted flatly that, under Chang Chien's plan, no merchant would be foolish enough to conform to the new specifications only to be eliminated in a few years when the full government-monopoly scheme would go into effect.[94] Despite some cogent arguments presented by this pamphlet, the real reason for the salt merchants' opposition—that they wanted to remain free from any outside interference in the continued operation of a lucrative monopoly—was carefully concealed under a mass of minor objections to Chang Chien's plan.

From 1912 on the continued fight of Chang Chien and Ching Pen-po for salt reform became thoroughly enmeshed in the intricate political happenings of the time. Histories of this period have generally concentrated on the political aspects of the changing events to the neglect of other aspects. We must, therefore, resort once again to the writing of Ching Pen-po for an account of salt reform efforts as it affected the political scene.

Ching relates that in 1912 he accompanied Chang Chien to Peking to talk with Yüan Shih-k'ai and Chou Hsüeh-hsi, the Minister of Finance. Chou, a native of Anhwei, came from a wealthy gentry background and was himself an "enfranchised merchant" of the Liang-Huai district. In spite of these facts Chang Chien believed Chou would be sympathetic to his cause and appealed to Chou on patriotic grounds. Because Chang Chien had the backing of Yüan Shih-k'ai, Chou could not oppose Chang Chien openly. He saw to it, however, that details of Chang Chien's plan were leaked out prematurely to newspapers opposed to the plan, and when submission of the plan to the Parliament could no longer be put off, he submitted simultaneously a second plan, which resembled Chang Chien's plan in all except the few key points.[95]

Faced with these maneuvers of Chou, and realizing that Yuan Shih-k'ai was not deeply concerned with the salt problem as he had professed to be, Chang Chien decided to return to Nan-t'ung for the time being. On the eve of his departure he and Ching Pen-po held a long conversation. Ching believed that the cause of salt reform needed to be publicized. To that end he asked Chang Chien to support his efforts to organize a society and to publish a periodical. Chang Chien asked Ching if the latter was willing to devote three years of his life solely to the cause of salt reform. Ching replied that so long as the situation remained unimproved, he would never abandon his efforts. The two men then came to an agreement. Ching would remain in Peking to run the society and publish the periodical, while Chang Chien would provide the necessary financial support.[96]

The Salt Administration Discussion Society (Yen-cheng T'ao-lun Hui) was organized in December of 1912. The following month the first issue of the *Salt Administration Magazine (Yen-cheng Tsa-chih)* was published.[97] The society became the center of salt reform activities, and the periodical served as the vehicle by which the views of the salt reformers were made known throughout a large part of the country. No better evidence of the periodical's influence can be found than the publication of a rival periodical by the salt merchants of Chekiang, which had an identical format with that of the *Salt Administration Magazine*, even to the cover design. Known as the *Salt Discussion Miscellany (T'an-yen Ts'ung-pao)*, the publication featured articles designed to refute articles in the *Salt Administration Magazine*. This rival periodical did not last out its first year of existence. In contrast, the *Salt Administration Magazine* maintained publication even after Chang Chien had ceased to support it after 1914, and, with one short break, continued publication through the 1910s and 1920s.[98]

Meanwhile, in 1912, the struggle over salt policy did not end with the efforts of Chou Hsüeh-hsi to thwart reform efforts by the introduction of two salt reform schemes to Parliament. The Parliament was then the battleground upon which the T'ung-meng Hui, which soon became the Kuomintang, was opposed by the Kung-ho Tang (Republican Party) and a number of lesser parties. The salt issue soon became a bone of contention in party politics. Because Chang Chien was one of the organizers of the Kung-ho Tang, Chou Hsüeh-hsi joined the Kuomintang and attempted to introduce a counterscheme to Chang's plan under Kuomintang auspices. This move was vetoed by Sung Chiao-jen, the active parliamentary leader of the party. Chou then introduced a motion, calling for the retention of the Salt Bureau within the Ministry of

Finance, instead of being set up as an independent agency, as the reformers wished. He succeeded in making this a key issue between the Kuomintang and the Kung-ho Tang.[99]

At the same time another element entered into the struggle over salt reform. This was the Reorganization Loan negotiations between China and the five-power consortium. China wanted twenty-five million pounds to liquidate some of her most pressing financial obligations abroad and to stabilize her fiscal position. Negotiations had proceeded to a point where the question of securities came up. The only sizable source of unpledged income which China still had was the salt tax. If it was to be the security for the Reorganization Loan, direct foreign supervision could not be avoided. Chou Hsüeh-hsi saw in the successful conclusion of the loan agreement a way to remove the salt question from any further interference from the reformers. Accordingly he bent every effort to push through the loan. In this matter Chou was going with the interest of Yüan Shih-k'ai, who wanted the loan himself in order to be free from financial dependence upon the Parliament. With little regard for proper parliamentary procedures, Yüan signed the Reorganization Loan agreement on April 27, 1913.[100]

The signing of the Reorganization Loan brought to China a foreign inspector general of salt in the person of Sir Richard Dane. "Honest and independent of spirit, bluff and hearty in manner," Dane represented the best in the tradition of able British civil servants.[101] He had compiled an enviable record in India and had risen to be the first Inspector General of Excise and Salt in India before retiring in 1909. His appointment to China was a move inspired by the career of Sir Robert Hart, who had ably served as Inspector General of the Chinese Maritime Customs ever since 1863.[102]

For Chang Chien the signing of the Reorganization Loan and the appointment of Dane by no means represented the end of his salt reform efforts. In the latter part of 1913, soon after Hsiung Hsi-ling was chosen to be the premier and before he himself was appointed Minister of Agriculture and Commerce, Chang Chien wrote to Hsiung, pointing out that the salt tax was but one aspect of the entire salt question. He urged the speedy consolidation and supervision of salt-producing areas in order to check smuggling. He went on to add, "If the production of illegal salt is not stopped because the salt producing areas are not controlled, the foreigners would be sure to demand the power of supervision over the salt fields on the ground that it affects the salt revenue. It is permissible to allow the foreigners power over the salt tax, but if they control the production of salt, it would affect the livelihood of several millions of salters and the lives of four hundred million Chinese."[103] Soon after the sending of this letter, Chang Chien took on ministerial duties and had to devote his attention to other matters.

One of Dane's first acts upon arrival in his new post was the decision to introduce the Indian salt-tax system to China. This system was similar to the original proposal of Chang Chien. It called for the free sale of salt after the payment of one unified tax.[104] This scheme, however, ran counter to the wishes of the reformers, nearly all of whom favored the "government monopoly" scheme. Ching Pen-po held several long talks with Dane and finally convinced him of the necessity to conduct an extensive personal survey of the entire salt situation in China before committing himself to any one scheme.[105] Dane proposed to spend three years for the survey.

From 1913 to 1915 Dane had the good fortune to have Chang Hu as his Chinese colleague. A member of the Salt Administration Discussion Society, Chang Hu had been connected with some phase of the salt administration throughout most of his official career. One of his foreign contemporaries had characterized him as "brilliant, well-informed, and a versatile administrator."[106] Together he and Dane were largely responsible for raising the salt revenue from 19,000,000 yuan (about 13,500,000 taels) in 1913 to 60,000,000 yuan in 1914.[107] Chang Hu's progressive ideas, however, were not kindly received by the more conservative officials. When Chou Hsüeh-hsi was appointed to his second term of office as Minister of Finance in March, 1915, he set out to discredit Chang Hu. The latter was accused of malfeasance and corruption and finally forced to resign.[108]

The attempt of Yüan Shin-k'ai to make himself emperor in 1915 marked the end of the initial phase of salt reform efforts under the republic. The activities of the Salt Administration Discussion Society were suspended until 1922, when Ching Pen-po revived the organization.[109] Although Chang Chien's name was again prominently mentioned in the publications of the society, he himself had ceased to associate actively with it. Strictly speaking, Chang Chien's efforts in salt reform terminated in 1915. Thus his years of struggle against the entrenched salt interests ended, devoid of immediate results. Through his support of Ching Pen-po, however, he contributed directly to the cause of salt reform. The publications and the activities of the Salt Administration Discussion Society served to publicize the need for salt reform to an increasingly larger group among the articulate segment of the population.

On the regional level, the limited success of the T'ung Jen T'ai Salt Company demonstrated the possibility of introducing improved methods of salt production in the Huai-nan area, but because production of salt was so closely related with other aspects of the salt business, the result of Chang Chien's efforts in the Huai-nan area was inconclusive. As it turned out, his land reclamation efforts held greater promise for that part of Kiangsu than his salt reform work. Nevertheless in land reclamation also, Chang Chien was hampered by the existence of an outmoded and inflexible salt administration. For if government supervision of land reclamation in Kiangsu had been placed under an independent government organ charged with this specific function, the result could conceivably have been quite different. Thus, for Chang Chien, the interrelation of land reclamation and salt reform remained crucial in the determination of their final success and failure.

CHAPTER SEVEN

Controlling the Huai

IN CHANG CHIEN's life several events made lasting impressions upon his memory. The Yellow River flood of 1887, which began with the breaking of the dykes at Cheng-chou, Honan, was one of them. He was then thirty-four, and had not yet begun his more active career. He had followed his patron, Sun Yün-chin, to K'ai-feng in May, 1887, upon Sun's appointment to be the prefect of that city. There were already indications then that the Yellow River might cause trouble again that year. In the course of consulting with Governor Ni Wen-wei on the possible means of averting the impending disaster, Sun brought up Chang Chien's name and prevailed upon Governor Ni to use him.[1]

As Sun well knew, Chang Chien had been interested in the problem of water conservancy for some time. He had read the writings of some of the greatest conservationists of former times, men like P'an Chi-hsün of the Ming dynasty and Chin Fu of the Ch'ing dynasty.[2] He was well acquainted with the number of times that the Yellow River had changed its course; the sixth and the most recent one had occurred only thirty-two years previously, in 1855. On that occasion it had abandoned its southern channel, which led due east from K'ai-feng to the sea, and had assumed a course which permitted it to flow northeastward to the Shantung coast. There was no certainly that it would not change its course once more.

Upon his assignment by Governor Ni, Chang Chien at once set out up and down the river to check on the situation in person. Almost at the very beginning he was aware of being handicapped by the complete lack of accurate data. He became convinced that no permanent solution could be reached without extensive surveys of the Yellow River. He wrote a series of letters to Governor Ni, setting forth his ideas. While the governor was still considering his proposals, the August rains came and continued without letup for a week. The water level of the Yellow River rose rapidly. On the seventh one of the tributaries which joined the Yellow River at Cheng-chou, upstream from K'ai-feng, overflowed its banks. By the tenth the flood crest of the Yellow River reached the critical mark of thirty-three feet above its normal level, and urgent messages for help streamed into the Governor's office at K'ai-feng. In the early hours on the morning of the thirteenth, the dykes at Cheng-chou broke along a mile-wide front, and the full fury of the angry water snuffed out thousands of lives in a matter of hours.[3] The released water quickly fanned out over the flat Honan countryside, where those who escaped the initial onslaught had to fend for themselves as best they could. Here and there could be seen "a long rope tying seven or eight elders, women, and children together, with a dog at the end; an infant in swaddling clothes; people crowding rooftops and tree branches, or hanging on to oxcarts, turning over and over with the swirling waters."[4] For days the full force of the flood water scoured the countryside. Most of the water drained into the Chia-lu River, thence to the Yin River, which in turn flowed into the Huai, causing further floods along the course of these rivers. It took fully a year to plug up the breach in the dykes at Cheng-chou and to turn the Yellow River into its northern course once again.

Chang Chien never forgot this experience. Years later he was to refer to it again and again. His interest in water conservancy acquired an added sense of urgency. He soon turned his attention, however, from the Yellow River to the Huai River. Although not as long as the Yellow River, the Huai was equally prone to periodic floods and had plagued the provinces of Anhwei and Kiangsu for centuries.

The Huai System

The source of the Huai is located near T'ung-pe on the Honan-Hupeh border, from whence it follows a course eastward through Honan, Anhwei, into Kiangsu.[5] As a series of mountain ranges run nearly parallel to the Huai south of the river, its southern tributaries are short and comparatively unimportant. In contrast, its northern tributaries are sizable rivers in themselves. From the source of the Huai eastward, a number of northern tributaries flow through the central, southern, and eastern parts of Honan and northern Anhwei, forming a network which, together with a number of shorter southern tributaries of the Huai, makes up the Huai watershed.

Since 1855 the Huai has been without a natural outlet to the sea. A small part of the combined waters of the Huai and its tributaries, upon reaching Hung-tse Lake, is lost through evaporization. The remainder flows into the Yangtze through two routes. The greater portion leaves Hung-tse Lake at San-ho-k'ou, then flows eastward through San Ho (Three River) into the series of lakes known collectively as Kao-pao Lake, and from thence southward through several short distributaries into the Yangtze at San-chiang-ying. The other route of discharge leads northeastward through the Ch'ang-fu River to Ch'ing-k'ou, where it meets the waters of the Grand Canal, then southward through the latter to join the first outflow in discharging into the Yangtze at San-chiang-ying. The section of the Grand Canal between Ch'ing-k'ou and the Yangtze is commonly known as the Inner Grand Canal.

East of the Inner Grand Canal in Central Kiangsu there is a basinlike low area, which is dissected by a gridlike system of waterways collectively known as the Inner Lower Rivers (Li-hsia Ho). This system is connected with a number of shallow, winding streams running eastward to outlets on the coast. The coastal strip through which they flow has been gradually built up in the past thousand years as the sea receded. The land is so flat that during high tides seawater still penetrates deep inland, through such openings as She-yang-k'ou, Tou-lung-k'ou, and Wang-chia-kang. Between the low area and the coastal strip runs a north-south waterway called the Ch'uan-ch'ang River, which extends from the Yangtze northward almost to the former course of the Yellow River.

Northern Kiangsu contains two rivers which are generally considered as a part of the Huai system, although both have their own outlets to the sea. These are the Shu and the Yi, both of which originate in Shantung and follow a generally southward course before making wide turns northeastward into the sea. The outlet of the Shu is at Lin-hung-k'ou, while the Yi discharges its water through Kuan River at Kuan-ho-k'ou.

History of Huai Control

In ancient times the Huai ranked with the Yellow, the Chi, and the Yangtze as the four main rivers of East China.[6] As late as the Sung dynasty the Huai was still a busy artery of water transportation. At that time the Huai flowed free and clear directly into the sea.

In 1194, the Yellow River, after repeated usurpation of the lower Huai channel during floods, assumed this course permanently as its southern channel. Part of the Yellow River still flowed through a northern channel at that time, but in 1492 a series of disastrous floods on the northern channel caused Liu Ta-hsia, the Yellow River commissioner, to divert all the waters into the southern channel, sealing off the northern channel altogether. Henceforth the silt brought down by the Yellow River, which had begun to clog up the lower reaches of the combined Yellow-Huai channel, accumulated even faster. As a result the Huai began to back up around the village of Hung-tse, gradually forming a large but shallow lake.

Toward the end of the sixteenth century the problem of sedimentation had reached such an acute stage that two opposing solutions were offered in coping with the situation. These two schemes of river control were respectively championed by two famous conservation officials, P'an Chi-hsün and Yang I-k'uei. P'an's proposal, summarized in the phrase "Build up the Ch'ing (Huai River) to scour the Huang (Yellow River)," consisted of containing the Huai with a system of dykes and deepening its junction with the Yellow River at Ch'ing-k'ou, so that the force of the accelerated Huai water would help carry the silt into the sea. For fourteen years (1578–92) P'an occupied the post of Director of Water Conservancy and labored hard to put his plan into effect. He was never entirely successful, as recurrent floods on the Huai would break through various sections of the dykes from time to time. A series of particularly bad floods led to the removal of P'an and the installation of Yang I-k'uei in his place. Yang's ideas, that of "separating the Huang and guiding the Huai," was to open new outlets for the Yellow River to reach the sea, while diverting much of the Huai water away from joining the Yellow River at Ch'ing-k'ou, and leading it down several of the Inner Lower Rivers and thence to the sea. This plan also failed to achieve complete success.

After the fall of the Ming dynasty, the Manchus inherited the task of dealing with the Huai and the Yellow rivers. The K'ang-hsi Emperor was deeply concerned with the problem, ranking it with the maintenance of grain transportation and the crushing of the revolt of Wu San-kuei as the three foremost tasks of his reign. He chose Chin Fu for the job of controlling the rivers. Chin's plans were essentially the same as those of P'an Chi-hsün. He was largely successful in carrying them out, but later became involved in a controversy with Yü Ch'eng-lung concerning the best method for the draining of the low area in central Kiangsu. Chin Fu died before the controversy could be settled. His successor, Chang P'eng-ho, continued his policy in controlling the Huai and the Yellow River with good results.

In spite of these efforts, the increase of silt on the lower reaches of the Yellow River continued. By the time of the Tao-kuang Emperor (1821–51), the excess water of the Huai began to flow into the Yangtze. Henceforth the Huai became more and more a tributary of the Yangtze. This process reached its ultimate stage in 1855, when the Yellow River once again changed its course, from the southern to the northern channel. Without the force of Yellow River's water maintaining even a shallow channel, that portion of the Yellow River from Ch'ing-k'ou to the sea rapidly dried up. From that time on the Yangtze became the Huai's sole outlet; only during the flood season would a portion of the Huai water escape to the sea through its old channel.

In the nineteenth century two scholars in particular were deeply concerned with the problem of the Huai. Feng Tao-li of Tung-t'ai, Kiangsu, published in 1839 the *Illustrated Discourse on the Water Conservancy of the Huai and the Yangtze*,[7] in which he called attention to the seriousness of the problem. In 1866 Ting Hsien of Shan-yang, Kiangsu, advocated returning the Huai to its old course and the creation of a Huai River Control Commission.[8] Neither man was in the official capacity to carry out his ideas. Among the Liang-Kiang governors-general of late Ch'ing time, Tso Tsung-t'ang gave evidence of his concern over the long-term implications of the Huai problem, but he was shifted to another post and official concern died with his departure.

Efforts to Tame the Huai

The ideas of P'an, Chin, Feng, and Ting all had considerable influence upon Chang Chien's thinking. For some time after the Yellow River Flood of 1887 he had no chance to apply himself to water conservancy work. By 1903 the increasing stability of his business and educational enterprises allowed him to turn his attention to other fields of endeavor. He began his water conservancy work with a small project to deepen and widen an extension of the

Inner Lower Rivers which flowed through Nan-t'ung and Hai-men. This was undertaken in conjunction with his land reclamation projects, but he thought of it in more than local terms. It was to be the first move in his efforts to provide outlets for the water of the Huai.[9]

In 1906 Tuan-fang became the newly appointed governor-general of Liang-Kiang. Recently returned from his trip to Europe and America as a member of the constitutional mission, Tuan-fang seemed to Chang Chien to belong to a small group of Manchu officials who were not totally devoid of initiative and energy. In the summer of 1907 another serious flood devestated Kiangsu. Prompted by this, Chang Chien approached Tuan-fang with the proposal of setting up a joint official-gentry corporation on the *kuan-tu shang-pan* model, whereby a government-supervised organization would be run primarily under private control, to be given the power to cope with the entire Huai problem.[10] This was a radical idea, since the power of river conservancy had traditionally belonged to the responsible officials or government agencies. Under the circumstances it was not surprising that Chang Chien's ideas met a cold reception. His further suggestion that surveying work on the Huai be initiated was accepted by Tuan-fang. There were other officials, however, who privately obstructed Chang Chien's efforts in this direction. Yang Wen-ting, the intendant of the Huai-Yang districts in Kiangsu, advised Tuan-fang to order the official surveyor to falsify the statistics obtained in order to make Chang Chien's proposals seem totally inadequate and thereby discredit his efforts.[11] It was apparent that Chang Chien's ideas were not popular with those officials who wished to see the *status quo* maintained.

Tuan-fang was reassigned to the governor-generalship of Chihli in 1909. That same year the Kiangsu Provincial Assembly was organized, in conformity with the plan adopted by the Ch'ing government for the limited reform of the Chinese political system. Chosen by the delegates to head the assembly, Chang Chien sought to relate river conservancy work with the assembly's activities by organizing the Kiang-Huai Water Conservancy Company under the auspices and supervision of the assembly. To make the arrangement attractive to assembly members, Chang Chien stipulated that 30 percent of the future profits from reclaimed and improved land should revert to the assembly. The company's first concern was to be surveying work.[12] At this point he was faced with a shortage of trained surveyors. He had anticipated this need several years before, and had added surveying courses to the curriculum of the Nan-t'ung Normal School. Now the group of forty graduates were put to work as a partial solution to the shortage,[13] and he went ahead with the establishment of a surveying bureau at Ch'ing-chiang-p'u, where the Grand Canal crosses the former course of the Yellow River. Operations started in 1911. The Kiang-Huai Water Conservancy Company was set up to operate over the Huai Basin in Anhwei as well as Kiangsu. Consequently Chang Chien took the step of obtaining the support of the Anhwei Provincial Assembly as well, but for the time being he depended solely on Kiangsu for financial support.[14] This question of support was to plague him for some time to come. The surveying bureau, which continued a precarious existence until 1926, had to suspend operations more often for lack of funds than for political disturbances in the field. There is no evidence that Anhwei ever supported it to any substantial extent. The surveying work which the bureau managed to accomplish, however, was of acceptable quality. Its efforts, together with the later surveying work done by the Kiang-pei Grand Canal Engineering Bureau, the Huai-Yang-Hsü-Hai Topographical Surveying Bureau, the Anhwei Water Conservancy Surveying Bureau, and the Shantung Grand Canal Engineering Bureau made the Huai the most completely surveyed river basin in China.[15]

Shortly after the fall of the Ch'ing dynasty, the Kiang-Huai Water Conservancy Company received some unfavorable publicity. In 1912 the American Red Cross Society had shown an interest in helping to cope with the Huai problem. Charles Davis Jameson, an American engineer who had been in China since 1895, had been asked by the society to make a preliminary survey of the situation. For some reason Jameson and Chang Chien developed an intense dislike for each other.[16] During the eight months Jameson was in the Huai region, he felt that he was given insufficient cooperation by Chang Chien.[17] Upon his departure he published a report criticizing the work of the surveying bureau, against which Chang Chien issued a characteristically vigorous rebuttal.[18]

This episode probably contributed to the promptness with which a petition was jointly submitted to the government by Ch'eng Te-ch'üan and Po Wen-wei, respectively the military governors of

Kiangsu and Anhwei, calling for the creation of an official agency for the control of the Huai to be headed by a director and two associate directors, one from each province.[19] The petition was actually written by Chang Chien, and he was duly appointed in December, 1912, the Director of the Central Bureau of Huai Control, with Po Wen-wei and Hsü Ting-lin as his associates. Po, a revolutionary of some years standing, had an abiding interest in ridding Anhwei of the menace of Huai floods. His ideas may even have influenced Chang Chien on certain points.[20] Hsü was an old friend of Chang Chien's, the two having often exchanged ideas on the Huai ever since 1906.[21]

Chang Chien's first move in his new position was to push for the creation of a National Water Conservancy Bureau, a move which was brought to success with his being chosen the Director General of Water Conservancy in December, 1913. In reality this position was so lightly regarded by the government that he was granted funds to add only six men to the existing staff of the Kiang-Huai Water Conservancy Company.[22] At that time he was also the Minister of Agriculture and Commerce, and this was generally considered the more important of the two positions he was occupying concurrently.

As Director General of Water Conservancy, Chang Chien announced the four projects which he hoped to carry out. They were: (1) the control of the Huai; (2) the building of a canal between the Liao and the Sungari rivers in Manchuria; (3) the creation of a hydraulic engineering school; and (4) the establishment of an agricultural bank.[23] The Liao-Sungari Canal project suggested itself to him as a result of his tour of Manchuria in 1911. It was designed primarily to facilitate the shipment of goods by water from the Amur-Sungari region to southern Manchuria and China. As for the establishment of an agricultural bank, it had a twofold purpose. Officially, the bank, to be jointly operated by government and private interests, was to provide the needed capital for river conservancy projects. At the same time it was to be a source of rural credit to those farmers who wished to improve their own lands.[24] Neither the Liao-Sungari Canal nor the agricultural bank projects were followed up. Instead Chang Chien concentrated his efforts toward controlling the Huai during his term of office.

The central core of his ideas on the Huai was set forth in a document which he made public in 1913. Basically he favored the dredging of a new outlet to the sea while retaining the outlet to the Yangtze at San-chiang-ying. For the new outlet he proposed to widen and deepen Kuan-ho-k'ou at the mouth of the Kuan River. This was a modification of both his original idea to return the Huai to its old course and his later two-outlet idea, with the sea outlet at Lin-hung-k'ou. He came to favor Kuan-ho-k'ou over Lin-hung-k'ou because the former would be more economical. One point remained unchanged. He continued to stress the importance of including the Yi and the Shu rivers in any comprehensive plan for the Huai basin.[25]

For the realization of his plans he needed more men trained and experienced in hydraulic engineering than those available at the time. Chang Chien recognized the necessity of relying heavily upon foreign engineers for the initial stages of any water conservancy project—he was particularly impressed with the achievements of the Dutch and preferred Dutch engineers to those of any other nationality[26]—but he believed that Chinese should be their assistants from the very beginning, so that with experience the Chinese would eventually be able to dispense with the service of foreigners. To supply these assistants, Chang Chien returned to an idea he had had for some time, the establishment of a hydraulic engineering school. This would be a special school opened to all qualified youths of the nation. Each year the provincial governors would appoint for entrance a total of one hundred graduates of middle schools, who, in exchange for three years of all-expenses-paid training, would agree to serve the nation for a stipulated number of years after graduation.[27] For the location of such a school Chang Chien considered a number of places in Nanking and Shanghai, finally deciding on the ready facilities of the Provincial Assembly buildings in Nanking, unoccupied since the dissolution of the assembly in 1912. When he tried to obtain the necessary approvals from the other departments of the government, he encountered the usual amount of inertia and procrastination. He managed to go ahead with the establishment of the school by reaching an agreement with the responsible officials of Chihli, Shantung, Chekiang, and Kiangsu, each to contribute annually 7,000 yuan (5,000 taels) to the support of the school.[28] This school merged with several other schools to form the National Central University in 1927.[29]

Meanwhile, early in 1914 Chang Chien began negotiations with the American Red Cross for a loan to finance the Huai Project. This was contrary to his original wish to steer clear of contracting foreign loans, but he was forced to it by the difficulties he had in trying to obtain funds from official and private sources. The negotiations, conducted through the good office of the American Minister Paul Reinsch, were prolonged by the insistence of Chang Chien on certain detailed stipulations.[30] He was extremely careful to eliminate the slightest possibility that Jameson might be placed in the position of chief supervising engineer. He had nothing but the greatest distrust for Jameson.[31] Further complications came in the form of objections from the Ministry of Foreign Affairs, which favored a loan from Belgium rather than from the United States. These obstacles proved to be surmountable, but the negotiations really bogged down because Chang Chien and the American Red Cross had conflicting ideas about the manner in which the projected loan should be used. The Red Cross came to regard Chang Chien as an obstructionist.[32] In any case the negotiations had to be broken off in 1914 with the outbreak of World War I.

To familiarize himself with the actual conditions, Chang Chien interrupted the negotiations in April, 1914, and made his first systematic tour of the Huai basin. Accompanied by a Dutch engineer, he spent a whole month traveling over that area of the Huai from Huai-yuan, Anhwei, to the sea. One night while staying over at Ch'en-chia-kang on the coast, he "heard the reports of bandit gunfire," a not uncommon occurrence in the bandit-infested northern Kiangsu of the time.[33] On another occasion, while the party was sailing across Hung-tse Lake, they seemed to encounter only favorable winds. Whenever they changed their course, the wind would change directions with them. Even the Dutch engineer remarked upon this strange occurrence.[34] The trip increased Chang Chien's firsthand knowledge of the river which he hoped to tame. He returned to Peking on May 28.

As the flood season approached late in the summer of 1914, Chang Chien again asked and received permission to be relieved of his ministerial duties so that he could go south to Kiangsu once more.[35] At about that time the American Red Cross sent an engineering team over into the Huai danger area. The team, headed by Colonel William L. Sibert, who had just completed the Gatun lock and dam on the Panama Canal, included two other outstanding engineers, Professor Daniel W. Mead of the Ohio Flood Commission and Mr. Arthur P. Davis, chief engineer of the United States Reclamation Service.[36] They spent the months of August and September in the field, but were unable to visit northern Kiangsu because of renewed bandit activities. They did, however, request for and receive all of the pertinent data gathered by the successive survey organizations. Upon the termination of their visit, they issued a report, stating that they believed the existing single outlet to the Yangtze, if properly improved at a cost of thirty million dollars, would be sufficient to handle all of the Huai flow.[37] Chang Chien promptly voiced his criticism by publishing an article entitled "When Seeking a Solution to the Huai Problem It Is Necessary to Study Its History and Geography!"[38] This was a pointed reminder to the Red Cross-sponsored group that they were relatively late-comers among those who had sought a solution to the Huai problem.

In 1915 Chang Chien asked for permission to attend the International Water Conservancy Conference to be held in the United States. This would have allowed him to visit America for the first time, but his request was turned down by Yüan Shih-k'ai because of his advanced age.[39] As we have seen, he soon resigned all his official positions and returned to Nan-t'ung.

The year 1916 was marked by the most severe flooding of the Huai region in several decades, surpassing the havoc wrought by the 1914 flood. The effect of this disaster gave renewed emphasis to the need for a permanent solution. Chang Chien's own comprehensive plan appeared in 1918. A year later the Anhwei Water Conservancy Surveying Bureau issued its plan. This was in turn followed in 1920 by the plan of a well-known American engineer, John Ripley Freeman, who had been retained by the Chinese Government on a consulting basis.

Chang Chien's ideas were embodied in a lengthy, detailed plan which was drawn up at his direction by his associates in the Kiang-Huai Water Conservancy Surveying Bureau. Based on the latest data accumulated over a span of years, it went into great details concerning the financial and technical aspects of the enterprise. In essence, however, it modified the basic concepts of his previous recommendations only to the extent that, instead of locating the sea outlet of the Huai at Kuan-ho-k'ou, the Huai River was to reach the sea by way of the former course of the Yellow River.

Where sedimentation had raised the former riverbed so high as to make the cost of dredging prohibitive, an alternate channel was to be formed by constructing a new levee parallel to the old north-bank levee. The latter thus would be on the south bank of the new channel. Otherwise the double-outlet scheme remained substantially unchanged. Of the total volume of water discharged by the Huai into Hung-tse Lake, 20 percent would be retained in the lake, 56 percent would flow through the San Ho Channel, the Kao-pao Lakes, and into the Yangtze at San-chiang-ying, while the remaining 24 percent would then be discharged through the Ch'ang-fu River, the former Yellow River, into the sea. Thus Hung-tse Lake would become a retention basin, with only a portion of the lake turned into reclaimed land. The plan was projected on a nine-year basis, at an estimated annual cost of ten million yuan. Labor was to be supplied by the demilitarization of a million soldiers of the private armies who were then waging civil wars across the land. The bulk of the financial burden of the project would be paid out of the money saved from disbanding these armies. The eventual accumulation of income through the sale of reclaimed land and the taxation of land improved by the project, as well as transportation charges on increased water traffic, would repay the cost of the project severalfold. This plan did not encompass the improvement of the Huai above the Hung-tse Lake, but did include the improvement and control of the Yi and the Shu.[40]

The plan announced by the Anhwei Water Conservancy Surveying Bureau differed with Chang Chien's plans on the following points:

1. All of the Huai water was to be released through the two outlets, in the proportion of 30/37 to the Yangtze and 7/37 to the sea. With the dredging of two channels leading the water through Hung-tse lake, the remainder of the lake would all be drained and converted into farm lands.

2. The sea outlet would be located at the mouth of the She-yang River, south of the mouth of the former Yellow River. Water to be discharged here would be led through a portion of the lower Inner Rivers system.

3. The Yi and the Shu would have a joint outlet.

4. The estimated cost was eighty-eight million yuan. The eventual benefits were estimated to be nearly five times this amount.[41]

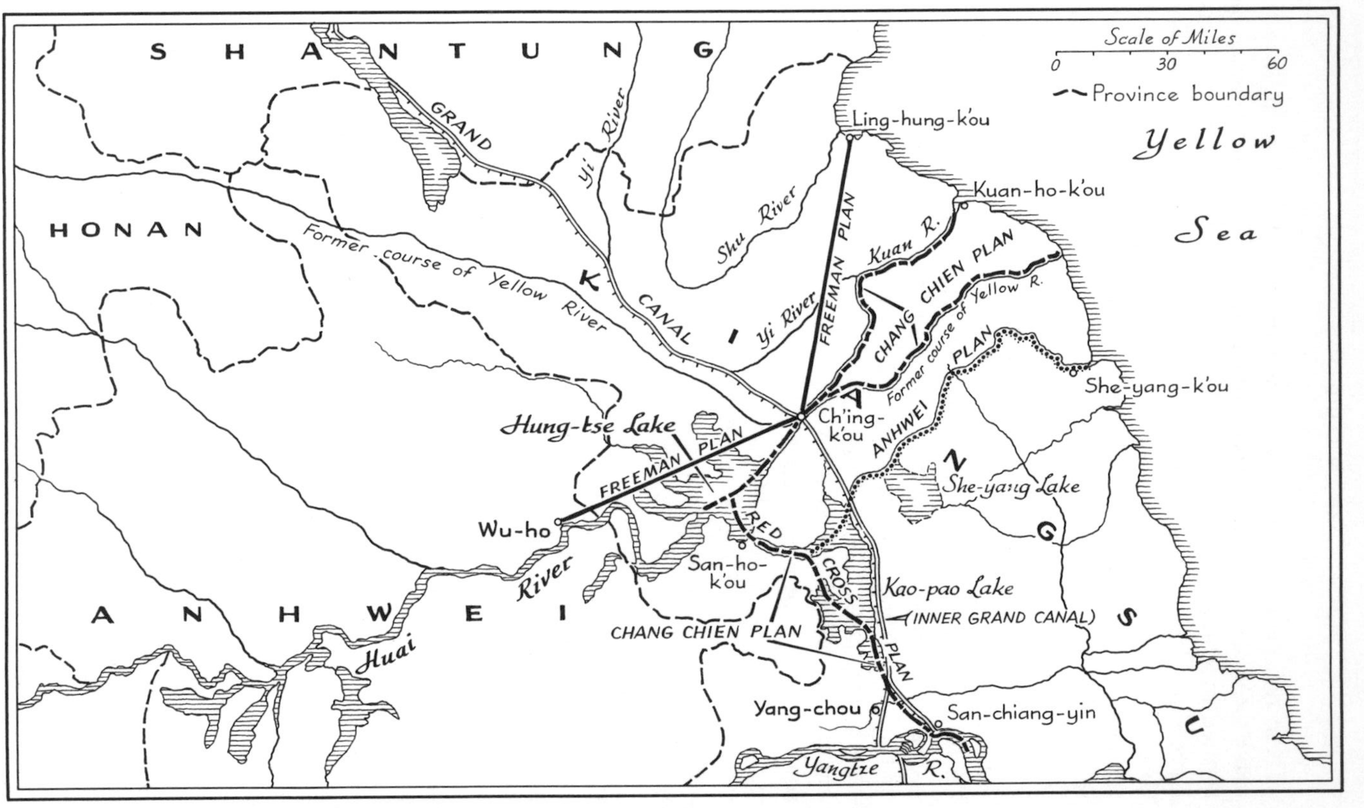

Map Two Huai Basin and Proposed Drainage Schemes

The boldest of the proposed solutions to the Huai problem was the Freeman Plan. John Ripley Freeman, an American engineer of wide experience on such major rivers as the Mississippi and the Colorado, was generally regarded as one of the world's leading experts on hydraulic engineering.[42] From 1917 to 1920 he served as Consulting Engineer to the Chinese Government on the improvement of the Grand Canal. His interest in the Huai was further heightened when Sung Hsi-shang, a graduate of the Nan-t'ung Normal School and one of Chang Chien's proteges, consulted him on the problem of the Huai.[43] In 1919 he made a trip of several months' duration to China. As a result of the trip, he drafted what he called a "tentative plan." He departed from all the other suggestions by calling for the dredging of an artificial channel from Wu-ho in Anhwei direct to the sea at Lin-hung-k'ou. The perfectly straight channel was to have only one slight change of direction, at the point where Ch'ang-fu River meets the Grand Canal. The channel was made straight so that the scouring action of the comparatively swift-moving current would keep the accumulation of sediment at a minimum. In order to obtain the desired swiftness of current, all of the Huai water was to be concentrated to flow through the channel; the Yangtze outlet would be sealed off. In addition, the waters of the Shu and the Yi, which ordinarily flow into the sea at Ling-hung-k'ou and Kuan-ho-k'ou respectively, would be diverted to the new channel. The northern half of Hung-tse Lake would be made into a reservoir, while the southern part would be reclaimed. Freeman believed no more than twelve million yuan would be required for the project.[44]

It is not within the scope of this study to judge the relative merits of these differing proposals. There was general agreement in the need to provide for the Huai's outflow. The key question was: Should there be one or two outlets? The proponents of the single-outlet solution were split between the Yangtze and the sea outlets, while those who favored two outlets disagreed as to the location of the sea outlet.

The single-outlet idea was generally attacked as inadequate for the passage of all the water of the Huai during flood season. Both the Red Cross Plan and the Freeman Plan were based on the peak flow figure—i.e., the maximum amount of water flowing past a given point—of 1914: 5,660 cubic meters per second, whereas later data showed that the figure could reach as high as 12,500 cubic meters per second, as it did in the floods of 1916.[45] As for the Anhwei Plan, its suggestion of locating the sea outlet at the mouth of the She-yang River received scant support. Chang Chien's ideas were in turn criticized by Freeman, who regarded the cost of the project as excessive and doubted whether anything less than the total flow of the Huai through the former channel of the Yellow River could keep the problem of sedimentation from getting out of hand.[46] Chang Chien himself admitted that he was induced to favor the former mouth of the Yellow River over Kuan-ho-k'ou as the sea outlet because of the outspoken opposition of the salt field owners of the Kuan-ho-k'ou area.[47]

None of the plans discussed above was actually carried out, but Chang Chien's efforts toward solving the problem of the Huai prompted the government to appoint him to the post of Director of the Grand Canal in Kiangsu in 1920, with his colleague Han Kuo-chün as Associate Director. From the very first he was faced with the old problem of the lack of operating funds. For although a budget of one million yuan was allotted to him for his three-year term, its expenditure had to be approved by the Ministry of Finance.[48] Most of the available fund was used for surveying work. When he submitted a comprehensive plan for improving the canal, he was told to continue his work of piecemeal improvement with a limited budget. Knowing that he would never be allowed to have a free hand, he handed in his resignation in 1921, but without success. He tried four more times to resign, but each time the government refused to release him from his post.[49]

In 1921 another disastrous flood ravaged Anhwei and Kiangsu. Both the Yangtze and the Huai were badly swollen, and reports of extreme conditions came from up and down the Huai River. Accompanied by Han Kuo-chün, Chang Chien, then in his sixty-eighth year, traveled widely over the threatened area, supervising the work of checking the flood. Meanwhile he was selected to go to the United States as one of the senior advisers to the Chinese delegation attending the Washington Conference, but he felt that his presence was needed in Kiangsu and declined the post.[50] On August 23 his official party arrived at Chao-kuan Dam, near Kao-yu, Kiangsu. There they were greeted by a mob of several thousand refugees, half of whom, those whose homes were upstream of the dam, demanded that the dam be fully opened, while the other half were equally determined to prevent this from happening and thereby further endangering their downstream homes. Both sides made representations to him, and the situation became extremely tense. He, however, held fast to his decision not to make a move before ascertaining the exact situation both upstream and downstream of the dam. When the official party moved on to Kao-yu, they were met by more people fleeing from disaster, clamoring that the dam be opened. They surrounded the temple in which the official party was staying, pressing their demands, and it was only with great difficulties that Chang Chien, Han Kuo-chün, and the others managed to get away without suffering bodily harm. Chang Chien finally decided against opening Chao-kuan Dam because the country downstream of the dam was already inundated by eight feet of water.[51]

This incident acted as a spur to his efforts to carry out a partial solution of the Huai problem. This was a plan, begun earlier in the year, to divert some of the Huai water from its course between Kao-pao Lake and the Yangtze through a side outlet to the sea. Such an outlet was to be provided by Wang-chia-kang. Water from Kao-pao Lake would flow eastward down the southernmost channel of the Inner Lower Rivers to the new outlet. As this route had very little gradient and was affected by the fluctuations of the tides, the work at Wang-chia-kang consisted of the straightening of the channel and the construction of a dam to allow the outward flow of water at low tide while holding back the high tides.[52] Chang Chien was able to complete the straightening of two thirds of the channel before funds ran out. Most of the financial support had been raised through his personal connections, including a loan of 10,000 yuan from the salt merchants of the Huai-nan area, but appeals to the provincial authorities were in vain. As a result, the remainder of his program, including the construction of the dam and a comprehensive scheme to create a secondary network of canals linked to the Ch'uan-ch'ang River, was never carried out.[53]

The winter of 1921–22 also saw him turn to the problem of the Yangtze. Impatient with the inaction of the provincial authorities, he issued a call for nine of the lower Yangtze localities in Kiangsu —Kiang-ying, Ch'ang-shu, T'ai-ch'ang, Pao-shan, Ch'ung-ming, Ch'ing-kiang, Ju-kao, Nan-t'ung, and Hai-men—to send representatives to a meeting held at Nan-t'ung on November 9 to discuss possible joint action. A second meeting was held in Shanghai in the spring of 1922, as a result of which the provincial authorities formed an agency to survey the Yangtze.[54] This was the extent of Chang Chien's efforts toward the Yangtze. He realized that a piecemeal solution to the Yangtze problem was unsatisfactory, and that the Yangtze must be treated as a whole. Consequently when his son, Chang Hsiao-jo, was appointed Chairman of the Yangtze Waterway Commission in 1926, he wrote to his son, with the hope that the latter would carry out some of his own ideas.[55]

Chang Chien's lifelong concern with China's perennial problem of flooding rivers was not untypical of conscientious officials and gentry throughout much of Chinese history. He was, however, one of the earliest to appreciate the value of applying Western technology to the task of river control. He pioneered in the establishment of a permanent agency for the systematic collection of scientific data. In his writings he demonstrated a capacity for combining the experience gained by successful conservationists of the past with the method of control based on the most up-to-date information. He did not hesitate to consult qualified foreign engineers—his own plan for controlling the Huai was submitted to Freeman for critical appraisal—but he had little use for those who ignored the regional particularities presented by the problem. His greatest difficulty was the shortage of funds, as his private resources were completely inadequate for such vast undertakings. He sought to obtain government support for his projects by being appointed to official positions, but the unstable political situation in the early years of the republic deprived him of any real financial backing from the government.

In summary it seems clear that Chang Chien's efforts to tame the Huai ended in failure. Despite the grandiose schemes made and the number of survey maps drawn, precious little actual result accrued over the entire span of years during which he worked to promote the control of the Huai. This troublesome river continued to ravage the countryside periodically. The reason for this state of affairs is not difficult to pin down. The Huai flowed through Honan, Anhwei, and Kiangsu on its way to its meeting with the waters of the Yangtze. Control of the Huai would require cooperation among the three provinces, something which was beyond the power of Chang Chien to ensure. He was fully aware of the fact that it required a national agency with adequate power and funds to do the job. This was what he sought to achieve when he attained the post of Director General of Water Conservancy in 1913. Unfortunately he was never given the proper backing by Yüan Shih-k'ai, and any hope he had of raising funds through the good office of the American Red Cross was completely dashed when World War I broke out. The failure of Chang Chien to tame the Huai remained one of his bitterest regrets to the end of his life.

CHAPTER EIGHT

The Modernization of Nan-t'ung

WE HAVE traced Chang Chien's career as an industrialist, an educator, a conservationist, and a government official. It has been indicated that patriotism was the underlying motivation which prompted him to undertake his various endeavors. The account would not be complete, however, if his civic and philanthropic efforts in Nan-t'ung were not related to the rest of his career. More than anything else, they emphasized the tenor of his life and his accomplishments.

To Chang Chien all he undertook reflected his interest in his native district. His establishment of the Dah Sun Cotton Mill was due in part to the fact that Nan-t'ung was a cotton-producing district. After Dah Sun yarn became a commercial success, he did not institute machine weaving on a large scale, because home weaving was an important subsidiary occupation in Nan-t'ung. His educational effort was directed primarily toward providing Nan-t'ung with a complete school system. His conservation efforts in water conservancy, land reclamation, and salt reform, though they were to achieve national significance, originated out of his concern with the welfare of his native district. In short, throughout his manifold career, Chang Chien was guided by his desire to reach a specific objective: achieving "local self-government" for Nan-t'ung.

It may be argued that there appears to be a logical inconsistency here: that if patriotism was Chang Chien's basic motivation, his primary concern for his native district would seem to be a contradiction. In reality the apparent inconsistency arises only through a difference in the usage of the term "local self-government," which we associate with local political independence from the central authority. Chang Chien used the term *tzu-chih* (self-government or local rule) in a much broader sense. It embraced every aspect of "self-strengthening" on the local level, including industry, education, conservation, philanthropy, and public works. His efforts in these directions were not designed to build up Nan-t'ung at the expense of the nation as a whole. On the contrary, he was firmly convinced that only through the improvement of each locality could the nation as a whole be effectively strengthened. In 1915, when he made a move to put all his local projects on a self-sustaining basis, he aptly summed up this point of view:

> I believe that national strength is based on local self-government. Local self-government in turn is dependent upon industry and education. And in order to make up for the inadequacies in the society, we must rely on philanthropy. From 1895 on I concerned myself with industry. From 1901 on I was occupied with education. It was not until 1907 that I took up philanthropy. For if nothing is done for the people who are uneducated and uncared for, their effect on local self-government may be slight, but their effect on national welfare would be very great.[1]

Civic and Philanthropic Enterprises

The majority of Chang Chien's many civic and philanthropic projects in Nan-t'ung were realized after 1912. This was due as much to his preoccupation with industrial and educational efforts in the early part of his active career as to the fact that the replacement of the Ch'ing dynasty by a politically unstable republic in effect gave him a free hand in Nan-t'ung. His interest in promoting local welfare, however, may be traced as far back as 1883. At that time he had just returned from Korea, declining all proffers of official appointments. He had not yet won his *chü-jen* degree. So in the course of preparing for further scholastic advancement, he concerned himself with local affairs. The first matter that engaged his attention was the traditionally heavy commodity tax which was levied on the native cloth produced in Nan-t'ung. Largely due to the effort of Chang Chien and Shen Hsieh-chün (who was later to become one of his staunchest supporters in the establishment of Dah Sun), the tax was reduced.[2] In 1884 he was responsible for the erection in his birthplace of Ch'ang-lo village of a public granary, in which surplus grain was kept for use in lean years.[3] Three years later Chang Chien sought to aid in the reestablishment of the P'u-shan T'ang, a benevolent institution for the relief of the destitute, in Hai-men. The people of Hai-men had sought official permission for its reestablishment in vain for three years, when

Chang Chien decided to lend a hand. He also found the official red tape almost insuperable, and the matter was not favorably settled until 1897.[4]

Until 1908 Chang Chien was primarily occupied by Dah Sun and the beginnings of a school system in Nan-t'ung. Whenever he had time, however, he would turn his attention to matters of local welfare. He realized that further efforts toward the improvement of Nan-t'ung must be preceded by the completion of a comprehensive survey and mapping of the locality. This was essential not only for his plans to establish a system of primary schools in Nan-t'ung, but also for his proposed network of paved roads. Accordingly, he added a course on surveying in the normal school. By 1908 he had obtained the required number of competent surveyors to initiate the project. Up to eight groups of surveyors were sent out to cover the district. Altogether 400 days were spent for the actual fieldwork. Another additional 240 days were required to complete the maps. Two sets of maps were produced, scaled at 5,000:1 and 20,000:1 respectively, at a cost of some 33,000 yuan (about 23,500 taels), most of which went for salaries. As a result Nan-t'ung was the most completely mapped locality of its size in the country and one of the few localities that had been surveyed up to that time.[5]

The survey maps proved to be of immediate benefit, for one of the pressing problems which plagued Nan-t'ung at the time was the rapid rate of erosion which threatened the district's Yangtze River front. In 1909 Chang Chien seized on the opportunity of a visit by Governor-general Tuan-fang to point out to him the seriousness of the situation. That same year he attempted unsuccessfully to borrow 500,000 taels from the official government bank to finance the project of building an embankment along the river front.[6] The following year he requested the provincial officials to forward his petition for a local exemption of the tax on cotton yarn to finance the project, but this request also met with a refusal. By that time the erosion had reached such a point that the river front came to within two miles of Nan-t'ung city, whereas thirty years before the river and the city were separated by four times that distance.[7] Chang Chien then turned to a foreign bank in Shanghai to obtain the necessary 500,000 taels through a twenty-year loan at 6 percent annual interest, pledging the 2,600 acres of river-front land as securities, but again officials failed to approve the transaction.[8]

With the end of the imperial government, Chang Chien hoped that the new republican regime would be more sympathetic toward the plight of Nan-t'ung. Accordingly, he renewed his request for tax exemption, stating that it would be used as part payment for the proposed long-term bank loan. To his disappointment, the new government also failed to give its consent for the tax exemption.[9] Chang Chien then made one more attempt to settle the financial aspect of the project by arranging for a new loan of 500,000 taels at 5.5 percent interest per annum from the Bank of Belgium, through the good offices of the Belgian Consul in Peking. Since negotiations for Belgium to back the Huai River project were still in progress at the time, the consul insisted on the inclusion of this loan in the Huai River discussion in order to benefit from the expert advice of Western engineers. The failure of the Huai River discussion thus brought this to nought also.[10]

In 1909 Chang Chien turned to the problem of improving the local prison. Like prisons throughout the country at the time, the one in Nan-t'ung was dark, dank, and filthy. Seven years were to elapse before the remodeling of the prison. The new prison was a two-storied brick structure, with over one hundred rooms for the inmates and eight prison workshops, ranging from soap and print shops to tailoring and carpentry shops. To finance the remodeling, Chang Chien had to borrow 30,000 yuan (about 21,000 taels) over the years. Eventually the financial load of maintaining the upkeep of the prison became too much for him, and he had to request the provincial government in 1920 to assume its maintenance.[11]

Chang Chien's interest in improving the prison was more a reflection of his desire to alleviate the lot of the unfortunate rather than an interest in police matters. Nevertheless he deemed it important that Nan-t'ung should have its own law-enforcement agency. The plant guard which he set up with the establishment of the Dah Sun Cotton Mill in 1899 became the Nan-t'ung, T'ai-chou, Hai-men Industrial Police Guard.[12] He also set up police training schools to provide basic training for the raw recruits, who had little knowledge of the most elementary police procedures. By 1920 the local force had proved its worth. Under the command of Chang Jen, son of Chang Ch'a, it successfully fought off incursions by a gang of Shanghai rowdies in 1914 and bandits in 1916.[13] Police expenses, however, like the cost of maintaining the prison, proved beyond the capacity of Chang Chien. Having paid over 100,000 yuan (about 71,000 taels) to provide for police barracks, police stations, the prison, and other public buildings, he had to ask the provincial government to take over the financial burden. The significant point here is that, until 1920, both the national and the provincial authorities apparently pursued a "hands-off" policy in regard to Nan-t'ung. In contrast, other cities in Kiangsu, such as Huai-yin and T'ung-shan (Hsü-chou), received full government subsidy for their local law-enforcement agencies.[14]

Chang Chien's chief philanthropic efforts centered around several institutions in which he took an early interest, an interest which he maintained throughout his life. These institutions were: a foundling home, homes for the aged, workshops for the poor, a medical clinic, a home for the disabled and a school for the blind and dumb.

The institution of the foundling home had existed in traditional China. The original foundling home in Nan-t'ung was established in 1664. Since 1774 a number of other foundling homes came into existence, so that by 1875 there were no less than six, some of which were in the outlying sections of Nan-t'ung district.[15] By the end of the nineteenth century, however, most of the foundling homes had fallen upon hard times through poor management and the lack of funds. In 1906, at the prompting of his wife, Chang Chien completed at a cost of 23,400 yuan (about 16,700 taels) his new foundling home, a one-story brick structure in T'ang-chia-cha. Upwards of 1200 children could be provided for.[16] The infants were either illegitimate or from destitute families. Since most of the children were abandoned there by unidentified parents at night, the home bowed to convenience and provided an ingenious receptacle outside the door. It was connected to a bell, so that the receptacle need only be turned around to alert the home that another infant had been left in its care.[17] The foundlings, most of them girls, were cared for either at the home itself or farmed out to families until they reached the age of ten. Children from four to seven were taught in a kindergarten attached to the home. When they reached seven years of age, they were sent to the nearby lower primary schools. At ten they were sent either to higher primary schools or directly to the various factories.[18] The foundling home was supported largely from Chang Chien's private funds. On a number of occasions, from 1907 on, he sold samples of his calligraphy to finance the home.[19] This was a common method of raising contributions for charity in those days. Chang Chien had no great difficulties in obtaining the necessary funds because his fine calligraphy was well known.

The end of the Ch'ing dynasty gave fresh impetus to Chang Chien in his philanthropic activities. Plans for the first home for the aged were drawn up in the early part of 1912, and the institution accepted its first inmate in November of 1913. Built at a cost of 6,000 yuan (about 4,300 taels) largely from the money which his friends contributed on his sixtieth birthday, the home stood on three acres of land and accommodated over a hundred men and women.[20] Another home was established in 1922.[21]

The year 1913 saw the establishment of workshops for the poor and a small medical clinic. The 66,000 yuan (about 47,000 taels) that went into the establishment of the workshops came from Chang Chien's salary as the Liang-Huai salt commissioner, which he declined to use himself and allocated for this purpose instead.[22] Three workshops were set up: one in I-cheng, one in Tung-t'ai, and one in Nan-t'ung.[23] The latter was established in October, 1914. A number of handicrafts were carried on in these shops, notably carpentry, tailoring, and weaving. The main idea of the workshops was to provide some kind of work relief to the destitute and the homeless until they were able to stand on their own feet again.

The medical clinic was an establishment attached to the medical school. By 1920 it had acquired X-ray and operating facilities, under the general direction of a German physician, Dr. Hans Scheidermann, who served until 1924.[24] By then the clinic had grown into a hospital of four wards and five clinics, with eight doctors and twenty nurses, caring for as many as a hundred patients monthly.[25]

Still another of Chang Chien's philanthropic projects which received its impetus in 1912 was a home for the disabled. The original plans had to be delayed while he was serving as Minister of Agriculture and Commerce in Peking. After his resignation in 1915 he took up the project once again, building the home near the foot of Lang Shan (Wolf Hill). In March, 1916, the home was formally opened with the acceptance of forty-nine inmates. By 1920 the institution was caring for 123 persons. The initial cost of 6,000 yuan (about 4,300 taels) and the cost of maintenance, like the support of the foundling home, came from periodical sales of his calligraphy.[26]

One project which appealed particularly to Chang Chien because it was both philanthropic and educational was the school for the blind and dumb. He first broached the subject to a Kiangsu provincial official as early as 1907, hoping for government support for the project. Apparently he did not succeed, for five years later he took up this project personally. First he instituted training in the method of teaching the blind and the dumb. Then in 1916 he established the school itself, which taught the handicapped by means of a modified braille system. In an article written when he first instituted training for the teachers of the handicapped, Chang Chien deplored the fact that no Chinese school of that type existed at the time. He emphasized their importance by citing the figure of 0.2 percent as being the percentage of the blind and dumb in the population in the West. Applying the figure to China, he estimated that there were 800,000 people who were thus handicapped in the country.[27]

As a result of all these philanthropic endeavors, Nan-t'ung was singularly free of beggars, which were found in every other locality of its size in China. A resident in Nan-t'ung, writing in the periodical *Education and Vocation* (*Chiao-yü yü Chih-yeh*) in 1926, reported this fact, and went on to add that, with the possible exception of the school for the blind and dumb, all other institutions were enjoying a flourishing existence.[28]

Institutions like the foundling home and the workshops for the poor were worthy projects, but their establishment merely carried on the tradition set by some of the more public-spirited gentry members in various localities in the country. Chang Chien, however, did not stop with their establishment. He wanted to provide Nan-t'ung with all the public services and institutions which befit a modern urban center. To this end he founded in Nan-t'ung a publishing house, a museum, a library, a meteorological station, and a theater with an attached dramatic school.

The Han Mo Lin Publishing House was founded in 1904 as a direct result of the establishment of the normal school. The original function of the publishing house was to supply the normal school's needs for textbooks and other printed matter. Later on it was put under the management of a Korean scholar who, out of his hatred for the Japanese, had fled his country to seek refuge in Nan-t'ung. Under the direction of this Mr. Kim, who was to spend the remaining thirty years of his life in Nan-t'ung, the publishing house expanded its activities to serve the needs of the entire community.[29]

Another institution which began as an adjunct of the normal school was the museum. Six acres of land near the school were set aside for its establishment in late 1905. Chang Chien contributed to the museum much of his personal collection, such as the ceremonial robe awarded to him by the Korean king in 1882, and invited others to send their collections to the museum. A three-storied structure was built to house the accumulated objects, with separate floors given over to the display of each of three categories of exhibits: natural objects, objects of historical interest, and works of art. Altogether, nearly 3,000 items had been acquired by 1914, the year of its opening. The grounds surrounding the museum were utilized to exhibit a variety of plants, and a small zoo and aviary was attached to the institution. When the fossil skeleton of a marine creature, measuring over forty feet in length, was unearthed on the grounds of T'ung Hai Reclamation Company, it was housed in a separate building constructed on the museum grounds.[30]

Adjoining the museum grounds stood the library, occupying what was once a Buddhist temple. Chang Chien initiated the project in 1908, writing to the provincial authorities for permission to convert the temple into a library.[31] He apparently failed to receive this permission at the time, for he had to wait until 1912 before putting his plan into effect. The work of remodeling the temple and the addition of a second building were completed in 1917, at a total cost of 26,243 yuan (18,745 taels), all from Chang Chien himself.[32] By 1924 the library contained 150,000 *chüan* of Chinese books, 600 Western-language books, and 300 Japanese books.[33] Two thirds of the books were donated by Chang Chien himself, with the rest coming from Chang Ch'a and other contributors in Nan-t'ung and the surrounding localities.[34] It is interesting to note that, according to the library's first catalogue issued in 1914, all the Western-language books were contributed by the Association for Research in Constitutionalism (Hsien-fa Yen-chiu Hui) and naturally consisted mostly of books in the field of political science. Some of its titles were: Aristotle's *Treatise on Government*,[35] Bentham's *Principles of Morals and Legislation*, Blackstone's *Commentaries on Law of England*, Malthus' *Principles of Population*, and Veblen's *Theory of the Leisure Class*.[36] For a city of Nan-t'ung's size the library was a fine one. Unfortunately it was not a free library and was seldom visited by readers. Although it stayed open from 8 A.M. to 5 P.M. daily, the admission charge of twenty fen (a fifth of a yuan) apparently kept many potential readers away. This was illustrated by the fact that, for the entire year of 1918, only a little over one hundred readers used the library.[37]

The meteorological station was another project which took several years to realize. Chang Chien had long regarded accurate weather reporting as essential for the improvement of farming. In early 1913 he began the construction of a station on the summit of Chün Shan (Army Hill). However, it was not fully operative until December of 1916.[38] It received radio weather reports twice daily from the Ziccawei meteorological station near Shanghai. Readings of instruments measuring the climate and atmosphere were taken eight times a day, and reports issued accordingly.[39] The station also served as a training school for aspiring meteorologists. In the summer of 1919 the first class of seven trainees was graduated.

One other project contributed to the cultural life of the community. This was the theater for Chinese opera and the attached dramatic school. In this matter Chang Chien's own love of opera was a strong motivating force. To provide the proper setting for the staging of performances, he built a three-storied auditorium with a capacity of 1200 in 1919 at a cost of 70,000 yuan (50,000 taels).[40] The following year a dramatic school was established as a step in the maintenance of a permanent opera company. The school, however, was more than just a vocational institution; courses in science and languages were offered in addition to music and drama. Under the direction of Ou-yang Yü-ch'ien, an outstanding opera star, the school offered five years of free training for any deserving youth in return for two years of service with the opera company after graduation.[41] Started at a cost of 20,000 yuan (about 14,000 taels), the school at its most flourishing stage had over fifty students. The school went through ups and downs and finally closed along with the theater in 1925, but during its existence it produced a number of competent performers.[42]

An interesting sidelight of Chang Chien's venture in establishing the theatre was his effort to introduce modern rules of etiquette among the theater-going crowd. The seats at the theatre were all numbered and reservation was required for attendance. Moreover, he introduced the practice of applauding as a sign of appreciation rather than the standard practice of vocal approval. Those were innovations at the time, and their introduction indicated Chang Chien's concern for the behavior of the inhabitants of what he fondly regarded as his "model district."[43]

Within the city of Nan-t'ung Chang Chien went to great lengths to beautify the place by the improvement of the existing park and the addition of new ones. By late 1917 five parks had been opened to the public. First of all, the old park was improved and renamed North Park. By its attractive lake were added tennis courts and a rifle range. Next a brand new East Park was constructed, designed with the children in mind. Its playgrounds were installed with swings, slides, and spins for their enjoyment. South Park was characterized by its beautiful lily pond. In this park was erected a pavilion called "Yü-chung T'ang," the equivalent of a local hall of fame, in which were placed the names of all the local sons who had distinguished themselves throughout history. The fourth park, West Park, was given over to active recreation. It had playgrounds, drill fields, and swimming pools, as well as a boat dock where boats used on the adjoining lake were kept. For the children a collection of animals was kept in a small zoo. The Nan-t'ung Clubhouse was later built just outside West Park. Finally, there was Central Park, built on the site of a local scenic spot. In this park no less than half a dozen pavilions, offering varied views of the surrounding lake, were located amongst beds of flowers and rare plants.[44] Upon the completion of Central Park in September, 1917, Nan-t'ung held a celebration to commemorate the event.

Chang Chien also saw to the public improvement of Nan-t'ung in other ways. Outside the city of Nan-t'ung he promoted a tree-planting campaign in 1917 to alleviate the generally denuded condition of the countryside. This was carried on as a part of the school program to teach the students the importance of conservation. In the city itself he added to the usefulness and good appearance of public structures by repairing the district office building and the courthouse building.[45] In early 1915 he completed what became the outstanding landmark of the entire Nan-t'ung district, an eighty-foot clock tower which served the additional function of a fire tower.[46] Through these projects the city of Nan-t'ung gradually took on the appearance of a modern municipality.

Of Nan-t'ung's water conservancy projects, the Yao-wang Harbor project ranks next in importance only to the Yangtze river-front embankment project. The building of the seven sluice gates at Yao-wang Harbor was begun in November, 1918, under the general supervision of a young Dutch hydraulic engineer, Hendrik C. de Reike. It was completed in December, 1919, at a cost of 140,000 yuan (100,000 taels), paid for entirely by the funds of the T'ung Hai Land Reclamation Company. Unfortunately de Reike did not see the completion of the project. He died in September, 1919, of cholera contracted while supervising the project.[47]

De Reike was born in Japan, where his father had been the supervising engineer in the building of Yokohama harbor. Following in his father's footsteps, he had been employed on the Whangpoo Water Conservancy Project before coming to Nan-t'ung in 1916 at the invitation of Chang Chien. He was placed in charge of all construction projects in the district. In the short period of three years he supervised the construction of ten sections of the river embankments, two sluice gates, and a bridge. At the time of his death he had already drawn up plans for the construction of five locks, seven weirs, and three roads. His tragic death was a keenly felt loss to Chang Chien, who, after informing the Dutch Consul at Shanghai of de Reike's death, requested that he be duly honored.[48] He was buried at the foot of Chün Shan.

One of Chang Chien's proudest achievements was the building of a network of paved motor roads radiating from the city of Nan-t'ung to the outer reaches of the district. He prepared for the construction of this road system in 1914. Four years later, he announced the plan to build two main roads, one leading eastward from the city of Nan-t'ung to the seacoast, one leading northward to the Ju-kao line. In addition, a secondary road would be built from the city of Nan-t'ung in the direction of the town of Hai-men, together with five shorter roads connecting the city of Nan-t'ung with T'ang-chia-cha, T'ien-sheng Harbor, and Lang Shan (Wolf Hill). Chang Chien foresaw the need for the erection of a total of thirty large bridges and 120 smaller bridges, the total cost of which would amount to 60,000 yuan (about 43,000 taels).[49] With the concurrence of his brother, Chang Chien in 1918 allotted 1 percent of the total capital from all the enterprises in Nan-t'ung, including Dah Sun, T'ung Hai, and T'ung Jen T'ai, for the financing of road construction. This sum came to 75,000 yuan (about 54,000 taels). Later on another 42,000 yuan (30,000 taels) were raised.[50] The actual construction of the entire network of roads was entrusted to a local Board of Highway Construction, which owned three steam rollers, as well as a fleet of eleven American-made buses. Part of the materials for paving the roads was provided by tearing down the wall of the city of Nan-t'ung. In February, 1921, the first section of the east-west main road, between Nan-t'ung and Chang Chien's native village of Ch'ang-lo, was opened to traffic. Two years later the entire length was completed. As he rode on the new highway, Chang Chien could not refrain from comparing the three hours which it now took to travel from Nan-t'ung to the seacoast with the condition of twenty years before, when T'ung Hai was first organized. Then the same trip took three days to complete.[51]

The buses of the local Board of Highway Construction were all purchased by Dah Sun through its Shanghai office. Beginning in June, 1920, regular service was instituted to Lang Shan and to the docks at T'ien-sheng Harbor.[52]

For the streets of the city of Nan-t'ung Chang Chien introduced gas illumination at night before 1910, switching to electric streetlights in 1917. Electricity was provided by the four 50-kilowatt generators of the T'ung Ming Electric Light Company, established with a capital of 60,000 taels in 1917. The facilities permitted the transmission of 4,000 volts up to a distance of two miles.[53] Unfortunately T'ung Ming's generators did not produce sufficient electricity to provide the power for Nan-t'ung's numerous industries. It was one of Chang Chien's lifelong regrets that his master plan of a two-million-yuan, joint private-government electric company was never realized.[54]

Efforts to Maintain the Institutions

It has been noted that nearly all of the many civic and philanthropic institutions were financed solely by Chang Chien and his brother, Chang Ch'a. As the Chang brothers approached their seventies they were well aware that the various institutions would not be permanent unless they put them on a self-sustaining basis. All attempts to acquire official support had failed. Both before and after the establishment of the republic, Chang Chien had failed to gain some measure of tax relief.[55] By 1915 the combined yearly expenses which the Chang brothers had to bear had reached the figure of 270,000 yuan (about 193,000 taels).[56] That year he tried a new approach. Relying on his past association with Yüan Shih-k'ai, he wrote the president requesting that some 23,000 acres of wasteland in the neighboring district of T'ai-chou be set aside as endowment for the educational and philanthropic institutions of Nan-t'ung, promising to repay the full land price in twelve years.[57] This was duly approved. Subsequently the government canceled the debt,[58] but apparently the purchase of these wastelands did not solve the problem. In 1920 Chang Chien made another attempt to put the status of the various Nan-t'ung institutions on a permanent basis. He issued two million yuan (about 1.4 million taels) worth of local public bonds, payable either at 6 percent interest per annum in twenty years or at a graduated scale in less than twenty years.[59] We are unable to determine the results of this drive for funds because of a lack of information. Judging from the fact that most of the civic and philanthropic institutions failed to survive after the passing of the Chang brothers, we must assume that the scheme was not successful.

In 1920 Chang Hsiao-jo, Chang Chien's son, organized the Nan-t'ung Local Self-government Association. Since his return from the United States in 1918, Chang Hsiao-jo had been given increasing responsibilities by Chang Chien, who hoped that he would eventually take over most of the responsibilities resting upon his father and his uncle. Yet the establishment of the Local Self-government Association, according to Chang Hsiao-jo, originally did not meet with Chang Chien's full approval. Only after Chang Hsiao-jo repeatedly pressed for its establishment did Chang Chien give his consent.[60] For a while the association served the purpose of centralizing all local civic and philanthropic endeavors, but it never fully became the effective agency which Chang Hsiao-jo had hoped.

As he approached his seventieth birthday (according to Chinese calculation) in 1922, Chang Chien began making plans to hold an exhibition coinciding with the celebration of his birthday. The exhibition was to be a kind of summing up of Nan-t'ung's progress in the fields of industry, education, conservation, philanthropy, and public works during the previous quarter century. This would constitute his final report to the people of Nan-t'ung and to the world, after which he had every intention of entering full retirement. No pains were spared for the occasion. A special planning bureau was set up in 1921 to handle the details. Arrangements were initiated with the government to exempt imported items of exhibit from the regular custom duties. The exhibition was to last three months, beginning in late March of 1922.[61] Unfortunately while the preparations were still under way in August, 1921, another of the periodic typhoons hit Nan-t'ung severely for four days, ending August 22. The dikes and embankments suffered damages to the extent of 200,000 yuan (about 140,000 taels). If the local water conservancy problem was to be tackled thoroughly, another 200,000 yuan would be needed for the construction of dams and sluice gates. Due to this natural calamity, Chang Chien called off the exhibition and the attendant celebrations, leaving only a mass athletic meet to be held. He postponed the celebration to 1927, when Nan-t'ung would be commemorating the thirtieth anniversary since the start of its modernization.[62] Chang Chien's death in 1926 cut short this last hope.[63]

CHAPTER NINE

Chang Chien as a Modernizer

IF IT WAS Chang Chien's life goal to modernize his nation, the question must be asked whether he succeeded or failed in the main to achieve his objective. In 1929 the noted Chinese scholar Hu Shih wrote in his foreword to the biography of Chang Chien:

> No one can deny that in the history of modern China Chang Chien was a great but ultimately unsuccessful hero. He single-handedly blazed innumerable new trails and played the part of a pioneer for thirty years. He gained livelihood for millions, benefitted an entire region, and influenced the whole country. Yet because he embarked on so many projects and took upon himself such enormous tasks, he died with many plans uncompleted.[1]

This constitutes a fair reflection of the sentiment in which Chang Chien was held in the years immediately following his death. He was generally thought of with admiration and regret; admiration for all that he managed to accomplish in a quarter of a century, and regret that his career, remarkable though it was, generally ended in failure. This judgment of his being a "heroic failure" has held firm among his countrymen to the present. Recently two of his associates have published studies of his life. Liu Hou-sheng's *Chang Chien Chuan-chi*, published in 1958, concludes somewhat curiously with several negative conclusions: that Chang Chien was neither a political figure nor an industrialist, or for that matter, even an accomplished writer.[2] In 1963 Sung Hsi-shang, in the preface to his *Chang Chien ti Sheng-p'ing*, regrets that Chang Chien was unable to realize his hopes in any of his major endeavors.[3] From these judgments of people who have known Chang Chien's career best, the general conclusion that his failures far outweigh his successes seem inescapable.

Why was Chang Chien considered a failure? He was so considered for two reasons. One was the situation in Nan-t'ung after his death. The great accomplishments he effected there was not sustained. We have already seen how Dah Sun, the most important of Nan-t'ung's industries and the financial source of much of the district's civic and philanthropic enterprises, steadily lost money and became heavily indebted in the 1920s. Nan-t'ung as a whole declined along with Dah Sun.[4] This came about partly as a result of the generally unstable and stagnant situation in China as a whole in the 1920s and 1930s, but partly also as a result of factors inherent in the situation in Nan-t'ung itself. Chang Chien himself must share in the blame. Among his colleagues and associates, he chose to concentrate his hopes for a successor in the person of his son, Chang Hsiao-jo, but the younger Chang did not live up to his father's expectations.[5] He lacked his father's commanding personality, executive ability, and breadth of vision. It could almost be said that his greatest achievement was in finishing the task of editing of his father's collected works, and in writing the first biography of his father.

On a broader level, Chang Chien was considered a failure because his career was generally outside the mainstream of contemporary history. Throughout his life Chang Chien suffered from a degree of provincialism. In spite of his concern with national affairs, he was always isolated from the larger movements of his time. Politically, he was never affiliated, either before or after 1911, with the group which became dominant. During the Ch'ing dynasty he supported the government against the revolutionaries, yet his constitutional and self-government efforts were apart from government efforts in the same direction.[6] After the dynasty was overthrown, he was among the group which initially supported Yüan Shih-k'ai but later lost its influence when it withdrew its support as Yüan's imperial ambitions were revealed. Socially, also, some of the major changes which occurred in the first quarter of the twentieth century touched Chang Chien but lightly. His basic beliefs altered remarkably little from the time he first conceived of the idea of setting up a cotton mill to the day he died. He accepted few of the Western-inspired ideas, such as individualism, the equality of the sexes, and the pursuit of truth for its own sake. He remained basically a product of classical training. Intellectually, Chang Chien remained aloof from the ferment which stirred China during the latter part of his life. A wave of new ideas flowed in from the West, partly through books, but more through the efforts of returned scholars from abroad like Ts'ai Yüan-p'ei and Hu Shih. These men brought back with them new conceptual schemes and new methodologies, all profoundly influential in the minds of the rising younger generation. Chang Chien found himself out of touch with these new developments.

Both these indictments can be considered valid, but to judge the success and failure of Chang Chien's career solely on these two counts is to overlook the historical context under which he operated. When he first embarked on his modernizing career in 1895, the Ch'ing dynasty was beset by upheavals from within and agressions from without. When he died in 1926, even the partial measure of national unity which came as a result of the Northern Expedition of 1926–28 had not yet been realized. Throughout his life Chang Chien operated in an unstable political environment. Moreover, the slowness and unevenness with which the necessary economic and social factors for economic development came into existence in China must also be taken into account. At the time of Dah Sun's founding, the country did not possess even the rudimentary legal and social framework for the transaction of modern business. Laws governing corporate bodies were promulgated in 1904.[7] Such essential facilities as banking, insurance, and modern transportation were almost entirely concentrated in the treaty ports, and designed primarily to serve the foreign commercial interests in these ports. Outside the treaty ports they were practically nonexistent. These difficiencies in the economic sphere were symptomatic of Chinese society as a whole, in which many customs and beliefs quite incompatable with a modern society continued to hold sway throughout the period of Chang Chien's active career.

Chang Chien's accomplishments and failures must also be judged in the light of the inner makeup of the man as well. He was among the last generation of men nurtured in the traditional environment and classical training of the official-gentry class. The initial responsibility for coping with the challenge of the West had fallen on this elite group in Chinese society. And by the very nature of their training and experience, they were ill equipped to assume such a responsibility. The mainspring from which the beliefs of the official-gentry class flowed was Confucianism. Its moral concept and philosophy of life had been the guiding philosophy of the nation for centuries. To a follower of Confucius, moral superiority was of much greater import than mere technical knowledge. Since the concept of change and progress could be applied only to material things, it was therefore of secondary importance and had no effect upon the basic Confucian precepts of human conduct and human relationship. Even the so-called progressive officials like Tseng Kuo-fan, Tso Tsung-t'ang, Li Hung-chang, and Chang Chih-tung—men whose "enlightened" ideas have been much emphasized of late by scholars interested in China's reaction to the West—never seriously questioned the basic Confucian precepts which formed the guiding principles of their lives. Their outlook was summed up neatly in Chang Chih-tung's famous dictum of "Chinese learning for the foundation, Western learning for utilization." Chang Chien transcended the strictures of the Confucian view of life held by these contemporaries to the extent that he saw nothing incompatible with Confucianism in the introduction of industrialization, universal education, and local self-government into China. However, in his system of values and in his mode of thought, he remained steadfastly Confucian.

Given the historical conditions of the time and the inner makeup of the man, we should not be unduly surprised either by the fact that Chang Chien's successes were balanced by his failures or by the fact that some of his successes did not last. His failures, more often than not, were the reflection of larger failures on the national scene, while his achievements were primarily the results of his own vision, energy, and persistence. Nor can we say that his successes were important only for Nan-t'ung. The founding of Dah Sun and the creation of a modern school system, for example, were of national significance. These, and even some of his less successful ventures, such as land reclamation and salt reform, were known throughout the country and served as inspirations for men of the following generation.

The unique contribution of Chang Chien was that his career as a modernizer represented an alternative pattern to those of other reformers in modern China. The leading figures at the time, like K'ang Yu-wei and Sun Yat-sen, all concentrated on finding a political solution to the country's problems. It was their contention that without fundamental political change there was no hope of effecting basic social or economic changes in China. Moreover, in the impatience of trying to pull the country swiftly out of the morass, they assumed nothing significant could be achieved except at the national level, by efforts of the central government. Chang Chien was a living refutation to the exclusiveness of these assumptions. He did not scorn political action, but he chose to concentrate on basic problems in the areas of industry, education, and conservation, which were outside the immediate concerns of political reformers. Except for his brief terms of office, he carried out all of these basic reforms in the capacity of a private individual, on the local level.

Of course, he was not altogether free from official associations. In a country where the basic level of governmental administration operated through the local gentry, his high prestige as a top scholar guaranteed him a certain privileged status. Also through his scholastic attainments he gained the support of some of the most powerful officials of the realm. In any case, with the existing political structure of his time, he could not have operated entirely free from governmental interference even if he had wished to. Chang Chien, however, functioned as a modernizer largely outside of the official political structure. Although the government had permissive power over his projects, he was committed to carry them out on his own. Much of his difficulties in raising funds stemmed from the fact that he was not in a position to divert official funds to his projects, as Chang Chih-tung and Shen Hsüan-huai did. Instead he had to rely on his own reputation and achievement to acquire the needed capital. It must be admitted, however, that in his later years he wielded so much power in Nan-t'ung that for all practical purposes his position was close to that of a regularly appointed official.

Although Chang Chien confined most of his activities to the local scene, he never lost sight of his larger purpose, that of modernizing all of China. On one occasion, in a speech welcoming a group of Chinese visitors from Southeast Asia, he said that in building up Nan-t'ung his "aim was to gain self-government for one district, so that when foreigners saw it, they would know that China still has men with ideas."[8]

For most of his projects Chang Chien followed a realistic, down-to-earth approach. His course of action was determined by his practical nature. He wanted to start projects which would benefit the people of his native district, and which would show results within a reasonable period of time. He was always willing to tailor the means by which he intended to achieve his ends to the possible. His experience strengthened this tendency on his part. His greatest successes came in those areas where his own efforts, combined with favorable factors, were adequate to tackle the problem at hand. His sharpest failures were in projects where his own resources were inadequate. His approach was at all times pragmatic, and seldom followed a consistent and clearly defined doctrine. If he appeared at times to be a democrat, a champion of private enterprise, or a proponent of a decentralized system of education, it was because his experience taught him that such values and systems were practicable in China, not because he was ideologically wedded to these values and systems.

Chang Chien as a modernizer did not abandon the traditional values in which he was steeped. He was proud of China's heritage and never turned his back on it, as Liang Ch'i-ch'ao did for a time. Stripped of his material accomplishments, he betrayed a moral core of Confucianism which was a testament to the solid grounding of traditional training which he had undergone. He valued rationality and abhored violence. It was not weakness on his part that he failed to exalt the glory of fighting and dying for a cause; it was his belief that violence offered no solution to any problem. Only when patriotism was involved did he condone the taking up of arms as a necessity. His aversion to the use of force was matched by his distaste for social upheaval. Revolution in any form did not appeal to him. Wherever possible he introduced reforms without tearing down and destroying the old institutions. Politically he favored legitimism, and in 1911 it was not until events had gone to the length of bringing the republic into existence that he gave his support to the new regime.

Yet, despite his belief in Confucian principles, he was able to depart from the Confucian frame of reference in important respects. He entered the business world, engaged in the culturally despised vocation of commercial undertakings, and made a success of it. Without extensive experience abroad, he was able to overcome the ethnocentric bias of the cultured Chinese and to deal with foreigners on equal terms. He gained a great deal of knowledge in Western technology. By modern standards he did not thoroughly master much of his technical knowledge, but his deficiencies should be considered against the fact that his long years of training in classical studies scarcely prepared him for absorbing technical knowledge.

Thus, the secret of his success was his ability to transcend the bounds of his culture, without at the same time rejecting it altogether. In this respect, he was symptomatic of his times. Until the Revolution of 1911 doomed once and for all the efforts of the moderate reformers, the prevailing spirit of those who were concerned with

China's salvation was of the middle road. In Chang Chien's case it was at once his strength and his weakness. Ability to bridge the old and the new made it possible for him to accomplish what he did as a modernizer. That same combination of the old and the new made it difficult for him to sympathize with the rising generation which took over the country in the 1920s. In many ways Chang Chien can be thought of as the epitome of the transitional figure in modern China.

China in the twentieth century has seen an unmitigated series of calamities and frustrations, the occasional respites notwithstanding. A good measure of her troubles, to be sure, stemmed from external sources. Yet a closer examination betrays an internal deficiency which was quite as crucial as the country's external impotence. That was the repeated mistake, on the part of the Chinese people, to seek a panacea, a "single solution." First it was the unreasoning xenophobia of the Boxers, then the demand for a constitutional government. These were replaced by the adoption of the republican form of government in 1911, the failure of which led in turn to the one-party rule of the Kuomintang and the Communists. In the course of attempting to realize these successive illusory hopes, certain positive results were achieved, notably the literary reforms of the May Fourth Movement and the educational and industrial growth of the 1930s. By and large, however, the Chinese as a people have been caught up alternatively between the two poles of either a feeling of despairing resignation, or one of feverish adherance to some all-encompassing cause. In such a prevailing climate it is little wonder that the spirit and accomplishments of a man like Chang Chien would seem curiously out of place, that the outcome of his limited success, achieved largely at the local level, should be more pitied than praised. No one would deny that, for every country and society, rapid change cannot be accomplished without vision, direction, and energy on the national level. It is nonetheless true that the real accomplishments in modernization of a backward country, Japan for instance, depended also upon the countless and largely unknown people who did their part, large and small, to help bring about change and reform on the "grass-roots" level. Had China had more men like Chang Chien, his own career might not have seemed so unique and outstanding, but the country as a whole would have benefitted enormously in her attempts to find a place among the developed nations of the world.

Abbreviations

CC	Chang Hsiao-jo, *Nan-t'ung Chang Chi-chih Hsien-sheng Chuan-chi*
CL	Chang Chien, *Chang Chi-tzu Chiu-lu*
ESNL	*Erh-shih-nien-lai Chih Nan-t'ung*
Life	*Life of the Honorable Chang Chien: with an Account of the Enterprizes Inaugurated by Him*
NP	Chang Chien, *Seh-weng Tzu-ting Nien-p'u*
NTSY	*Nan-t'ung Shih-yeh Chiao-yü Tz'u-shan Feng-ching*
TCLS	*T'ung-chou Hsing-pan Shih-yeh Chih Li-shih*

The component sections of *CL* and *TCLS* are as follows:

CL (1)	Cheng-wen Lu	Politics
CL (2)	Shih-yeh Lu	Business
CL (3)	Chiao-yü Lu	Education
CL (4)	Tzu-chih Lu	Local Self-government
CL (5)	Tz'u-shan Lu	Philanthropy
CL (6)	Wen Lu	Essays
CL (7)	Shih Lu	Poems
CL (8)	Chuan Lu	Special Section
CL (9)	Wai Lu	Additional Section
TCLS (1)	Ta Sheng Sha-ch'ang	Dah Sun Cotton Mill
TCLS (2)	Ta Sheng Fen-ch'ang	Dah Sun Branch Mill
TCLS (3)	T'ung Hai K'en-mu Kung-ssu	T'ung Hai Land Reclamation Company
TCLS (4)	Kuang Sheng Yu-ch'ang	Kwan Sun Oil Mill
TCLS (5)	Ta Hsing Mien-ch'ang	Dah Sing Flour Mill
TCLS (6)	Han Mo Lin Shu-chü	Han Mo Lin Publishing House
TCLS (7)	Che Sheng Shui-li Kung-ssu	Che Sun Waterways Company

TCLS (8)	Che Sheng Shui-kang Kung-ssu	Che Sun Harbor Company
TCLS (9)	Ta Ta Lun-pu Kung-ssu	Dah Ta Pier Company
TCLS (10)	Ta Ta Nei-ho Lun-ch'uan Kung-ssu	Dah Ta Inland Navigation Company
TCLS (11)	Ta Sheng Lun-ch'uan Kung-ssu	Dah Sun Steamship Line
TCLS (12)	T'ung Jen T'ai Yen Kung-ssu	T'ung Jen T'ai Salt Company
TCLS (13)	Fu Sheng Chih-wu Kung-ssu	Fu Sun Sericulture Company
TCLS (14)	Tzu Sheng T'ieh Kung-ch'ang	Tze Sun Iron Works

Notes

Preface

1. See, for instance, Ssu-yü Teng and John King Fairbank, *China's Response to the West*, pp. 215–19; and George M. Beckmann, *The Modernization of China and Japan*, p. 154. Franz Michael and George Taylor, in their *The Far East in the Modern World*, have given due notice of Chang Chien's several other activities, but have neglected to mention his major contributions in education and conservation.

One. Introduction

1. The most recent study on this topic, Ping-ti Ho's *Studies on the Population of China*, 1368–1953, gives the figures 143, 411, 559 for the year 1741 and that of 429, 931, 034 for 1850. Ho, pp. 281–82. See also his discussion of these data in the same book, pp. 36–64.

2. Feng Kuei-fen (1809–74), a scholar from Kiangsu, served under Tseng Kuo-fan and was one of the first to recognize the importance of Western science. Arthur Hummel, *Emminent Chinese of the Ch'ing Period*, pp. 241–43. Kuo Sung-tao (1818–91), a close associate of both Li Hung-chang and Tseng Kuo-fan, served as the first Chinese minister abroad in 1876 and repeatedly urged the government to benefit from Western technology by the construction of railways and telegraph lines. Hummel, *Emminent Chinese*, pp. 438–39; Immanuel C. Y. Hsü, *China's Entrance into the Family of Nations: the Diplomatic Phase, 1858–1880*, pp. 180–85. See also David Hamilton's paper on Kuo in Harvard University, *Papers on China*, 15, 1–29. Hsüeh Fu-ch'eng (1838–94), one of Li Hung-chang's secretaries, served as an early diplomatic representative of China in England and France and was especially impressed with the political systems of these countries. Hummel, *Emminent Chinese*, pp. 331–32; Hsü, *China's Entrance*, p. 175. And Cheng Kuan-yin, a scholar who became a businessmen, wrote in the 1880s a treatise advocating modernization entitled "Warnings to the Seemingly Prosperous Age" (*Sheng-shih Wei-yen*), in which he advanced many then revolutionary ideas. Kung-chuan Hsiao, "Weng T'ung-ho and the

Reform Movement of 1898," *Tsing Hua Journal of Chinese Studies*, New Series I, No. 2, p. 222.

Two. Early life

1. The following account of Chang Chien's early life is primarily based on the biography of Chang Chien by his son and his own *nien-p'u* (chronological records). The *nien-p'u* contains certain material not found in the biography. Chang Hsiao-jo, *Nan-t'ung Chang Chi-chih Hsien-sheng Chuan-chi*, pp. 1–66; and Chang Chien, *Seh-weng Tzu-ting Nien-p'u*, I, *passim*. These two basic sources are cited as *CC* and *NP* respectively hereafter.

2. Wang P'ei-tang, *Chiang-su Sheng Hsiang-t'u Chih*, p. 475.

3. *Hai-men-t'ing T'u-chih*, XIX, 7a. See also Ping-ti Ho, *The Ladder of Success in Imperial China*, p. 310.

4. Chang Chien, *Chang Chi-tzu Chiu-lu, Chuan-lu*, III, 1a–11b. This basic source is cited as *CL* hereafter, with appropriate subsections numbered in sequence. See Abbreviations on page 183.

5. The civil service examination as found in the Ch'ing dynasty was modeled after that of the previous Ming dynasty. There were altogether nine specific examinations leading to the top, beginning with the *hsien* (district), *chou* (prefectural), and the *yüan* (one conducted by provincial literary examiners) examinations, the passing of which qualified one for the *hsiu-ts'ai* degree. Those who reached this level were officially called *kung-sheng*, and further divided into *lin-sheng* (who received certain stipends), *tseng-sheng*, or *fu-sheng*, depending on their rankings on the list of successful candidates. Following the three lower examinations came the *k'o* (departmental) and *hsiang* (provincial) examinations, usually held once every three years. A candidate who passed both these tests became a *chü-jen*, or to use its more esoteric designation, a *hsiao-lien*. For those who failed the *hsiang* examinations, a *shui* (annual) examination had to be taken the following year; while those who passed the *hsiang* examination would leave for the capital city of Peking to take the *hui* (metropolitan) examination which took place the spring following each *hsiang* examination. Those who succeeded in the *hui* examination were called *kung-shih* and took a second examination (*fu-shih*) immediately. The handful who managed to get through to this point were guaranteed the top degree, since the last test, the *tien* (palace) examination, served only to rank the candidates according to their talents. The top three scholars were honored with the respective titles of *chuang-yüan*, *p'ang-yen*, and *t'an-hua*.

All the *chin-shih* could expect some kind of official appointment as their reward. For further discussions of the examination system, see Pao Chao Hsieh, *The Government of China (1644–1911)*; and H. S. Brunnert and V. V. Hagelstrom, *Present Day Political Organization of China*, pp. 266–73.

6. *CC*, pp. 24–29.

7. These incidents are found in both Chang Chien's biography and his *nien-p'u*. See *CC*, pp. 19–21 and *NP*, I, 31a–32a. Unfortunately there are no corroborating statements concerning these incidents in the records of the principal examiners, such as Weng T'ung-ho's diary.

8. *CC*, p. 22. An unofficial source has related more of the behind-the-scene maneuverings leading to Chang Chien's success. One of the preliminary readers somehow was able to recognize his papers and noted some technical imperfections of the kind that had ruined his chances before. This examiner, knowing that Chang was Weng's favorite, corrected these imperfections before submitting the papers to the eight final judges. As was customary at the time, the final ranking of the top candidates was supposed to follow the seniority of the eight judges, each of whom would put forth a name. When Weng T'ung-ho, who ranked fourth, insisted on Chang Chien being chosen *chuang-yüan*; the senior judge refused to yield. The impasse was settled in Weng's (and Chang's) favor only by the timely support of another powerful official. See *Fan-t'ien-lu Ts'ung-lu*, VIII, 26b–27b. For further discussions of examination irregularities, see Shang Yen-liu, *Ch'ing-tai K'o-chü K'ao-shih Shu-lu*, Chapter VIII.

9. T. F. Tsiang, "Sino-Japanese Diplomatic Relations, 1870–1890," *Chinese Social and Political Science Review*, XVII, No. 1, pp. 107–69.

10. Chang Shu-sheng, *Chang Ch'ing-ta Kung Chou-i*, VI, 11b.

11. *CC*, p. 35. For the early relationship between Chang Chien and Yüan Shih-k'ai, see also Jerome Ch'en, *Yüan Shih-k'ai*, p. 15.

12. *NP*, I, 22b–23a; Chang, *Chang Ch'ing-ta Kung Chou-i*, VI, 11b.

13. *CC*, pp. 26–37.

14. *Ibid.* pp. 67–68.

15. *CL*(1), I, 7b.

16. Wang Yün-sheng, *Liu-shih-nien-lai Chung-kuo Yü Jih-pen*, I, 207.

Three. Dah Sun and Nan-t'ung Industries

1. *CL*(2), I, 14b and 18a.
2. Ralph M. Odell, *Cotton Goods in China*, p. 168.
3. Yen Chung-p'ing, *Chung-kuo Mien-yeh Chih Fa-chan*, p. 82.
4. *CL*(2), I, 7b.

5. Fang Hsien-t'ing, *Chung-kuo Chih Mien-fang-chih-yeh*, p. 1.

6. China, Imperial Maritime Customs, *Decennial Reports: on the Ports Open to Foreign Commerce in China and Corea and on the Conditions and Development of the Treaty Port Provinces, 1882–91*, Appendix, pp. xxii–xxiii.

7. *Ibid.*, p. 320.

8. China, Imperial Maritime Customs, *Decennial Reports, 1892–1901*, p. 477.

9. China, Imperial Maritime Customs, *Decennial Reports, 1882–91*, Appendix, p. xii.

10. The only source which gives P'eng's full name (in English transliteration without the original Chinese characters) is United States, Department of State, *Papers Relating to the Foreign Relations of the United States, 1883*, p. 140. P'eng held the title of an expectant magistrate of Hupeh, but was probably a member of the compradore class. See *Chung-kuo Chin-tai Kung-yeh Shih Tzu-liao*, I, 1037; also Yen Chung-p'ing, *Chung-kuo Mien-fang-chih Shih-kao*, pp. 98–101.

11. Yen, *Chung-kuo Mien-fang-chih Shih-kao*, pp. 98–101. For a contemporary notice of the founding of the Shanghai Weaving Bureau, see the February 21, 1879, issue of the *North China Herald.*

12. Yen, *Chung-kuo Mien-fang-chih Shih-kao*, pp. 102–6.

13. *Ibid.*, pp. 341–48.

14. *CL*(8), VII, 1a. On Shen Yün-p'ei, see *Chung-kuo Chin-tai Kung-yeh Shih Tzu-liao*, II, 939.

15. Chang Chih-tung, *Chang Wen-hsiang Kung Ch'üan-chi*, LXXVIII, 27a–28a; also *CL*(2), I, 16b.

16. Chang, *Chang Wen-hsiang Kung Ch'üan-chi*, XLIII, 15a–16a. Lu Jun-hsiang, like Chang Chien, enjoyed the distinction of winning the coveted *chuang-yüan* designation (in 1874). *Chung-kuo Chin-tai Kung-yeh Shih Tzu-liao*, II, 962.

17. *NP*, II, 3b.

18. *CL*(2), I, 16a.

19. *T'ung-chou Hsing-pan Shih-yeh Chih Li-shih, Ta-sheng Sha-ch'ang*, pp. 1–8. This source is cited as *TCLS* hereafter, with appropriate subsections numbered in sequence. See Abbreviations on pages 183-84.

20. *TCLS*(1), p. 9; *CL*(2), I, 16b.

21. *TCLS*(1), p. 2.

22. *Ibid.*, pp. 2–3.

23. *Ibid.*, p. 7; *NP*, II, 3b.

24. *TCLS*(1), pp. 4–7; *CL*(2), I, 16b.

25. *TCLS*(1), pp. 8–9; Chang, *Chang Wen-hsiang Kung Ch'üan-chi*, XLII, 11b–13a.

26. *TCLS*(1), pp. 10–11.

27. *NP*, II, 3b; *CL*(2), I, 16b.

28. Chang, *Chang Wen-hsiang Kung Ch'üan-chi*, XLIII, 13a–15b.

29. Yen, *Chung-kuo Mien-yeh Chih Fa-chan*, pp. 81–82.
30. *TCLS*(1), pp. 12–13.
31. *Ibid.*, pp. 14–15.
32. *Ibid.*, p. 23.
33. *Ibid.*, pp. 23–24.
34. *Ibid.*, pp. 15–16.
35. *Ibid.*, pp. 113–14.
36. *Ibid.*, pp. 16–17.
37. *Ibid.*, pp. 15–17; *CL*(2), I, 16b.
38. *TCLS*(1), pp. 20–23.
39. *CL*(2), I, 16b.
40. *TCLS*(1), p. 24.
41. *NP*, II, 4b.
42. *TCLS*(1), pp. 26–27.
43. *Ibid.*
44. *Ibid.*, pp. 27–28.
45. *Ibid.*, p. 32.
46. *Ibid.*
47. *Ibid.*, pp. 31–34.
48. *Ibid.*, p. 34.
49. *Ibid.*, p. 35.
50. *Ibid.*, pp. 37–40.
51. *Ibid.*, pp. 41–42 and 117.
52. *Ibid.*, p. 36.
53. *Ibid.*, pp. 36–37.
54. *Ibid.*, p. 37.
55. *CL*(8), VII, 4a.
56. *NP*, II, 5a.
57. *CL*(2), I, 10b–11b; Sheng Hsüan-huai, *Yü-chai Ch'un-kao*, XXVIII, 11b–12a.
58. *CL*(2), I, 17a.
59. *Ibid.*, 10a–10b.
60. See Chapter IV.
61. *NP*, II, 6b.
62. *Ibid.*
63. *Ibid.*, 8a.
64. Liu K'un-i, *Liu Chung-ch'eng Kung I-chi*, *Shu-tu*, XII, 54b.
65. *NP*, II, 8a.
66. *CL*(2), I, 14b.
67. *TCLS*(1), pp. 43–45; *CL*(2), I, 10b–11b.
68. *TCLS*(1), pp. 45–46.
69. *Ibid.*, pp. 46–47.
70. *Ibid.*, pp. 47–48; *CL*(2), I, 11b. In January, 1899, Governor-general Liu demonstrated his continuing trust in Chang Chien by designating him as one of two leading gentry members to establish the central commerce bureau for the region in Shanghai. Liu, *Liu Chung-ch'eng Kung I-chi*, *Chou-shu*, XXIX, 56a–57a.
71. *TCLS*(1), p. 49.
72. *Ibid.*, pp. 49 and 119.
73. *Ibid.*, p. 49.
74. *Ibid.*
75. *Ibid.*, p. 50.
76. *Ibid.*
77. *Ibid.*, pp. 52 and 54.
78. *CL*(2), I, 14b–15a.
79. *NP*, II, 8b.
80. *Ibid.*, 8b–9a.
81. *TCLS*(1), p. 119.
82. *NP*, II, 9a.
83. *TCLS*(1), p. 64.
84. *NP*, II, 9a.
85. *CL*(2), IV, 1a.
86. *TCLS*(1), pp. 58–59; *CL*(2), I, 15b–16a. For Liu's report of Chang Chien's efforts, see Liu, *Liu Chung-ch'eng Kung I-chi*, *Chou-shu*, XXXII, 53a–55b.

87. *CL*(2), I, 17b.
88. *Ibid.*
89. *Ibid.*, 17a.
90. Yen, *Chung-kuo Mien-fang-chih Shih-kao*, p. 119.
91. *CL*(2), II, 18a–19a.
92. *Ibid.*, 19a–21a; *TCLS*(2), p. 82.
93. *CL*(2), V, 8a.
94. *Ibid.*, IV, 3a.
95. *Ibid.*
96. Yen, *Chung-kuo Mien-fang-chih Shih-kao*, p. 159.
97. *CL*(2), V, 12a–12b.
98. *Ibid.*, IV, 3a.
99. *Ibid.*; see also King-kung Wong, *Chang Chien, A Case Study of Attempts at China's Modernization by the Traditional Gentry*, p. 96.
100. *CL*(2), V, 8b.
101. *Chung-kuo Chin-tai Kung-yeh Shih Tzu-liao*, II, 1076–77.
102. *TCLS*(1), pp. 134–36.
103. Wu Ch'eng-lo, *Chin-shih Chung-kuo Shih-yeh T'ung-chih*, II, 96.
104. The following figures on Dah Sun's number of spindles, capitalization, and net profit are compiled from various sources, the most important being the annual reports of Dah Sun up to 1909, *TCLS*(1), pp. 185–272, and *TCLS*(2), pp. 97–124.
105. *Erh-shih-nien-lai Chih Nan-t'ung*, II, 2. This source is cited as *ESNL* hereafter.
106. Compiled from all major sources, including *ESNL*; Yen, *Chung-kuo Mien-yeh Chih Fa-chan*, p. 119; annual reports in *TCLS*; and the report to the stockholders on the twentieth anniversary of the founding of Dah Sun, *CL*(2), VI, 1a–1b. Data on net profit after 1913 are not available.
107. *CL*(2), VII, 34b; Yen, *Chung-kuo Mien-fang-chih Shih-kao*, p. 347.
108. *CL*(2), VIII, 34b–35a.
109. Yen, *Chung-kuo Mien-fang-chih Shih-kao*, pp. 138, 141, and 143.
110. Odell, *Cotton Goods*, p. 168.
111. *Ibid.*
112. *Ibid.*
113. *Ibid.*, p. 169.
114. *Chung-kuo Chin-tai Kung-yeh Shih Tzu-liao*, II, 1228.
115. Odell, *Cotton Goods*, p. 184.
116. Yen, *Chung-kuo Mien-fang-chih Shih-kao*, p. 142; also Wong, *Chang Chien*, p. 98.
117. Liu Hou-sheng, *Chang Chien Chuan-chi*, p. 257.
118. Yen, *Chung-kuo Mien-yeh Chih Fa-chan*, p. 118; also letter from Dr. George L. Hagman, March 6, 1957. Dr. Hagman was a long-time resident in Nan-t'ung as a missionary who first went there in 1914. In response to my request, both Dr. and Mrs. Hagman were kind enough

to search their memories for relevant information concerning Chang Chien and Nan-t'ung.

119. Liu, *Chang Chien Chuan-chi*, p. 283.

120. *Ibid.*, p. 257.

121. See Chapter VIII.

122. Liu, *Chang Chien Chuan-chi*, p. 258.

123. Wong, *Chang Chien*, p. 103.

124. See Chapter VI.

125. Wong, *Chang Chien*, p. 103.

126. *Ibid.*, pp. 103–4.

127. *Ibid.*, p. 106.

128. *Ibid.*

129. Yen, *Chung-kuo Mien-fang-chih Shih-kao*, p. 347; also Wong, *Chang Chien*, p. 106.

130. See Chapter VI.

131. *TCLS*(4), pp. 1–3; Chang Ch'ao-han and Ho Ssu-ch'ing, "Nan-t'ung Kung-yeh Chih Tiao-ch'a" (Part 1), *Shih-yeh Tsa-chih*, No. 52, p. 61.

132. *TCLS*(4), pp. 21–25.

133. *Chung-kuo Chin-tai Kung-yeh Shih Tzu-liao*, II, 808.

134. *Life of the Honorable Chang Chien with an Account of the Enterprizes Inaugurated by Him*, p. 62. This source is cited as *Life* hereafter.

135. Chang and Ho, "Nan-t'ung Kung-yeh Chih Tiao-ch'a" (Part 1), *Shih-yeh Tsa-chih*, No. 52, pp. 61–62.

136. *TCLS*(1), p. 167.

137. *TCLS*(5), pp. 1–2.

138. Chang and Ho, "Nan-t'ung Kung-yeh Chih Tiao-ch'a" (Part 1), *Shih-yeh Tsa-chih*, No. 52, p. 63.

139. *Ibid.*

140. *Life*, p. 60.

141. Chang and Ho, "Nan-t'ung Kung-yeh Chih Tiao-ch'a" (Part 1), *Shih-yeh Tsa-chih*, No. 52, pp. 64–65.

142. *Ibid.*, p. 65; *Life*, p. 60.

143. Shih-yeh Pu, Kuo-chi Mao-i Chü, *Chung-kuo Shih-yeh Chih, Chiang-su Sheng*, pp. 41–42.

144. *TCLS*(11), pp. 1–2.

145. *Ibid.*

146. *Ibid.*, p. 17.

147. *ESNL*, II, 72.

148. Chiao-t'ung T'ieh-tao Pu, *Chiao-t'ung Shih, Hang-cheng Pien*, pp. 319–20.

149. *TCLS*(10), pp. 4–14.

150. *CL*(2), II, 22a–22b.

151. Chiao-t'ung T'ieh-tao Pu, *Chiao-t'ung Shih, Hang-cheng Pien*, pp. 320–21.

152. *Ibid.*

153. *CL*(2), II, 21a–22a.

154. *TCLS*(7), pp. 1–6.

155. *TCLS*(9), p. 2.

156. *CL*(2), IV, 10b.

157. *Ibid.*; Chang and Ho, "Nan-t'ung Kung-yeh Chih Tiao-ch'a" (Part 2), *Shih-yeh Tsa-chih*, No. 55, p. 49.

158. *ESNL*, II, 17.

159. Chang and Ho, "Nan-t'ung Kung-yeh Chih Tiao-ch'a" (Part 2), *Shih-yeh Tsa-chih*, No. 55, p. 55.

160. *Ibid.*

161. *Life*, p. 64; Shih-yeh Pu, Kuo-chi Mao-i Chü, *Chung-kuo Shih-yeh Chih, Chiang-su Sheng*, pp. 41–42.

162. *TCLS*(1), pp. 168–69.

163. *Chung-kuo Chin-tai Kung-yeh Shih Tzu-liao*, II, 1076–77.

164. *TCLS*(1), pp. 134–36.

165. *Chung-kuo Chin-tai Kung-yeh Shih Tzu-liao*, II, 1076–77.

166. *CL*(2), VIII, 30b.

167. *TCLS*(1), pp. 64–104.

168. *Ibid.*, pp. 64–70.

169. *Ibid.*, pp. 70–104.

170. *Ibid.*, p. 65.

171. *CL*(2), IV, 3a–3b.

172. *Ibid.*, 1a.

173. *TCLS*(1), p. 137.

174. Chao Feng-t'ien, *Wan-ch'ing Wu-shih-nien Ching-chi Ssu-hsiang Shih*, pp. 34–40, 84–88, and 142–46; Hsia Yen-teh, *Chung-kuo Chin-pai-nien Ching-chi Ssu-hsiang*, pp. 92–100.

175. *CL*(1), I, 20a–20b.

176. *CL*(2), III, 5a.

177. *CL*(8), IV, 33a; see also Wong, *Chang Chien*, pp. 85–87.

178. *CL*(3), III, 20a.

179. *CL*(2), III, 17a–18a.

180. See Chapter VI.

181. *CL*(1), II, 10b–11a; *CL*(2), II, 1a.

182. Chao, *Wan-ch'ing Wu-shih-nien Ching-chi Ssu-hsiang Shih*, p. 39; Hsia, *Chung-kuo Chin-pai-nien Ching-chi Ssu-hsiang*, p. 96. See also Wong, *Chang Chien*, p. 86.

183. *ESNL*, p. 8.

184. *Ibid.*

185. *CL*(1), VII, 3b; Hsia, *Chung-kuo Chin-pai-nien Ching-chi Ssu-hsiang*, pp. 92–100.

186. *CL*(1), IX, 3b–5b.

187. Joseph A. Schumpeter, *Capitalism, Socialism and Democracy*, pp. 131–34.

188. Harvard University, Research Center in Entrepreneurial History, *Change and the Entrepreneur*, p. 88. The following brief discussion of Chang Chien as an entrepreneur owes a great deal to the concepts worked out at the Research Center in Entrepreneurial History. However, so much of Chang Chien's career lies outside the strict confines of his role as an entrepreneur that it has not been thought useful to compare him directly with other entrepreneurs.

Four. Involvement in National Affairs

1. He had already resigned all official posts, but participated in this examination out of reverence for the wishes of his deceased father. Wong, *Chang Chien*, p. 12.

2. *NP*, II, 6a.

3. Weng's diary records instances of long conversations with Chang Chien, without mentioning the substance of the conversations, on five separate occasions between May 20, 1898, and June 20, 1898, as cited in *CC*, p. 65.

4. *Ibid.*

5. *Ibid.*, p. 64.

6. Kung-chuan Hsiao, "Weng T'ung-ho and the Reform Movement of 1898," *Tsing Hua Journal of Chinese Studies*, New Series I (hereafter N. S. I), No. 2, p. 171; Chester C. Tan, *The Boxer Catastrophe*, pp. 16–17.

7. Excerpts from Weng's diary in Chung-kuo Shih-hsüeh Hui, *Wu-hsü Pien-fa*, I, 507. See also Hsiao, "Weng T'ung-ho and the Reform Movement of 1898," *Tsing Hua Journal of Chinese Studies*, N. S. I, No. 2, p. 169.

8. Hsiao, "Weng T'ung-ho and the Reform Movement of 1898," *Tsing Hua Journal of Chinese Studies*, N. S. I, No. 2, pp. 170–71.

9. Tan, *The Boxer Catastrophe*, p. 18; Hummel, *Emminent Chinese*, II, 860.

10. Tan, *The Boxer Catastrophe*, p. 18.

11. *NP*, II, 2a; *CC*, p. 64.

12. *NP*, II, 7a.

13. Hsiao, "Weng T'ung-ho and the Reform Movement of 1898," *Tsing Hua Journal of Chinese Studies*, N. S. I, No. 2, pp. 179–89.

14. *CC*, p. 65.

15. *Ibid.*; Hsiao, "Weng T'ung-ho and the Reform Movement of 1898," *Tsing Hua Journal of Chinese Studies*, N. S. I, No. 2, p. 160.

16. *CC*, p. 65.

17. In the early part of 1900, Ho Ssu-k'un warned Chang Chien of the drive then going on to round up all of K'ang Yu-wei's former associates. Ho advised him to "flee far away," which he declined to do. *NP*, II, 10b.

18. Chang Chien's own preface to poem referring to the events of 1898; *CC*, p. 66.

19. Ping-ti Ho, "Weng Tung-ho and the 'One Hundred Days of Reform,' " *Far Eastern Quarterly*, X, 125–35; Hsiao, "Weng T'ung-ho and the Reform Movement of 1898," *Tsing Hua Journal of Chinese Studies*, N. S. I, No. 2, pp. 166–79.

20. Hsiao, "Weng T'ung-ho and the Reform Movement of 1898," *Tsing Hua Journal of Chinese Studies*, N. S. I, No. 2, pp. 196–98.

21. Tan, *The Boxer Catastrophe*, pp. 237–39.

22. Sheng Hsüan-huai, holding the post of Director of Railway and Telegraph, was not a provincial official. Yüan Shih-k'ai was governor of Shantung, which was generally regarded as a northern province. For the sake of simplicity, however, they will both be included in the term "southern officials" hereafter.

23. *NP*, II, 10b–11a.

24. Hsi-yin, "Keng-tzu Ch'üan-huo Tung-nan Hu-pao Chih Chi-shih," *Jen-wen*, II, 1–7.

25. The ten articles of the second set of agreements, referred to in Article Two of the first set: "The stipulations setting forth the joint duties of protecting Shanghai by the Powers have been set forth elsewhere," can be found in Kuo Pin-chia, "Keng-tzu Ch'üan-luan," *Wen-che*, VI, No. 1, 159–60.

26. George Nye Steiger, *China and the Occident; the Origin and Development of the Boxer Movement*, pp. 249–50.

27. Tan, *The Boxer Catastrophe*, pp. 83–91.

28. *CL*(1), I, 23b–24a.

29. Tan, *The Boxer Catastrophe*, pp. 116–20.

30. *CL*(1), I, 24a–24b.

31. Tan, *The Boxer Catastrophe*, pp. 170–98.

32. Telegram from Liu to Sheng, March 6, 1901, in Chin Chia-jui and Liu Shu-hui, "Yu-kuan 'Tung-nan Hu-pao' Tzu-liao," in *I-ho T'uan*, ed. by Chien Po-chan, III, 360.

33. *CL*(1), I, 24b and 25b.

34. Tan, *The Boxer Catastrophe*, pp. 210–14.

35. Ssu-yü Teng and John King Fairbank, *China's Response to the West*, p. 196.

36. *CL*(1), II, 1a–26b.

37. *Ibid.*, 1b–2a and 5a–5b.

38. Teng and Fairbank, *China's Response*, pp. 197–205. See also Wong, *Chang Chien*, pp. 33–37.

39. *NP*, II, 12b.

40. *CC*, p. 106. See also his diary of his trip to Japan in *CL*(8), IV, 1a–33a.

41. *CC*, p. 106.

42. *CL*(8), VII, 12a.

43. *Ibid.*

44. *Ibid.*, 12b.

45. Li Chien-nung, *Chung-kuo Chin-pai-nien Cheng-chih Shih*, p. 233. Another translation of the letter appears on page 199 of Ssu-yu Teng

and Jeremy Ingalls' English version of Li's book, entitled *The Political History of China 1840–1928*.

46. Marius B. Jansen, *The Japanese and Sun Yat-sen*, pp. 78–81.

47. Feng Tzu-yu, *Chung-hua Min-kuo K'ai-kuo-ch'ien Ko-ming Shih*, I, 52.

48. *CL*(8), VII, 13b.

49. Feng, *Chung-hua Min-kuo K'ai-kuo-ch'ien Ko-ming Shih*, I, 211.

50. E-tu Zen Sun, "The Chinese Constitutional Missions of 1905–1906," *Journal of Modern History*, XXIV, 251–57, 265.

51. *Ibid.*, pp. 257–64.

52. Li, *Chung-kuo Chin-pai-nien Cheng-chih Shih*, pp. 250–51.

53. The following account of the constitutionalist movement among the gentry is based largely on Li, *Chung-kuo Chin-pai-nien Cheng-chih Shih*, pp. 265, 278–286.

54. Yang Chia-lo, *Min-kuo Ming-jen T'u-chien*, XII, 67; also Hsiao, "Weng T'ung-ho and the Reform Movement of 1898," *Tsing Hua Journal of Chinese Studies*, N. S. I, No. 2, pp. 206 and 223.

55. Fan Yin-nan, *Tang-tai Chung-kuo Ming-jen Lu*, p. 411; Chia I-chün, *Chung-hua Min-kuo Ming-jen Chuan*, VIII, 38.

56. Hsieh Ping, *Min-kuo Cheng-tang Shih*, p. 26.

57. *NP*, II, 20a.

58. *CL*(1), III, 13b–14a.

59. Wu Ching-hsiung and Huang Kung-chüeh, *Chung-kuo Chih-hsien Shih*, I, 21; Li, *Chung-kuo Chin-pai-nien Cheng-chih Shih*, pp. 262–65.

60. Chou Pi-ping and Lo Chih-yüan, *Chung-kuo Hsien-cheng Fa-chan Shih*, pp. 9–14; Li, *Chung-kuo Chin-pai-nien Cheng-chih Shih*, pp. 265–68.

61. The following brief account of Chang Chien's efforts on behalf of the Kiangsu Provincial Assembly is taken from his biography and *nien-p'u*. *CC*, pp. 140–44; *NP*, II, 22a–25a.

62. *CC*, p. 142.

63. *NP*, II, 23b.

64. *Ibid.*

65. *Ibid.*, 22b.

66. *Ibid.*, 33a.

67. Li, *Chung-kuo Chin-pai-nien Cheng-chih Shih*, p. 282.

68. *Ibid.*

69. *Ibid.*

70. *Ibid.*, pp. 283–84.

71. *Ibid.*, p. 283.

72. *CL*(1), III, 28b–30a.

73. For additional details concerning the Exposition, see *Chinese Recorder and Missionary Journal*, XIL, 501–2, 697.

74. *CL*(1), IV, 13a; Robert Dollar, *Private Diary of Robert Dollar on His Recent Visits to China*, pp. 68–69.

75. For the role of Lei Feng, who accompanied Chang Chien and

argued decisively that Chang Chien should not miss this opportunity of talking with Yüan, see Liu Hou-sheng, *Chang Chien Chuan-chi*, p. 180.

76. *CC*, p. 145. A contemporary periodical reported that in Peking Chang Chien was "welcomed by the United Association of Provincial Assemblies, by the members of the National Assembly and by other representative bodies. He has been recommended by Viceroy Jui Cheng and the Ministry of Education to be the president of the Central Board of Education to be formed in Peking shortly. He has been recommended by Tuan Fang and Jui Cheng as competent to be Co-Director of the Government Railways, He was also specially mentioned by Viceroy Chao Erh-sun, during the latter's farewell audience, for the Commissionership in Manchuria for the Development of Industries and Agricultural Schemes. He was to be presented to the Prince Regent on June 13." *North China Herald*, June 17, 1911, pp. 755–56.

77. *CL*(8), VII, 19a.

78. *NP*, II, 26b.

79. *CL*(1), III, 36b–37b.

80. *NP*, II, 27b.

81. *CL*(8), VII, 20a.

82. E-tu Zen Sun, *Chinese Railways and British Interests*, p. 25.

83. *NP*, II, 27b–28a. For Sheng's views on Szechwan railroads, see his *Yü-chai Ch'un-kao*, XVIII, 19a–22b, 31a–36b.

84. *NP*, II, 28a–28b.

85. See below, pages 82-86.

86. *CL*(8), VII, 21a. See also *Chung-kuo Chin-tai Kung-yeh Shih* Tzu-liao, II, 583.

87. *NP*, II, 29b.

88. *CL*(8), VII, 21a.

89. *Ibid.*

90. *Ibid.*

91. *Ibid.*

92. *Ibid.*, 21a–21b.

93. *Ibid.*, 21b.

94. *CL*(1), III, 37b–38b.

95. *Ibid.*, 41a.

96. *CL*(8), VII, 21b.

97. *Ibid.*

98. *Ibid.*

99. *Ibid.*, 22a.

100. *CL*(1), III, 39b.

101. *Ibid.*, IV, 1a–1b; *CL*(8), VII, 22a.

102. Li, *Chung-kuo Chin-pai-nien Cheng-chih Shih*, pp. 308–13. For Yüan's role at this crucial juncture, see Jerome Ch'en, *Yüan Shih-k'ai*, Chapter VII.

103. *CL*(1), III, 40a–41a.

104. *Ibid.*, 41a–42a.

105. Hu Han-min's letter, as quoted in *CC*, pp. 154–55. For the events of the abdication ceremony and Yüan's role in assuming supreme power, see Ch'en, *Yüan Shih-k'ai*, pp. 128–31.

106. *CC*, pp. 164–65.

107. *NP*, II, 31b–32a. See also Chapter VI, page 134.

108. Li, *Chung-kuo Chin-pai-nien Cheng-chih Shih*, pp. 321–24.

109. *CL*(1), IV, 2a–3b.

110. *NP*, II, 32a.

111. *CC*, pp. 170–71. See also Chün-tu Hsüeh, *Huang Hsing and the Chinese Revolution*, pp. 131–32.

112. Emphasis mine. *CL*(1), IV, 5a–6a.

113. Hsieh, *Min-kuo Cheng-tang Shih*, pp. 15–16.

114. Shen T'ing-kuo, *Chi Chang T'ai-yen Hsien-sheng*, p. 58.

115. *NP*, II, 32a.

116. Yang Yu-chiung, *Chung-kuo Cheng-tang Shih*, p. 53.

117. *Ibid.*, pp. 53–56.

118. Hsieh, *Min-kuo Cheng-tang Shih*, p. 45.

119. Yang, *Chung-kuo Cheng-tang Shih*, p. 58.

120. Tuan-sheng Ch'ien, *The Government and Politics of China*, p. 348.

121. *CL*(1), IV, 8b–9a.

122. *CL*(8), VII, 23b–24a.

123. Li, *Chung-kuo Chin-pai-nien Cheng-chih Shih*, pp. 384–89. See also Ch'en, *Yüan Shih-k'ai*, pp. 160–63.

124. *CL*(1), IV, 9a–11a.

125. Hsieh, *Min-kuo Cheng-tang Shih*, pp. 53–54.

126. *Ibid.*, pp. 55–59.

127. See Chapters VI and VII.

128. *CL*(1), IV, 7a–8b.

129. *CC*, p. 162.

130. *CL*(8), VII, 25a.

131. Li, *Chung-kuo Chin-pai-nien Cheng-chih Shih*, p. 402.

132. *Ibid.*, pp. 402–3.

133. *CC*, p. 180.

134. *Ibid.*

135. *CL*(1), VII, 1a–4a.

136. *CC*, pp. 183–84.

137. *Ibid.*, pp. 184–85.

138. *Ibid.*, pp. 186–88.

139. *CL*(8), VII, 26b.

140. See Chapter VII.

141. Li, *Chung-kuo Chin-pai-nien Cheng-chih Shih*, pp. 421–25.

142. *CL*(8), VII, 29a. Chang Chien's lack of sympathy for Yüan's imperial ambitions did not prevent Yüan from including Chang among his "four Friends of Mount Sung." Ch'en, *Yüan Shih-k'ai*, p. 213.

143. *NP*, II, 37a–42a.

Five. Chang Chien and Educational Reforms

1. *CL*(3), III, 15b.

2. For a fuller discussion of the T'ung-wen Kuan and other new-style schools, see Knight Biggerstaff, *The earliest Modern Government Schools in China.*

3. Biggerstaff, *Government Schools*, pp. 136–39.

4. Hummel, *Emminent Chinese*, I, 402–5.

5. Biggerstaff, *Government Schools*, pp. 228–41.

6. Li, *Chung-kuo Chin-pai-nien Cheng-chih Shih*, p. 131; Teng and Fairbank, *China's Response*, p. 86.

7. P. W. Kuo, *The Chinese System of Public Education*, pp. 69–86.

8. Lo Shao-chi, *Chung-kuo Hsien-tai Chiao-yü*, pp. 28-32, 45–51.

9. An example of a provincial timetable, that of Kiangsu, can be found in Chiang-su Hsüeh-wu Kung-so, *Chiang-su Hsüeh-wu Wen-tu*, unpaginated pages following document dated "twelfth day of the seventh Month of the Second Year of Hsüan-t'ung" [August 16, 1910].

10. Alice Henrietta Gregg, *China and Educational Autonomy: the Changing Role of the Protestant Educational Missionary in China, 1807–1937*, pp. 11, 20.

11. *Ibid.*, pp. 24–25, 43.

12. *Ibid.*, pp. 25–28, 48–54.

13. Lu-dzai Djung, *A History of Democratic Education in Modern China*, pp. 28–32, 45–51.

14. Teng and Fairbank, *China's Response*, pp. 197–205.

15. *CC*, p. 91.

16. *NP*, II, 14a. In 1903 he placed the support of the school on a regular basis by persuading the stockholders of Dah Sun to set aside a stipulated portion of the profits annually for the support of the school. *TCLS*(1), p. 124.

17. *CL*(3), II, 11b.

18. *Ibid.*, I, 13a–14b.

19. Ting Chih-p'ing, *Chung-kuo Chin-ch'i-shih-nien-lai Chiao-yü Chi-shih*, p. 6.

20. *ESNL*, I, 41.

21. *CL*(8), VII, 14b; *CL*(3), II, 20a.

22. *CL*(3), VI, 16a–16b.

23. *Ibid.*, II, 18a–19a. The modern schools in China at the time were designated as follows:

Ch'u-teng hsiao-hsüeh	Lower primary school
Kao-teng hsiao-hsüeh	Higher Primary school
Ch'u-teng chung-hsüeh	Lower middle school
Kao-teng chung-hsüeh	Higher middle school
Hsüeh-yüan	College
Ta-hsüeh	University

Normal schools were on the same level as middle schools. Those schools containing both the lower and the higher grades have been termed "combined schools" in this study.

24. *Ibid.*

25. *Ibid.*, 19a–20a.

26. *ESNL*, I, 74; Ch'i-chih, "Nan-t'ung P'ing-min Sheng-huo Chuang-k'uang," *Chiao-yü Yü Chih-yeh*, No. 72, pp. 117–22.

27. *CL*(3), II, 15b–17b.

28. The "five district" in the name of the school included Ching-hai village. Administratively a part of Nan-t'ung district, it was probably mentioned for historical reasons.

29. *ESNL*, I, 67–71.

30. Letter from Dr. George L. Hagman, March 6, 1957.

31. *Chien-p'u* at the front of *CL*, 4b–5a.

32. *Ibid.*, 5b.

33. *ESNL*, I, 27. For Chang Chien's land reclamation work, see Chapter VI.

34. Chiao-yü Pu, *Ti-erh-tz'u Chung-kuo Chiao-yü Nien-chien*, p. 729; also letter from Dr. George L. Hagman, March 6, 1957.

35. *CL*(3), V, 29a.

36. *Ibid.*, 13b–14b.

37. *Ibid.*, IV, 8a–9a; also letter from Dr. George L. Hagman, March 6, 1957. The relationship between the elderly Chang Chien and the younger Shen Shou has been the basis of gossip for years. As recently as 1961, the Hong Kong periodical *Ch'un-ch'iu*, a magazine devoted to popular and unofficial accounts of historical events, ran a two-part series on this supposed romance. *Ch'un-ch'iu*, No. 104 (October 16, 1961), pp. 10–11, 27; and No. 105 (November 1, 1961), pp. 13–15. Shen Shou's great talent as an embroiderer first came to the attention of Chang Chien when she exhibited one of her masterpieces at the Southern Industrial Exposition in Nanking in 1910. She was at that time unhappily married to Yü Chüeh, who had two other concubines and was indifferent to Chang Chien's wish to bring Shen Shou to Nan-t'ung to be head of the embroidery school. There is no question of Chang Chien's genuine affection for Shen Shou as a person. He has left us a number of poems written both before and after her death, an event which affected Chang Chien deeply. Subsequent to his arrangement for Shen Shou to be buried in Nan-t'ung, Yü Chüeh began a series of accusations against Chang Chien, claiming that Chang had been primarily responsible for improper relationships with his wife. Tso Shun-sheng, *Chung-kuo Hsien-tai Ming-jen I-shih*, pp. 64–71. Sung Hsi-shang, one of Chang Chien's protegees, has defended his patron's relationship with Shen Shou as nothing more than the natural affection of an older person for a younger person of great talent. Sung cites the great disparity in their ages and Shen Shou's chronic frail health as two factors ruling out any possible liaison between them. Sung Hsi-shang, *Chang Chien Ti Sheng-p'ing*, pp. 379–383.

38. *CL*(3), IV, 14b–15a.
39. *Ibid.*, 15b–16b.
40. *Ibid.*, V, 3b–4b.
41. *Ibid.*, 18b–21a.
42. *Ibid.*, VI, 6b–8a.
43. *Ibid.*, 1a–3b.
44. The following information is found in Chiao-yü Pu, *Min-kuo Liu-nien Shih-ch'a P'u-t'ung Hsüeh-hsiao Pao-kao Hsüan-lu*, pp. 29–32.
45. Ch'ien Kung-p'u, "Nan-t'ung Hsien Hsüeh-wu Ts'an-kuan Chi," *Chiao-yü Tsa-chih*, VIII, "Fu-lu," p. 27.
46. *CL*(3), II, 12a–13a.
47. The following information is found in Chiao-yü Pu, *Min-kuo Liu-nien Shih-ch'a P'u-t'ung Hsüeh-hsiao Pao-kao Hsüan-lu*, pp. 45–48.
48. The following information is based on Li Yüan-heng, "Nan-t'ung Tai-yung Ssu-fan Fu-shu Hsiao-hsüeh Kai-lan," *Chiao-yü Tsa-chih*, VI, "Cheng-chi," pp. 1–5.
49. Figures derived from several tables in Chiao-yü Pu, *Chung-hua Min-kuo Ti-wu-tz'u Chiao-yü T'ung-chi T'u-piao*. Unfortunately the figures for the primary schools, particularly the lower primary schools, probably include an indeterminate number of old-style schools.
50. Chiao-yü Pu, *Chung-hua Min-kuo Ti-wu-tz'u Chiao-yü T'ung-chi T'u-piao*, *passim*.
51. The above comparison is based on Chiao-yü Pu, *Min-kuo Liu-nien Shih-ch'a P'u-t'ung Hsüeh-hsiao Pao-kao Hsüan-lu*, *passim*.
52. *CC*, p. 114.
53. *Ibid.*
54. *Ibid.*
55. *CL*(8), VII, 16b.
56. *CL*(3), V, 17a–18b. See also Chapter VII.
57. *CL*(1), II, 12a–16a.
58. *CL*(3), III, 16a–18b.
59. *Ibid.*, II, 21b–22b.
60. *Ibid.*, 22b–25b.
61. *Ibid.*, III, 11a–12a.
62. *Ibid.*, 6a–6b.
63. *NP*, II, 17b.
64. *CL*(3), II, 2a.
65. *Ibid.*, 2a and 11b.
66. *Ibid.*, 17b. See also Wong, *Chang Chien*, pp. 143–45.
67. Chuang Yü, "Chang Chi-chih Hsien-sheng Chiao-yü T'an," *Chiao-yü Tsa-chih*, IX, "Yen-lun," p. 34.
68. P'eng Tse-i, "Chang Chien Ti Ssu-hsiang Chi Ch'i Shih-yeh," *Tung-fang Tsa-chih*, XL, p. 57.
69. *CL*(3), VI, 4a–4b.
70. *Ibid.*, I, 17b–18a.
71. *Ibid.*, II, 26b–27a.
72. Chuang, "Chang Chi-chih Hsien-sheng Chiao-yü T'an," *Chiao-yü Tsa-chih*, IX, "Yen-lun," p. 34.
73. *CL*(3), I, 14b–15a.
74. *Ibid.*, 15a–16b.
75. *Ibid.*, IV, 10b–11b.

76. Dewey's comment on Chang Chien, John Dewey, *Impressions of Soviet Russia and the Revolutionary World: Mexico—China—Turkey*, p. 249.
77. *CL*(3), V, 21b–22a.
78. Letter from Dr. P. W. Kuo, February 29, 1956.
79. *CL*(3), I, 18b.
80. *Ibid.*, III, 12b.
81. *Ibid.*, IV, 16b–18b.
82. *CC*, pp. 99–100.
83. *CL*(3), I, 8b–13a.

Six. Land Reclamation and Salt Reform

1. *CL*(2), VI, 20a–20b.
2. *CL*(2), VIII, 8a.
3. *Ibid.*, 30a.
4. *Ibid.*, 30b.
5. *Ibid.*
6. *Ibid.*, II, 2a–2b.
7. Liu K'un-i, *Liu Chung-ch'eng Kung I-chi, Chou-shu*, XXXV, 72a–73a.
8. *NP*, II, 11b.
9. *CC*, pp. 75–76.
10. *CL*(2), II, 1a–9b. Both the official title of the company and the original prospectus indicated that the company would be involved in animal husbandry, but nothing was ever done in this direction. For the original plan, see *CL*(2), II, 6a.
11. *CL*(8), VII, 9b.
12. *CL*(2), VIII, 7a–8b.
13. Shih-yeh Pu, *Chung-kuo Shih-yeh Chih, Chiang-su Sheng*, pp. 262–63.
14. *CL*(2), IV, 31a.
15. *Ibid.*, 28a.
16. *Ibid.*, 30b; Liu, *Chang Chien Chuan-chi*, p. 249.
17. *CL*(2), IV, 31a–31b.
18. *Ibid.*
19. *Ibid.*
20. *Ibid.*, VIII, 10b.
21. *Ibid.*
22. *Ibid.*, IV, 31b.
23. *Ibid.*, VIII, 14b.
24. *Ibid.*, 10b.
25. *Ibid.*, II, 26a–26b.
26. *Ibid.*, 27b–28b.
27. *Ibid.*, VIII, 11a.
28. *Ibid.*
29. *Ibid.*
30. *Ibid.*, V, 16a.
31. *Ibid.*, IV, 14a–19a.
32. *Ibid.*, V, 16a.
33. Lo Kung, "Chang Chi-chih Yü Huai-nan Yen-k'en," *Yen-wu Yüeh-pao*, V, No. 8, pp. 45–47.
34. *Ibid.*
35. Shih-yeh Pu, *Chung-kuo Shih-yeh Chih, Chiang-su Sheng*, p. 264.
36. *ESNL*, II, 42–50.
37. Li Chi-hsin, "Cheng-li Chiang-su Hai-pin Yen-k'en Chih Kuan-chien," *Chung-kuo Chien-she*, I, pp. 116–18.
38. Shih–yeh Pu, *Chung-kuo Shih-yeh Chih, Chiang-su Sheng*, p. 276.
39. *Ibid.*
40. *Ibid.*, p. 277.

41. *Ibid.* 42. *Ibid.*, p. 280.
43. *Ibid.*, p. 264.
44. Hsing-cheng Yüan, Nung-ts'un Fu-hsin Wei-yüan Hui, *Chiang-su Sheng Nung-ts'un Tiao-ch'a*, pp. 57–58.
45. *Ibid.* 46. *Ibid.*
47. *Ibid.*
48. Kung Shan-fu, "Ta Feng Yen-k'en Kung-ssu Chien-tsu Chi," *Chiang-su Yen-chiu*, I, No. 2, nonconsecutive pagination.
49. *Ibid.* 50. *Ibid.*
51. Lo, "Chang Chi-chih Yü Huai-nan Yen-k'en," *Yen-wu Yüeh-pao*, V, No. 8, 49–51.
52. Lu Yang-hao, "T'o-chan Su-peh K'en-chih," *Chiang-su Yen-chiu*, I, No. 1, nonconsecutive pagination.
53. *CL*(1), VIII, 8a–13b; *CC*, p. 185.
54. *CC*, pp. 188–91.
55. *Yen-cheng Tz'u-tien*, ed. by Lin Chen-han, Part XII, p. 1; Yen-wu Chi-ho Tsung-so, *Chung-kuo Yen-cheng Shih-lu*, I, 10.
56. Yen-wu Chi-ho Tsung-so, *Chung-kuo Yen-cheng Shih-lu*, I, 10. See also Esson McDowell Gale, *Salt for the Dragon, a Personal History of China, 1908–1945*, p. 99.
57. *CL*(2), III, 7b. 58. *Ibid.*, II, 12b.
59. *Ibid.*, 15a. 60. *Ibid.*, III, 22b.
61. *CL*(8), VII, 13a; *CL*(2), III, 7b, 19a.
62. *CL*(2), II, 17a, 22b. 63. *Ibid.*, III, 7b.
64. *Ibid.*, 22a. 65. *Ibid.*, IV, 11b.
66. *Ibid.*, II, 26b. 67. *Ibid.*, III, 8a.
68. *Ibid.*, IV, 13a.
69. Tseng Yang-feng, *Chung-kuo Yen-cheng Shih*, pp. 8–11.
70. *Ibid.*, p. 23. 71. *Ibid.*, pp. 23–28.
72. *Ibid.*, p. 23. 73. *Ibid.*, pp. 25–29.
74. Hu Hsiang-yün (ed.), *Ch'üan-kuo Tsui-chin Yen-ch'ang Lu*, *passim.*
75. *CL*(1), XVII, 1a–7a.
76. Ching Pen-po, *Yen-wu Ko-ming Shih*, pp. 3–6.
77. *Ibid.* 78. *Ibid.*
79. *Ibid.* 80. *CL*(1), XVII, 13a–19a.
81. Yen-wu Chi-ho Tsung-so, *Chung-kuo Yen-cheng Shih-lu*, IV, Chronology, 98.
82. *Ibid.*, 119. 83. *CL*(1), XVIII, 1a.
84. *Ibid.*, 4a–5a. 85. *CL*(1), XVIII, 8b–9a, 10a.
86. *Ibid.*, 10a. 87. *Ibid.*, 10a–10b.

88. *Ibid.*, 10b–11b.
89. *Ibid.*, 15a–15b.
90. *Ibid.*, XIX, 11b.
91. "Mei-shih Chia-lo-heng Chih Chang Chi-chih Hsien-sheng Han," *Yen-cheng Tsa-chih*, No. 3, "Tsa-lu," pp. 1–3.
92. "Chang Chi-chih Hsien-sheng Fu Mei-shih Chia-lo-heng Han," *Yen-cheng Tsa-chih*, No. 4, "Tsa-lu," pp. 1–6.
93. Ching, *Yen-wu Ko-ming Shih*, pp. 9–10.
94. T'ung-kuo Yen-yeh Lien-ho I-hui, *Po Chang Chien Chün Kai-ko Ch'üan-kuo Yen-cheng Chi-hua Shu T'iao-i*, pp. 1–44.
95. Ching, *Yen-wu Ko-ming Shih*, pp. 10–20. See also Marion Joseph Levy and Kuo-heng Shih, *The Rise of the Modern Chinese Business Class*, p. 35. For Chou Hsüeh-hsi's background, see *Chung-kuo Chin-tai Kung-yeh Shih Tzu-liao*, II, 931–33.
96. Ching, *Yen-wu Ko-ming Shih*, pp. 10–20.
97. *CC*, p. 192.
98. Ching, *Yen-wu Ko-ming Shih*, pp. 10–20.
99. *Ibid*.
100. *Ibid*. See also Ch'en, *Yüan Shih-k'ai*, pp. 156–58.
101. Gale, *Salt for the Dragon*, p. 134.
102. *Ibid.*
103. *CL*(1), XIX, 9a.
104. Yen-wu Chi-ho Tsung-so, *Chung-kuo Yen-wu Shih-lu*, IV, 22.
105. Ching, *Yen-wu Ko-ming Shih*, pp. 10–20.
106. Gale, *Salt for the Dragon*, p. 136.
107. *Ibid.*, p. 129.
108. Yen-wu Chi-ho Tsung-so, *Chung-kuo Yen-wu Shih-lu*, IV, 61.
109. Ching, *Yen-wu Ko-ming Shih*, pp. 10–20.

Seven. Controlling the Huai

1. *CL*(8), VI, 19b–20a.
2. *Ibid.*, 20a; *CL*(1), X, 34b–35a.
3. *NP*, I, 12a.
4. *CL*(1), X, 1b.
5. The following description of the Huai region is based on Lu Yang-hao, "Chiang-peh Shui-li Chi-yao," *Chiang-su Yen-chiu*, I, Nos. 3, 5, 6, nonconsecutive pagination; and Hu Huan-yung, *Liang-huai Shui-li*.
6. The following history of the Huai and its control is based on Cheng Chao-ching, *Chung-kuo Shui-li Shih*, pp. 132–68; and the excellent maps in Wu T'ung-chü, *Huai-ssu Nien-piao Ch'üan-pien*.
7. Feng Tao-li, *Huai-yang Shui-li T'u-shuo*.
8. Ting Hsien, *Fu-huai Ku-tao T'u-shuo*.
9. *CL*(1), X, 7b–10a.
10. *Ibid.*, 10a–11a, 18b–23a.

11. *Ibid.*, XV, 20a.
12. *Ibid.*, X, 27a–30a.
13. *Ibid.*, XI, 8b, 16b.
14. *Ibid.*, 11a; XII, 1b.
15. Tao-huai Wei-yüan Hui, *Tao-huai Kung-ch'eng Chi-hua*, p. 1.
16. The depth of feeling on the part of the two protagonists can be gauged by what they had to say about each other. Jameson wrote: "Mr. Chang Chien, about whom I was so enthusiastic when I first met him last year, has shown himself an obstructionist and in other works a great grafter. He came very near blocking all the famine relief work." Department of State Files, National Archives, Washington, D.C, No. 893.81/88, enclosure in Dispatch No. 909 from E. T. Williams, Jameson to G. W. Davis, July 30, 1912. Both Paul Reinsch, the American Minister, and his assistant E. T. Williams shared Jameson's doubt of Chang Chien's integrity. Reinsch did not believe Chang Chien to be "corrupt," but stated that Chang was not totally "free from the deviousness and looseness in financial methods common in Chinese officials." State Department Dispatch No. 893.81/109, Confidential Dispatch No. 86 from Paul Reinsch. Chang Chien's feelings about Jameson is well indicated by his efforts to exclude Jameson from any future role in Huai affairs. *CL*(1), XII, 7b–8a. Liu Hou-sheng, writing years later, recalled that Chang Chien stated that Jameson was only five years out of college and had prevailed upon the American Red Cross to send him to China in the hopes of making a personal windfall acting as the middleman. Liu, *Chang Chien Chuan-chi*, p. 274. Actually Jameson had graduated from Bowdoin College in 1877, had been in Mexico and Panama, and had served as a professor of railway engineering at M.I.T. and head of the engineering department at the State University of Iowa prior to coming to China. State Department Dispatch No. 893.81/89.
17. Department of State files, National Archives, Washington D.C., No. 893.81/88, Jameson to E. T. Williams, June 19, 1913.
18. *CL*(1), XI, 1a–1b.
19. *Ibid.*, 1b–3b.
20. Preface by Chung Chia-lu in Sung Hsi-shang, *Shuo Huai.*
21. On Hsü Ting-ling, see *Chung-kuo Chin-tai Kung-yeh Shih Tzu-liao*, II, 939.
22. *CL*(1), XII, 1a.
23. *Ibid.*, XI, 5b–10b.
24. *Ibid.*
25. *Ibid.*, 10b–16a.
26. *Ibid.*, 3a; Liu, *Chang Chien Chuan-chi*, p. 274.
27. *CL*(1), XI, 8b–9a.
28. *Ibid.*, 16b–19a.
29. *CL*(3), V, 17a–18b.
30. Paul Samuel Reinsch, *An American Diplomat in China*, p. 81.
31. *CL*(1), XII, 7b–8a.

32. United States, *Papers Relating to the Foreign Relations of the United States, 1914*, pp. 111–15.

33. *NP*, II, 38a.

34. *CC*, p. 205.

35. *CL*(8), VII, 28a.

36. Mabel Thorp Boardman, *Under the Red Cross Flag at Home and Abroad*, pp. 201–3.

37. *Ibid.*

38. *CL*(1), XII, 3a–7a.

39. *Ibid.*, 21b–22b; *CL*(8), VII, 29a.

40. *CL*(1), XIII, 1a–41b.

41. Chien-she Wei-yüan Hui, *Cheng-li Tao-huai T'u-an Pao-kao*, pp. 42–43.

42. Vannavar Bush, "John Ripley Freeman, 1855–1932," *National Academy of Sciences, Biographical Memoirs*, XVII, 171–87.

43. Sung, *Chang Chien Ti Sheng-p'ing*, pp. 358–59.

44. John Ripley Freeman, *Fei-li-men Chih-huai Chi-hua Shu*, translated by Yü Ming-teh and Ch'i Ch'un, *passim*. Freeman has included a summary of his Huai control plan in his article, "Flood Problems in China," *American Society of Civil Engineers, Transactions*, LXXXV, 1405–60.

45. Chien-she Wei-yüan Hui, *Cheng-li Tao-huai T'u-an Pao-kao*, p. 47.

46. Freeman, *Fei-li-men Chih-huai Chi-hua Shu*, pp. 130–33.

47. *CL*(1), XV, 26b.

48. *Ho-wu Chi-pao*, No. 5, "Wen-tu," pp. 8–9.

49. *CL*(1), XV, 18a; XVI, 9a, 21b.

50. *CL*(8), VII, 35a.

51. *NP*, II, 48b–49a.

52. Wu Chün-mien (ed.), *Li-hsia Ho Shu-t'i Kuei-hai Lun-chi*, pp. 12–20.

53. *CL*(1), XVI, 1a–9a.

54. *Ibid.*, 9b–16b.

55. *Ibid.*, 24a–25a.

Eight. The Modernization of Nan-t'ung

1. *CL*(4), II, 9b. Sung Hsi-shang stated that Chang Chien was influenced in his thinking by an early conversation with Timothy Richard, who hoped that a few districts might set the example for the entire nation. Sung, *Chang Chien Ti Sheng-p'ing*, p. 204.

2. *CL*(8), VI, 17a.

3. *Ibid.*, 17b.

4. *CC*, pp. 50–52.

5. *CL*(4), I, 18b–19b.

6. *Ibid.*, 17a–18a; *NP*, II, 24b.

7. *CL*(4), I, 17a–17b.

8. *Ibid.*, II, 2a–2b.

9. *Ibid.*, III, 6a–6b.

10. *Ibid.*, II, 2b–3b.

11. *Ibid.*, 23b–25b.

12. *Nan-t'ung Shih-yeh Chiao-yü Tz'u-shan Feng-ching*, p. 33. This source is cited as *NTSY* hereafter.

13. *CL*(4), II, 21a–23b.

14. *Ibid.* Contemporary observors agreed that local government officials generally bowed to Chang Chien's wishes, in deference to his scholarly reputation and local achievements. One of the instruments by which Chang Chien worked his will in Nan-t'ung was the person of the police chief, Yang Wei-seng. It is not clear whether Yang was a direct protegee of Chang, or whether he came under Chang's influence. Dr. Hagman has characterized Yang as "unusually alert," and Frederick Sites, a Shanghai visitor to Nan-t'ung, coroborated Dr. Hagman on this point, adding that Yang was especially friendly to foreigners. Letter from Dr. George L. Hagman, March 6, 1957, and Frederick Sites, "Chang Chien," *Asia*, XVIII, 589.

15. *T'ung-chou Chih-li-chou Chih*, III, 62–64.

16. *NP*, II, 20a; *CL*(5), 3b–4b.

17. Ch'ien, "Nan-t'ung Hsien Hsüeh-wu Ts'an-kuan Chi," *Chiao-yü Tsa-chih*, VIII, "Fu-lu," 27.

18. *NTSY*, p. 65.

19. *CC*, p. 103; *NP*, II, 21a.

20. *CL*(5), 11a–12b.

21. *NP*, II, 51a.

22. *Ibid.*, 34a.

23. *CC*, pp. 361–62.

24. *NTSY*, pp. 58–59; letter from Dr. George L. Hagman, March 6, 1957.

25. *ESNL*, I, 40.

26. *NTSY*, p. 64.

27. *CL*(3), III, 14b–15a.

28. Ch'i-chih, "Nan-t'ung P'ing-min Sheng-huo Chuang-k'uang," *Chiao-yü Yü Chih-yeh*, No. 72, pp. 117–22.

29. *TCLS*(6), p. 1; *CC*, p. 478.

30. *CL*(3), III, 3a–4a; Ch'ien, "Nan-t'ung Hsien Hsüeh-wu Ts'an-kuan Chi," *Chiao-yü Tsa-chih*, VIII, "Fu-lu," 27.

31. *CL*(3), III, 1a.

32. *Ibid.*, IV, 5b.

33. *ESNL*, I, 96.

34. *CL*(3), IV, 5b.

35. As listed in the library catalogue. Probably Aristotle's *Politics*.

36. Nan-t'ung T'u-shu-kuan, *Ti-i-tz'u Mu-lu*, unpaginated.

37. *Chiao-yü Tsa-chih*, X, "Fu-lu," 40.

38. *NP*, II, 43a.

39. *NTSY*, pp. 98–99.

40. *NP*, II, 45b.

41. *NTSY*, p. 54.

42. *Ibid.*

43. *CC*, p. 230.

44. *CL*(4), II, 12a–14b; *NTSY*, pp. 77–84.

45. *CL*(4), II, 23a.

46. *NTSY*, p. 67.

47. *Ibid.*, p. 32; Sung, *Chang Chien Ti Sheng-p'ing*, pp. 351–54.

48. *CL*(4), II, 26a–26b.

49. *Ibid.*, III, 2b–4a.

50. *Ibid.*, IV, 15a–15b.

51. *CL*(8), VII, 37b.

52. *NTSY*, p. 102. By the early 1920s Nan-t'ung had over a hundred automobiles, considerably more than most city of its size in China at the time. *ESNL*, I, 20–21.

53. *NTSY*, p. 27.

54. *CC*, p. 379.

55. There is a reference to a local supplementary tax which netted more than 100,000 yuan toward the support of the various local institutions, but further details are lacking. *CL*(4), III, 4b. See also Wong, *Chang Chien*, p. 80.

56. *CL*(4), II, 9b–11a.

57. *Ibid.; NP*, II, 40a; *CC*, p. 227.

58. *CC*, p. 227. See also Wong, *Chang Chien*, p. 81.

59. *CL*(4), III, 4a–5a.

60. *CC*, pp. 394–99.

61. *CL*(4), II, 14b–16b.

62. *Ibid.*, 19a–20a.

63. Sung Hsi-shang has vividly described Chang Chien's last illness and death. Sung, *Chang Chien Ti Sheng-p'ing*, pp. 367–70.

Nine. Chang Chien as a Modernizer

1. Hu Shih's foreword in *CC*.

2. Liu, *Chang Chien Chuan-chi*, pp. 282–83.

3. Sung, *Chang Chien Ti Sheng-p'ing*, pp. 8–9.

4. Tso, *Chung-kuo Hsien-tai Ming-jen I-shih*, p. 63.

5. Interviews with Dr. P. W. Kuo, April 2, 1956, and with Sung Hsi-shang, January 14, 1962.

6. As a part of the program toward greater liberalization of the government, the Ch'ing government issued in 1909 a series of regulations for local self-government. These were based on Japanese models. Chao Ju-heng, *Ti-fang Tzu-chih Chih Li-lun Yü Shih-chi*, pp. 46–50.

7. The first modern commercial laws in China were promulgated on January 21, 1904. Laws governing bankruptcy procedures did not come into effect until three years later. *Ta-ch'ing Kuang-hsü Hsin Fa-ling, Shih-yeh*, pp. 1, 13.

8. *CL*(3), IV, 10a–10b. Just as Chang Chien was not limited by space in his ideas, so was he equally unlimited by time. Answering one of Liu Hou-sheng's comments concerning the apparent failure of his land reclamation schemes, he said: "It is always most difficult to initiate a project. If presently I do not take advantage of my good health

and advantageous position to build the foundations, no one else will do it after my death. If I did manage to make a start, then it will probably be continued later. To maintain is always easier than to initiate. I do not insist on my seeing the projects through to their completion, nor do I think there will be no one to carry on my work. My successor need not be of the Chang family, or even natives of Nan-t'ung or Hai-men. As long as my goals are realized, I do not have to see the final results myself, nor would I insist on getting the credit." Liu, *Chang Chien Chuan-chi*, p. 251.

Glossary

Chang Ch'a 張詧
Chang Chien 張謇
Chang Chih-tung 張之洞
Chang Ching 張警
Chang Ching-ju 張敬孺
Chang Chiung 張駉
Chang Hsiang-tsu 張襄祖
Chang Hsiao-jo 張孝若
Chang Hsün 張勳
Chang Hu 張弧
Chang Jen 張仁
Chang Jen-chün 張人駿
Chang Mo 張謩
Chang P'ei-lun 張佩綸
Chang P'eng-ho 張鵬翮
Chang P'eng-nien 張彭年
Chang Ping-lin 章炳麟
Chang Po-hsi 張百熙
Chang Po-ling 張伯齡
Chang Shih-tsu 張怡祖

Chang Shu-sheng	張樹聲
Chang-teh	彰德
Chang Yu-tsu	張佑祖
Chang Yü	張譽
Chang Yü-ts'ai	張育才
Chang Yün-t'i	張雲梯
Ch'ang-fu	長福
Ch'ang-lo	長樂
Ch'ang-lu	長盧
Ch'ang-shu	常熟
Chao Er-sun	趙爾巽
Chao Feng-ch'ang	趙鳳昌
Chao-kuan	昭關
Chao P'eng-yüan	趙彭淵
Chao Pin-yen	趙濱彥
Chao Ping-chün	趙秉鈞
Che Sun	澤生
Ch'en Ch'i-mei	陳其美
Ch'en-chia-kang	陳家港
Ch'en San-li	陳三立
Ch'en-tan	震旦
Ch'en Te-ch'üan	程德全
Ch'en Wei-yung	陳維鏞
Cheng-chou	鄭州

Cheng Hsiao-hsü 鄭孝胥

Cheng Kuan-ying 鄭觀應

Cheng-wen She 政聞社

Chi 濟

Chiang Hsi-shen 蔣錫紳

Chiang-su Chiao-yü Tsung-hui 江蘇教育總會

Chiang-su Hsüeh-hui 江蘇學會

Chiang-su Sheng Chiao-yü Hui 江蘇省教育會

Chiang Tao-min 江導岷

Ch'iang-hsüeh Hui 强學會

Ch'ien-fo Shih 千佛寺

Chin Fu 靳輔

Chinkiang 鎮江

Chin-pu Tang 進步黨

chin-shih 進士

Ching Hsüeh-ch'ien 景學鈐

Ching Pen-po 景本白

Ching-shih Ta-hsüeh-t'ang 京師大學堂

Ch'ing (Prince) 慶(親王)

Ch'ing-chiang-p'u 清江浦

Ch'ing-kiang 靖江

Ch'ing-k'ou 清口

chou 州

Chou Fu 周馥

Chou Hsüeh-hsi	周學熙
Chou Shu-mo	周樹模
Ch'ou-an Hui	籌安會
Chu Chia-pao	朱家寶
Chu Pao-san	朱寶三
chü-jen	舉人
Ch'uan-ch'ang	串場
Ch'uan-hung	川洪
Ch'uan-sha	川沙
chuang-yüan	狀元
chüan	卷
Ch'un (Prince)	醇(親王)
Chün Shan	軍山
Chung-hua Min-kuo Lien-ho Hui	中華民國聯合會
Chung-kuo Kung-hsüeh	中國公學
Ch'ung-ming	崇明
Dah Lung	大隆
Dah Sing	大興
Dah Sun	大生
Dah Ta	大達
Ewo	怡和
Fan Fen	樊芬
Fan Hsiang	范祥
Fan Tseng-hsiang	樊增祥

fang	方
Feng Kuei-fen	馮桂芬
Feng-t'ien	奉天
fu	府
fu-sheng	附生
fu shih	覆試
Fu Sun	阜生
Futan	復旦
Hai-fu-cheng	海復鎮
Hai-men	海門
Han Kuo-chün	韓國鈞
Hanlin	翰林
Han Mo Lin	翰墨林
Han-yeh-p'ing	漢冶萍
Ho Feng-shih	何逢時
Ho Ssu-k'un	何嗣焜
Ho-tung	河東
hsiang (school)	庠
hsiang (village)	鄉
hsiao-lien	孝廉
hsien	縣
Hsien-cheng Ch'ou-pei Hui	憲政籌備會
Hsien-cheng Kung-hui	憲政公會
Hsien-cheng Pien-ch'a Kuan	憲政編查館

Hsien-fa Yen-chiu Hui 憲法研究會
Hsin-min Ts'ung-pao 新民叢報
Hsing-hua 興化
hsiu-ts'ai 秀才
Hsiung Hsi-ling 熊希齡
Hsü 徐
hsü 序
Hsü-chou 徐州
Hsü Hsien-min 徐顯民
Hsü Pao-shan 徐寶山
Hsü Shih-ch'ang 徐世昌
Hsü Shih-lin 徐石麟
Hsü Ting-lin 許鼎霖
Hsüan-ch'ing 選青
hsüeh 學
Hsüeh Chi 學記
Hsüeh Fu-ch'eng 薛福成
Hu Han-min 胡漢民
Hu-kwang 湖廣
Hu Shih 胡適
Hua Ch'eng 華成
Hua Hsin 華新
Huai 淮
Huai-nan 淮南

Huai-peh 淮北

Huai-yang 淮揚

Huai-yin 淮陰

Huai-yüan 懷遠

Huang Hsing 黃興

Huang Tsun-hsien 黃遵憲

Huang Yen-p'ei 黃炎培

hui 會

Hung-tse 洪澤

Hung Yüan 鴻源

I-cheng 儀徵

Jen Tsung 仁宗

Ju-kao 如皋

Jung-ch'ing 榮慶

K'ai-feng 開封

K'ailan 開灤

Kan-yü 贛榆

K'ang Yu-wei 康有為

Kao Ch'ing 高清

Kao-pao 高寶

Kao-yu 高郵

K'ao-ch'a Cheng-chih Kuan 考查政治館

K'ao-kung Chi 考工記

Kiang-Huai 江淮

Kiang-nan	江南
Kiang-ning	江寧
Kiang-yin	江陰
Kiukiang	九江
k'o	科
Kuan-ho-k'ou	灌河口
kuan-li	官利
kuan-tu shang-pan	官督商辦
Kuang-fang-yen Kuan	廣方言館
Kuang-fu Hui	光復會
Kuei Sung-ch'ing	桂嵩慶
K'un-shan	崑山
kung-chieh yü-li	公積餘利
Kung-chin Hui	共進會
Kung-ho Chien-she T'ao-lun Hui	共和建設討論會
Kung-ho Tang	共和黨
Kung-ho T'ung-i Tang	共和統一黨
kung-sheng	貢生
kung-shih	貢士
kung-ssu	公司
Kuo Hsün	郭勳
Kuo-hui Ch'in-yüan Tai-piao T'uan	國會請願代表團
Kuo-hui Ch'in-yüan T'ung-chih Hui	國會請願同志會
Kuo-min Hsieh-chin Hui	國民協進會

Kuo-min Tang 國民黨

Kuo Sung-tao 郭嵩燾

Kwan Sun 廣生

Lang Shan 狼山

Laou-Kung-Mow 老公茂

Lei Feng 雷奮

Li Chi 禮記

Li-hsia Ho 裏下河

Li Hung-chang 李鴻章

Li Shen-chih 李審之

Li Sheng-to 李盛鐸

Li Yüan-hung 黎元洪

Liang-Che 兩浙

Liang Ch'i-ch'ao 梁啓超

Liang-Huai 兩淮

Liang-Kiang 兩江

Liang-Kwang 兩廣

Liang Ting-fen 梁鼎芬

Lin-hung-k'ou 臨洪口

Lin Shao-nien 林紹年

lin-sheng 廩生

Lin Tse-hsü 林則徐

Liu-ch'iu 琉球

Liu Hou-sheng 劉厚生

Liu Kuei-hsing 劉桂馨
Liu K'un-i 劉坤一
Liu Ta-hsia 劉大夏
Liu Yen 劉晏
Lo Shu-yün 羅叔蘊
Lu Cheng-hsiang 陸徵祥
Lu Jun-hsiang 陸潤庠
lü 閭
Lü-ssu 呂四
Ma-an Shan 馬鞍山
Ma Chien-chung 馬建忠
Mao Sun 懋生
Meng Seng 孟森
mien-t'ieh chu-i 棉鐵主義
Min-chu Tang 民主黨
Min-kuo Kung-hui 民國公會
Min Pao 民報
Min She 民社
ming 名
Nan-huai 南滙
Nan-t'ung 南通
Nan-yang Ch'üan-yeh Hui 南洋勸業會
Nan-yang Ta-hsüeh 南洋大學
Ni Wen-wei 倪文蔚

Nien 捻

Ou-yang Yü-ch'ien 歐陽予倩

P'an Chi-hsün 潘季馴

P'an Hua-mou 潘華茂

P'an Tsu-yin 潘祖蔭

pang-yen 榜眼

pao 包

Pao-shan 寶山

Po Wen-wei 柏文蔚

P'u-k'ou 浦口

P'u-shan T'ang 普善堂

San-chiang-ying 三江營

San-ho (outlet) 三和

San-ho (river) 三河

San-ho-k'ou 三河口

san-kuan 散館

Sha Yüan-pin 沙元炳

Shan-yang 山陽

Shang Ch'i-heng 尚其亨

Shao-ying 紹英

She-yang-k'ou 射陽口

Shen En-fu 沈恩孚

Shen Hsieh-chün 沈燮均

Shen Lin-shen 沈林森

Shen Tseng-chih 沈曾植

Shen Yün-p'ei 沈雲沛

Sheng Hsüan-huai 盛宣懷

Shih Chi 史記

Shih-tai 石埭

Shu 沭

shu (number) 數

shu (school) 塾

Soy-chee 瑞記

Su Lun 蘇綸

sui 歲

Sun Hung-i 孫洪伊

Sun Pao-ch'i 孫寶琦

Sun Yün-chin 孫雲錦

Sung Chiao-jen 宋教仁

Sung Hsi-shang 宋希尚

Sung-kiang 松江

Sung P'u-chai 宋璞齋

Ta Feng 大豐

Taku 大沽

Ta Shun 大純

Ta Wei 大維

Ta Yu Chin 大有晉

Tai Hung-tz'u 戴鴻慈

Tai-wen-kun 大院君

T'ai-ch'ang 太倉

T'ai-chou 泰州

T'ai-hsing 泰興

T'ai-p'ing 太平

t'an-hua 探花

T'an Yen-k'ai 譚延闓

tang 黨

T'ang-chia-cha 唐家牐

T'ang Ching-ch'ung 唐景崇

T'ang Hua-lung 湯化龍

T'ang Shao-i 唐紹儀

T'ang Shou-ch'ien 湯壽潛

T'ao Shu 陶澍

Teng Ch'eng-hsiu 鄧承修

Teng-chou 登州

T'ieh-liang 鐵良

tien shih 殿試

Ting Cheng-to 丁振鐸

Ting Ju-ch'ang 丁汝昌

Ting Li-ying 丁立瀛

Tou-lung-k'ou 鬥龍口

Tsai-tse 載澤

Ts'ai Yüan-p'ei 蔡元培

Tseng Kuo-fan 曾國藩
tseng-sheng 增生
Tso Tsung-t'ang 左宗棠
Ts'ui Ting 崔鼎
Tuan Ch'i-jui 段其瑞
Tuan-fang 端方
tung-shih 董事
Tung-t'ai 東臺
T'ung Chiu Yüan 通久源
T'ung-chou 通州
T'ung Hai K'en-mu Kung-ssu 通海墾牧公司
T'ung-i Kung-ho Tang 統一共和黨
T'ung-i Tang 統一黨
T'ung Jen T'ai 同仁泰
T'ung-kuo Yen-yeh Lien-ho I-hui 通國鹽業聯合議會
T'ung-meng Hui 同盟會
T'ung Ming 同明
T'ung-pe 桐柏
T'ung-shan 銅山
T'ung-wen Kuan 同文館
T'ung Yi Kung 通益公
Tze Sun 資生
tzu-ch'iang 自强
Tzu-chih Hui 自治會

Wang-chia-kang	王家港
Wang Chih	王制
Wang Pin	王賓
Wang Shu-t'ang	汪樹堂
Wang T'ao	王韜
Wei-hai-wei	威海衛
Wei Ju-kuei	衛汝貴
Wei Kuang-tao	魏光燾
Wen-cheng	文正
Wen Shih-lin	溫世霖
Wen Wang Shih Tzu	文王世子
Weng T'ung-ho	翁同龢
Wo-jen	倭仁
Wu-ch'ang	武昌
Wu Ch'ang-ch'ing	吳長慶
Wu Hsi-lin	吳熙麟
Wu-hu	蕪湖
Wu San-kuei	吳三桂
Wusih	無錫
Wu Yüeh	吳樾
Yang-chou	揚州
Yang I-k'uei	楊一魁
Yang Ju	楊儒
Yang T'ing-tung	楊廷棟

Yang Wen-ting	楊文鼎
Yao-wang	遙望
Yeh Ch'in	業勤
Yen An-lan	晏安瀾
Yen-cheng T'ao-lun Hui	鹽政討論會
Yen-ch'eng	鹽城
Yen Fu	嚴復
yen-hu	鹽戶
Yi	沂
Yih Sun	頤生
ying	穎
Ying-chou	瀛洲
Yü Ch'eng-lung	于成龍
Yü Chin	裕晉
Yü Chüeh	余覺
Yü-chung T'ang	輿衆堂
Yü-pei Li-hsien Kung-hui	預備立憲公會
Yü Shen Shou	余沈壽
Yü T'ung	裕通
Yü Yüan	裕源
yüan	院
Yüan Shuang-ch'iu	袁爽秋
Yüan Shih-k'ai	袁世凱
Yung Wing	容閎
Ziccawei	徐家匯

Bibliography

A. Chinese and Japanese Sources

I. BASIC SOURCES

Chang Ch'ao-han and Ho Ssu-ch'ing. "Nan-t'ung Kung-yeh Chih Tiao-ch'a" [Investigation of Nan-t'ung Industries], *Shih-yeh Tsa-chih*, No. 52 (February, 1922), 54–66, and No. 55 (May, 1922), 49–56.

張朝漢 何思清 南通工業之調查

Detailed descriptions of some of Chang Chien's most important industrial enterprises.

Chang Chien. Chang Chi-tzu Chiu-lu [The Nine Records of Chang Chien]. Ed. by Chang Hsiao-jo. Shanghai, 1931. 80 chüan.

張謇 張季子九錄 張孝若

The indispensable basic source to the study of Chang Chien's life, this collection of his writings is divided topically. Within each topical section the sources are arranged in chronological order. The editor has made no attempt to present any background information. This, together with the fact that many of Chang Chien's letters are included without the related correspondence from the persons involved, makes this source a cumbersome one to use. Consultation with other works is necessary to render the material contained meaningful.

——— Seh-weng Tzu-ting Nien-p'u [Self-compiled Chronological Records of Chang Chien]. Nan-t'ung, 1925. 2 chüan.

嗇翁自訂年譜

Detailed chronological record of Chang Chien's life, kept by him until his seventieth year and completed by his son. A rich basic source.

Chang Hsiao-jo. Nan-t'ung Chang Chi-chih Hsien-sheng Chuan-chi [Biography of Mr. Chang Chien of Nan-t'ung]. Shanghai, 1930. 522 pp.

張孝若 南通張季直先生傳記

This is a highly useful biography of Chang Chien, written by his son. Many facets of Chang Chien's career and personality are presented in their favorable light. A pioneer work of its kind at the time of its publication, this book suffers through loose organization and superficial treatment of several of Chang Chien's more important contributions.

Ch'i-chih. "Nan-t'ung P'ing-min Sheng-huo Chuang-k'uang" [Living Conditions of the Masses in Nan-t'ung], *Chiao-yü Yü Chih-yeh*, No. 72 (February, 1926), 117–22.

啓之 南通平民生活狀況

Ch'iao Ch'i-ming. Chiang-su K'un-shan Nan-t'ung An-hui Su-hsien Nung-tien Chih-tu Chih Pi-chiao I-chi Kai-liang Nung-tien Wen-t'i Chih Chien-i [A Comparison of the Land Tenancy System of K'un-shan and Nan-t'ung in Kiangsu and Su-hsien in Anhwei, and a Proposal on the Question of Land Tenancy Reform]. Chin-ling Ta-hsüeh Nung-lin Ts'ung-k'an [Nanking University, Department of Agriculture and Forestry Series], No. 30. Nanking, 1926. 79 pp.

喬啓明

江蘇崑山南通安徽宿縣農佃制度之比較以及改良農佃問題之建議

Ch'ien Kung-p'u. "Nan-t'ung Hsien Hsüeh-wu Ts'an-kuan Chi" [Account of an Inspection of Educational Affairs in Nan-t'ung], *Chiao-yü Tsa-chih*, VIII (November, 1916), "Fu-lu" [Appendix], 27.

錢公溥 南通縣學務參觀記

Chuang Yü. "Chang Chi-chih Hsien-sheng Chiao-yü T'an" [Interview with Mr. Chang Chien on Education], *Chiao-yü Tsa-chih*, IX (January, 1917), "Yen-lun" [Pronouncements], 33–39.

莊俞 張季直先生教育談

Erh-shih-nien-lai Chih Nan-t'ung [Nan-t'ung Since Two Decades Ago]. Nan-t'ung (?), 1924 (?). ii, ii, xvi, vi, 114, 148 pp.

二十年來之南通

Written by an anonymous native of Nan-t'ung just shortly before Chang Chien's death, this is the latest available detailed account of Nan-t'ung's industrial and educational institutions.

Hai-men T'ing T'u-chih [Illustrated Gazetteer of Hai-men]. Compiled by Liu Wen-ch'e. Ed. by Chou Chia-lu. Hai-men (?), 1900. 20 chüan.

海門廳圖志 劉文澈 周家祿

Hsü P'eng-nien and K'ung Jung-chao (eds.). Chang Nan-t'ung Hsien-sheng Jung-ai Lu [The Record of Tributes Tendered to Mr. Chang Chien]. Shanghai, 1931. 10 chüan.

許彭年 孔容照 張南通先生榮哀錄

Ku Kung-i (ed.). Chang Seh-an Hsien-sheng Chiu-lu Lu [Abstract from Nine Records of Mr. Chang Chien]. Nan-t'ung, 1947. 10 chüan.

顧公毅 張嗇菴先生九錄錄

Selected portions from all sections of Chang Chi-tzu Chiu-lu, compiled under the auspices of the Chang family.

Li Yüan-heng. "Nan-t'ung Tai-yung Ssu-fan Fu-shu Hsiao-hsüeh Kai-lan" [Survey of the Elementary School Attached to the Nan-t'ung Normal School], *Chiao-yü Tsa-chih*, VI (May, 1914), "Ch'eng-chi" [Accomplishments], 1–5.

李元衡 南通代用師範附屬小學概覽

Liu Hou-sheng. Chang Chien Chuan-chi [Biography of Chang Chien]. Peking (?), 1958 (?). v, xxxviii, 288 pp.

劉厚生 張謇傳記

This is written by one of the last surviving business associates of Chang Chien. In spite of the title, Mr. Liu unfortunately has chosen to concentrate on the political events of the time and touches upon Chang Chien only incidentally.

Minami Manshū Tetsudō Kabushiki Kaisha Shanhai Jimusho Chōsashitsu [South Manchurian Railway. Shanghai Office. Research Bureau]. Kōsoshō Nantsūken Nōson Jittai Chōsa Hōkokusho [Report of Investigation into the Actual Situation of Villages in Nan-t'ung District of Kiangsu Province]. Shanghai (?), 1941. 186 pp.

南滿洲鐵道株式會社上海事務所調查室
江蘇省南通縣農村實態調查報告書

Nan-t'ung-chou Wu-shan Ch'üan-chih [Gazetteer of the Five Mountains of Nan-t'ung]. Compiled by Liu Ming-fang. No place of publications, 1751. 5 ts'e.

南通州五山全志 劉名芳

Nan-t'ung Shih-yeh Chiao-yü Tz'u-shan Feng-ching [Industry, Education, Philanthropy, and Scenic Sites of Nan-t'ung]. Nan-t'ung, 1920. 108 pp.

南通實業教育慈善風景

A profusely illustrated book. Many facts of Chang Chien's handiwork can be gleaned from both the pictures and the captions.

Nan-t'ung Ti-fang Tzu-chih Shih-chiu-nien Chih Ch'eng-chi [Result of Nineteen Years of Local Self-government in Nan-t'ung]. Nan-t'ung (?), 1915 (?). 88, 198 pp.

南通地方自治十九年之成績

Similar in organization but different in contents from Erh-shih-nien-lai Chih Nan-t'ung, this work contains useful information, but some of it is superceded by the later work.

Nan-t'ung T'u-shu-kuan [Nan-t'ung Library]. Nan-t'ung T'u-shu-kuan Ti-i-tz'u Mu-lu [First Catalogue of Nan-t'ung Library]. Nan-t'ung, 1914. 6 ts'e.

南通圖書館 南通圖書館第一次目錄

Sung Hsi-shang. Chang Chien Ti Sheng-p'ing [Life and Career of Chang Chien]. Taipei, 1963. 498 pp.

宋希尚 張謇的生平

This is the most recent account of Chang Chien's life. Mr. Sung has written less a biography than an annotated collection of source materials, drawn largely from Chang Chi-tzu Chiu-lu, supplemented by personal rememberances.

T'ung-chou Chih-li-chou Chih [Gazetteer of Nan-t'ung]. Compiled by Liang Yüeh-hsing and Mo Ch'iang-chih. Edited by Ku Tseng-huan and Ku Tseng-hsüan. Nan-t'ung, 1875. 16 chüan.

通州直隸州志 梁悅馨 莫祥芝
顧曾煥 顧曾烜

T'ung-chou Hsing-pan Shih-yeh Chang-ch'eng [Documents of the Establishment of Nan-t'ung Industries]. Rev. ed. Nan-t'ung, 1905. 4 ts'e.

通州興辦實業章程

An earlier version of the following work.

T'ung-chou Hsing-pan Shih-yeh Chih Li-shih [History of the Establishment of Industries in Nan-t'ung]. 3d ed. Nan-t'ung, 1910. Nonconsecutive pagination.

通州興辦實業之歷史

A basic source. This collection of original documents includes correspondences, articles, records of stockholders' meetings, and annual reports of all major enterprises in Nan-t'ung.

T'ung Hai K'en-mu Kung-ssu K'ai-pan Shih-nien Chih Li-shih [Decennial History of T'ung Hai Land Reclamation Company]. Nan-t'ung (?), 1911 (?). Unpaginated.

通海墾牧公司開辦十年之歷史

Mostly charts and photographs, with a brief account.

T'ung-kuo Yen-yeh Lien-ho I-hui [National Salt Business Federation]. Po Chang Chien Chün Kai-ko Ch'üan-kuo Yen-cheng Chi-hua Shu T'iao-i [Detailed Refutation of Chang Chien's Salt Reform Plan]. No place of publication, no date. 1 ts'e.

通國鹽業聯合議會

駁張謇君改革全國鹽政計劃書條議

II. DOCUMENTS AND MAJOR PRIMARY SOURCES

Chang Chih-tung. Chang Wen-hsiang Kung Ch'üan-chi [Complete Works of Chang Chih-tung]. Edited by Wang Chin-ch'ing. Peiping, 1948. 228 chüan.

張之洞 張文襄公全集 王晋卿

Chang Shu-sheng. Chang Ching-ta Kung Chou-i [Memorials of Chang Shu-sheng]. No place of publication, no date. 8 chüan.

張樹聲 張靖達公奏議

Chiang-su Hsüeh-wu Kung-so [Kiangsu Office of Education]. Chiang-su Hsüeh-wu Wen-tu [Documents of Kiangsu Educational Affairs]. No place of publication, 1910. 2 chüan.

江蘇學務公所 江蘇學務文牘

Chiang-su Shih-yeh T'ing [Kiangsu Bureau of Industry]. Chiang-su Sheng Fang-chih-yeh Chuang-k'uang [Condition of the Textile Industry in Kiangsu Province]. Wusih, 1919. Nonconsecutive pagination.

江蘇實業廳 江蘇省紡織業狀況

This source gives many otherwise unavailable facts and figures on cotton spinning and weaving mills in Kiangsu, where the center of China's cotton textile industry was located.

Chiao-t'ung T'ieh-tao Pu [Ministry of Communication and Railway]. Chiao-t'ung Shih, Hang-cheng Pien [History of Communications: Water Transportation]. No place of publication, 1931. 7 vols.

交通鐵道部 交通史航政編

One of six components of the comprehensive history of communications in China, this section contains a wealth of information on coastal and inland shipping. The other sections deal with mail service, air transportation, highways, tele-communications, and general administration respectively.

Chiao-yü Pu [Ministry of Education]. Chung-hua Min-kuo Ti-wu-tz'u Chiao-yü T'ung-chi T'u-piao [Fifth Statistical Survey of Education in China]. Peking, 1917. 5 ts'e.

教育部 中華民國第五次教育統計圖表

——— Min-kuo Liu-nien Shih-ch'a P'u-t'ung Hsüeh-hsiao Pao-kao Hsüan-lu [Selected Documents from the 1917 Report on Schools]. Peking, 1918. 338 pp.

民國六年視察普通學校報告選錄

One of the few available sources giving a qualitative as well as a quantitative comparison of selected elementary, secondary, and normal schools in the country.

——— Ti-erh-tz'u Chung-kuo Chiao-yü Nien-chien [The Second China Education Year Book]. Shanghai, 1948. 1645 pp.

第二次中國教育年鑑

A voluminous official source covering every aspect of education in China.

Ching Pen-po. Yen-wu Ko-ming Shih [History of the Revolution in Salt Affairs]. Nanking, 1929. 32, 206 pp.

景本白 鹽務革命史

Written by a man who was intimately involved in most of the salt reform efforts of the time, this short account relates certain events not generally covered by standard historical accounts. The bulk of the book is devoted to an appendix containing important documents on salt reforms.

Ch'ing-chi Hsüeh-hsiao Chang-ch'eng Hui-ch'un [Collected Documents on Schools in Ch'ing Times]. Peking, 1905–1906. 12 ts'e.

清季學校章程彙存

Pamphlets on education kept together at the East Asian Library of Columbia University.

Freeman, John Ripley. Mei-kuo Kung-ch'eng-shih Fei-li-men Chih-huai Chi-hua Shu [The Huai Control Plan of the American Engineer Freeman]. Translated by Yü Ming-teh and Ch'i Ch'ün. No place of publication, 1922. 135 pp.

美國工程師費禮門治淮計劃書

Hsing-cheng Yüan, Nung-ts'un Fu-hsing Wei-yüan Hui [Executive Yüan. Commission on Rural Reconstruction]. Chiang-su Sheng Nung-ts'un Tiao-ch'a [Investigation of Villages in Kiangsu]. Shanghai, 1934. 245 pp.

行政院農村復興委員會 江蘇省農村調查

Li Hung-chang. Li Wen-chung Kung Ch'üan-chi [Complete Works of Li Hung-chang]. Shanghai, 1921. 100 ts'e.

李鴻章 李文忠公全集

Liang Ch'i-ch'ao. Yin-ping-shih Ho-chi [Collected Works of Liang Ch'i-ch'ao]. Shanghai, 1936. 40 ts'e.

梁啓超 飲冰室合集

Liu K'un-i. Liu Chung-ch'eng Kung I-chi [Remaining Works of Liu K'un-i]. No place of publication, 1921. 66 chüan.

劉坤一　劉忠誠公遺集

Rare until reprinted in the following edition.

———. Liu K'un-i I-chi [Remaining Works of Liu K'un-i]. Peking, 1959. 2813 pp.

劉坤一遺集

Nei-wu Pu, Ch'üan-kuo Ho-wu Yen-chiu Hui [Ministry of Interior. National Waterways Research Association]. *Ho-wu Chi-pao* [Waterways Quarterly]. Peking, 1919–　. Quarterly.

內務部. 全國河務研究會　河務季報

Nung-kung-shang Pu [Ministry ot Agriculture, Labor, and Commerce]. Nung-kung-shang Pu T'ung-chi Piao [Statistical Tables of the Ministry of Agriculture, Labor, and Commerce]. Peking (?), 1908. 2 ts'e.

農工商部　農工商部統計表

Nung-kung-shang Pu Hsien-hsing Chang-ch'eng [Current Regulations of the Ministry of Agriculture, Labor, and Commerce]. Peking (?), 1909. 4 ts'e.

農工商部現行章程

Nung-shang Pu [Ministry of Agriculture and Commerce]. Nung-shang Fa-kuei Hui-pien [Collection of Agricultural and Commercial Laws]. Peking (?), 1914. 2 ts'e.

農商部　農商法規彙編

Sheng Hsüan-huai. Yü-chai Ts'un-kao [Extant Writings of Sheng Hsüan-huai]. Shanghai, 1939. 100 chüan.

盛宣懷　愚齋存稿

Shih-yeh Pu, Kuo-chi Mao-i Chü [Ministry of Industry. Bureau of Foreign Trade]. Chung-kuo Shih-yeh Chih, Chiang-su Sheng [Chinese Industries: Kiangsu Province]. No place of publication, 1933.

實業部
國際貿易局　中國實業志. 江蘇省

One of several provincial handbooks published by the Ministry of Industry, this source thoroughly covers the industries of Kiangsu.

Ta-ch'ing Kuang-hsü Hsin Fa-ling [New Laws of Kuang-hsü Period]. Shanghai (?), 1909. 20 ts'e.

大清光緒新法令

Tuan-fang. Tuan Chung-min Kung Chou-kao [Memorials of Tuan-fang]. No place of publication, 1918. 16 chüan.

端方 端忠敏公奏稿

Weng T'ung-ho. Weng Wen-kung Kung Jih-chi [Diary of Weng T'ung-ho]. Shanghai, 1925. 40 ts'e.

翁同龢 翁文恭公日記

Yen-wu Chi-ho Tsung-so [Central Office of Salt Investigations]. Chung-kuo Yen-cheng Shih-lu [Veritable Records of Chinese Salt Administration]. No place of publication, 1933. 4 vols.

鹽務稽核總所 中國鹽政實錄

A massive compendium of facts and figures on every aspect of salt administration.

III. OTHER MATERIALS

Chang Chih-tung. Ch'üan-hsüeh P'ien [Exhortation to Learning]. No place of publication, 1898. 2 chüan.

張之洞 勸學篇

Chang Chung-yüan and Yang Chün-ju. "Kao Chih-yen Hsien-sheng Pan-li Ts'un-cheng Shih-chi" [An Account of the Rural Reform Efforts of Mr. Kao Chih-yen]. *Hsien-hsiang Tzu-chih*, IV (June, 1934), 61–63.

張中元
楊駿儒 高志巖先生辦理村政事蹟

Chao Feng-t'ien. Wan-ch'ing Wu-shih-nien Ching-chi Ssu-hsiang Shih [Economic Thought During the Last Fifty Years of the Ch'ing

Period]. Yen-ching Hsüeh-pao Monograph Series, No. 18. Peiping, 1939. 320 pp.

趙豐田　　晚清五十年經濟思想史
燕京學報

Chao Ju-heng. Chiang-su Sheng-chien [Kiangsu Province Gazette]. Shanghai, 1935. 2 vols.

趙如珩　　江蘇省鑑

———. Ti-fang Tzu-chih Chih Li-lun Yü Shih-chi [The Theory and Practice of Local Self-government]. Shanghai, 1933. vii, 568 pp.

地方自治之理論與實際

Ch'en I-lin. Tsui-chin San-shih-nien Chung-kuo Chiao-yü Shih [History of Chinese Education in the Last Thirty Years]. Shanghai, 1930. 380 pp.

陳翊林　　最近三十年中國教育史

Cheng Chao-ching. Chung-kuo Shui-li Shih [History of Water Conservancy in China]. Changsha, 1939. 347 pp.

鄭肇經　　中國水利史

Cheng Ho-sheng. Chin-shih Chung-hsi shih-jih Tui-chao Piao [Comparative Tables of Chinese and Western Dates for Recent Periods]. New ed. Taipei, 1962. iv, viii, 880 pp.

鄭鶴聲　　近世中西史日對照表

Cheng Kuan-ying. Sheng-shih Wei-yen [Warnings to the Seemingly Prosperous Age]. Reprinted ed. No place of publication, 1893. 6 chüan.

鄭觀應　　盛世危言

The most influential book of its kind, dealing with political, economic, educational, and other reforms.

Chia I-chün. Chung-hua Min-kuo Ming-jen Chuan [Biographies of Notables in the Republic of China]. Peiping, 1933. 2 vols.

賈逸君　　中華民國名人傳

Chiang I-hsüeh. "Chang Chien I-chuan" [Draft Biography of Chang Chien], *Shuo-wen*, III (September, 1942), 101–3.

蔣逸雪 張謇擬傳

Chiang Nai-yung. Yin-hua Fang-chih-jan Tz'u-tien "Anglo-Chinese Dictionary of Textile Terms." 2d ed. Chungking, 1947. 168 pp.

蔣乃鏞 英華紡織染辭典

Chiang-su Yen-chiu [Research on Kiangsu]. Shanghai, 1935– . Monthly.

江蘇研究

Chiang T'ing-fu. Chung-kuo Chin-tai Shih [History of Modern China]. Changsha, 1941. 128 pp.

蔣廷黻 中國近代世

Chiao-yü Tsa-chih (*The Educational Review*). Shanghai, 1908– . Monthly.

教育雜誌

Chiao-yü Yü Chih-yeh [Education and Vocation]. Shanghai, 1919– Monthly.

教育與職業

Chien Po-tsan, ed. I-ho T'uan [The Boxers]. Shanghai, 1951. 4 vols.

翦伯贊 義和團

Highly useful collection of source materials. The bibliography is especially valuable.

Chin Liang. Chin-shih Jen-wu Chih [Contemporary Personages]. Peiping, 1934. 366 pp.

金梁 近世人物志

Chou I-pin and Lo Chih-yüan. Chung-kuo Hsien-cheng Fa-chan Shih [History of Constitutional Developments in China]. Chungking, 1944. 319 pp.

周異斌 羅志淵 中國憲政發展史

Chu Ching-nung et al, ed. Chiao-yü Ta Tz'u-shu [Educational Dictionary]. Shanghai, 1930. Nonconsecutive pagination.

朱經農等 教育大辭書

Ch'üan Han-sheng. "Chia-wu Chan-cheng I-ch'ien Ti Chung-kuo Kung-yeh-hua Yün-tung" [The Movement for Industrialization in China Prior to the Sino-Japanese War of 1894]. *Kuo-li Chung-yang Yen-chiu Yüan Li-shih Yü-yen Yen-chiu So Chi-k'an*, XXV (1954), 59–80.

全漢昇

甲午戰爭以前的中國工業化運動

Chuang Yü and Ho Sheng-nai, eds. Tsui-chin San-shih-wu-nien Chih Chung-kuo Chiao-yü [Chinese Education in the Last Thirty-five Years]. Shanghai, 1931. 2 vols.

莊俞

賀聖鼐 最近三十五年之中國教育

Chung-hua Min-kuo Shih-san-nien-tu Tiao-ch'a Ch'üan-kuo Chih-yeh Chiao-yü Pao-kao [Report of Investigation of Vocational Education Throughout the Nation in 1924]. Special supplement of *Chiao-yü Yü Chih-yeh* (May, 1926). 26, 77 pp. 中華民國十三年度

調查全國職業教育報告

Chung-kuo Chien-she (*Construction of China*). Shanghai, 1930– . Monthly.

中國建設

Chung-kuo Chin-tai Kung-yeh Shih Tzu-liao [Sources for A History of Modern Chinese Industries]. Vol. 1, compiled by Wang Ching-yü. Vol. 2, compiled by Sun Yü-t'ang. Peking, 1957.

中國近代工業史資料 汪敬虞 孫毓棠

Extremely valuable compilation of relevant source materials on the establishment and growth of Chinese industries in the nineteenth and early twentieth centuries.

Chung-kuo Shih-hsüeh Hui [Chinese Historical Association]. Wu-hsü Pien-fa [Reform of 1898]. Shanghai, 1953. 4 vols.

中國史學會 戊戌變法

Has a useful bibliography.

Fan-t'ien Lu Ts'ung-lu [Collectenea of Fan-t'ien Studio]. No place of publication, no date.

梵天廬叢錄

Fan Yin-nan. Tang-tai Chung-kuo Ming-jen Lu [Outstanding Chinese of the Contemporary Period]. Shanghai, 1931. 460 pp.

樊蔭南　當代中國名人錄

Fang Hsien-t'ing. Chung-kuo Chih Mien-tang-chih-yeh [The Cotton Textile Industry of China]. Shanghai, 1934. 387 pp.

方顯廷　中國之棉紡織業

A standard work.

Feng Kang et al, eds. San-shui Liang Yen-sun Hsien-sheng Nien-p'u [a Chronological Records of Mr. Liang Shih-i of San-shui]. 2d ed. No place of publication, 1946. 2 vols.

鳳岡等　三水梁燕孫先生年譜

Feng Tao-li. Huai-yang Shui-li T'u-shuo [Illustrated Discourse on the Water Conservancy Program of the Huai and the Yangtze]. Tung-t'ai, Kiangsu, 1839. 17, 19 pp.

馮道立　淮揚水利圖說

Feng Tzu-yu. Chung-hua Min-kuo K'ai-kuo Ch'ien Ko-ming Shih [History of the Revolution Prior to the Establishment of the Republic of China]. Shanghai, 1928. 3 vols.

馮自由　中華民國開國前革命史

Hsi-yin [Chao Feng-ch'ang]. "Keng-tzu Ch'üan-huo Tung-nan Hu-pao Chih Chi-shih" [A True Account of the Maintenance of Peace in the Southeast during the Boxer Disaster of 1900], *Jen-wen*, II (September, 1931), 1–7.

惜陰〔趙鳳昌〕

庚子拳禍東南互保之紀實

Hsia Yen-teh. Chung-kuo Chin-pai-nien Ching-chi Ssu-hsiang [Chinese Economic Thought during the Last Hundred Years]. Shanghai, 1948. 202 pp.

夏炎德　中國近百年經濟思想

Hsiao Kung-ch'üan. Chung-kuo Cheng-chih Ssu-hsiang Shih [History of Chinese Political Thought]. Taipei, 1954. 6 vols.

蕭公權　中國政治思想史

Hsieh Pin. Min-kuo Cheng-tang Shih [History of Political Parties during the Republican Period]. Shanghai, 1926. 242 pp.

謝彬 民國政黨史

Useful for understanding the complex political situation of the first decade of the republican period. Complete listings of members of cabinets are included.

Hsien-cheng [Constitutional Government]. Chungking, 1944– . Monthly.

憲政

Hsien-cheng Tsa-shih [Constitutional Government Miscellany]. Shanghai, 1906– .

憲政雜識

An organ of the constitutionalists of Kiangsu.

Hsien-hsiang Tzu-chih [Rural Self-government]. Peiping, 1931– Monthly.

縣鄉自治

Hsü T'ung-hsin, ed. Chang Wen-hsiang Kung Nien-p'u [Chronological Records of Chang Chih-tung]. Chungking, 1944. 229 pp.

許同莘 張文襄公年譜

Hsü Ying. Tang-tai Chung-kuo Shih-yeh Jen-wu Chih [An Account of Contemporary Chinese Industrialists]. Shanghai, 1948. 202 pp.

徐盈 當代中國實業人物志

Hu Hsiang-yün, ed. Ch'üan-kuo Tsui-chin Yen-ch'ang Lu [Latest Account of Salt Fields in the Country]. Peking, 1915. Nonconsecutive pagination.

胡翔雲 全國最近鹽場錄

Hu Huan-yung. Liang-huai Shui-li [Water Conservancy in the Huai Region]. Shanghai, 1947. 92 pp.

胡煥庸 兩淮水利

Hua-shang Sha-ch'ang Lien-ho Hui [Federation of Chinese Cotton Mills]. Hua-shang Sha-ch'ang Lien-ho Hui Pao-kao Shu [Report of the

Federation of Chinese Cotton Mills]. Shanghai, 1934. 45 pp.

華商紗廠聯合會

華商紗廠聯合會報告書

Hua-shang Sha-ch'ang Lien-ho Hui Chi-k'an (*China Cotton Journal*). Shanghai, 1919– . Quarterly.

華商紗廠聯合會季刊

Huang Yen-p'ei. "Wo So Sheng-kuan Chih Chung-kuo Tsui-ch'u-ch'i Chi Tsui-chin-ch'i Hsien-cheng Yün-tung" [My Personal Acquaintance with the Earliest and the Most Recent Constitutional Movements in China], *Hsien-cheng*, No. 1 (January, 1944), 10–11.

黃炎培

我所身觀之中國最初期及最近期憲政運動

Jen Shih-hsien. Chung-kuo Chiao-yü Ssu-hsiang Shih [History of Chinese Educational Ideas]. Shanghai, 1937. 2 ts'e.

任時先　中國教育思想史

Jen-wen [Humanities]. Shanghai, 1930– . Monthly.

人文

Kung Chün. Chung-kuo Hsin-kung-yeh Fa-chan Shih Ta-kang [Outline History of the Development of Modern Industry in China]. Shanghai, 1933. 302 pp.

龔駿　中國新工業發展史大綱

Kung Shan-fu. "Ta Feng Yen-k'en Kung-ssu Chien-tsu Chi" [An Account of the Rent Reduction of Ta Feng Land Reclamation Company], *Chiang-su Yen-chiu*, I, No. 2 (June, 1935), nonconsecutive pagination.

龔善福　大豐鹽墾公司減租紀

Kuo-li Chung-yang Yen-chiu Yüan Li-shih Yü-yen Yen-chiu So Chi-k'an (*Bulletin of the Institute of History and Philology, Academia Sinica*). New Series. Taipei, 1951–

國立中央研究院歷史語言研究所集刊

Kuo Pin-chia. "Keng-tzu Ch'üan-luan" [Boxer Uprising of 1900], *Wen-che*, VI (1936), 135–82.

郭斌佳 庚子拳亂

Li Chi-hsin. "Cheng-li Chiang-su Hai-pin Yen-k'en Chih Kuan-chien" [Observations Gained from Supervising Land Reclamation along the Kiangsu Coast], *Chung-kuo Chien-she*, I (June, 1930), 115–35.

李積新 整理江蘇海濱鹽墾之管見

Li Chien-nung. Chung-kuo Chin-pai-nien Cheng-chih Shih [Political History of China in the Past Century]. 2d ed. Taipei, 1959. viii, 690 pp.

李劍農 中國近百年政治史

A standard account, expanded from an earlier version entitled Tsui-chin San-shih-nien Chung-kuo Cheng-chih Shih.

Li, Ting-i. Chung-kuo Chin-tai Shih [History of Modern China]. Taipei, 1953. 266 pp.

李定一 中國近代史

Lin Chen-han, ed. Yen-cheng Tz'u-tien [Dictionary of Salt Administration]. Shanghai (?), 1928. Nonconsecutive pagination.

林振翰 鹽政辭典

Lo Kung. "Chang Chi-chih Yü Huai-nan Yen-k'en" [Chang Chien and Reclamation of Salt Fields in Huai-nan], *Yen-wu Yüeh-pao*, V, No. 8 (August, 1946), 45–51.

羅恭 張季直與淮南鹽墾

Lu Shao-chi. Chung-kuo Hsien-tai Chiao-yü [Education in Contemporary China]. Shanghai, 1934. 176 pp.

盧紹稷 中國現代教育

Lu Yang-hao. "Chiang-pei Shui-li Chi-yao" [Summary of Water Conservancy Problems of North Kiangsu], *Chiang-su Yen-chiu*, I, No. 3 (July, 1935); I, No. 5 (September, 1935); and I, No. 6 (October, 1935); nonconsecutive pagination.

陸養浩 江北水利輯要

——— "T'o-chan Su-pei K'en-chih" [Expand Land Reclamation in Northern Kiangsu], *Chiang-su Yen-chiu*, I, No. 1 (May, 1935), nonconsecutive pagination.
拓展蘇北墾殖

Mo-hsin Fu-hsin Sheng-hsin Tsung-kung-ssu San-shih Chou-nien Chi-nien K'an "The Thirtieth Anniversary Memorial Book, 1898–1928, Mow Sing and Foh Sing Flour Mills and Sung Sing Cotton Mills." Shanghai, 1929. Nonconsecutive pagination.
茂新福新申新總公司三十週年紀念刊

Mu Hsiang-yüeh. Ou-ch'u Wu-shih Tzu-shu [Autobiography at Fifty]. Shanghai, 1926. 94, 226, 81 pp.
穆湘玥 藕初五十自述

P'eng Tse-i. "Chang Chien Ti Ssu-hsiang Chi Ch'i Shih-yeh" [Chang Chien's Ideas and Career], *Tung-fang Tsa-chih*, XL (July, 1944), 54–60.
彭澤益 張謇的思想及其事業

Shang Yen-liu. Ch'ing-tai K'o-chü K'ao-shih Shu-lu [An Account of the Ch'ing Civil Service Examinations]. Peking, 1958. xiv, 352 pp.
商衍鎏 清代科舉考試述錄

She-hui K'o-hsüeh (*The Social Sciences*). Peiping, 1935– . Quarterly.
社會科學

Shen Nai-cheng. "Ch'ing-mo Chih Tu-fu Chi-ch'üan Chung-yang Chi-ch'üan Yü 'T'ung-shu Pan-kung'" "On the Powers of the Viceroys and Governor of the Provinces in the Last Years of the Tsing Dynasty," *She-hui K'o-hsüeh*, II, No. 2 (January, 1937), 311–42.
沈乃正
清末之督撫集權,中央集權與'同署辦公'

Shen T'ing-kuo. Chi Chang T'ai-yen Hsien-sheng [Recalling Mr. Chang Ping-lin]. Shanghai, 1946. 90 pp.
沈廷國 紀章太炎先生

Shen Pao Kuan. Tsui-chin Chih Wu-shih-nien, Shen Pao Kuan Wu-shih Chou-nien Chi-nien [The Past Fifty Years, in Commemoration of the Shen Pao's Golden Jubilee]. A special supplement of the Shen Pao. Shanghai, 1923.

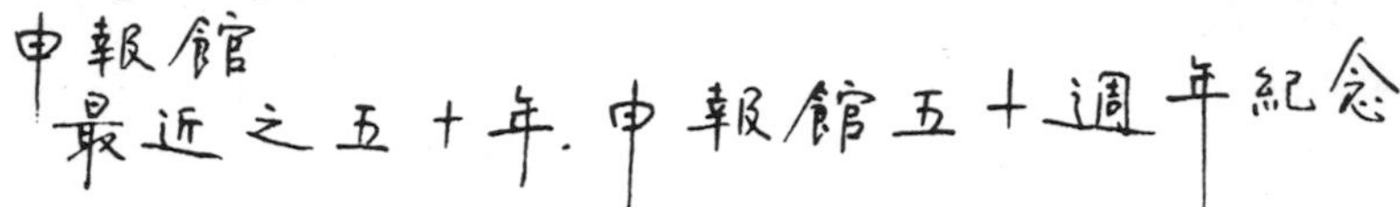

Shih-yeh Tsa-chih (*The Industrial Magazine*). Changsha, 1917– . Monthly.

實業雜誌

Shu Hsin-ch'eng. Chin-tai Chung-kuo Chiao-yü Shih-liao [Historical Materials on Modern Chinese Education]. Shanghai, 1923. 4 vols.

舒新城 近代中國教育史料

Shuo-wen. Shanghai and Chungking, 1939– . Monthly.

說文

Sonoda Ikki. Hsin Chung-kuo Jen-wu Chih [Personages in New China]. Translated by Huang Hui-ch'üan and Tiao Ying-hua. Shanghai, 1930. 578 pp.

園田一龜 新中國人物誌

Sung, Hsi-shang. Chang Chien Chuan [Biography of Chang Chien]. Taipei, 1954. i, ii, 50 pp.

宋希尚 張謇傳

A brief account.

——— Shuo Huai [On the Huai]. Nanking, 1929. 152 pp.

說淮

T'an-yen Ts'ung-pao [Salt Discussion Miscellany]. Shanghai, 1913–14. Monthly.

談鹽叢報

T'ang Tsu-p'ei. Min-kuo Ming-jen Hsiao-chuan [Brief Biographies of Famous personages of the Republican Period]. Hong Kong, 1953. 178 pp.

唐祖培 民國名人小傳

Tao-huai Wei-yüan Hui [Huai Control Commission]. Tao-huai Kung-ch'eng Chi-hua [Plans for Control of the Huai River]. Shanghai, 1931. 134 pp.

導淮委員會 導淮工程計劃

Ting Chih-p'ing, ed. Chung-kuo Chin-ch'i-shih-nien-lai Chiao-yü Chi-shih [Chronology of Chinese Education in the Last Seventy Years]. New ed. Taipei, 1961. 291, xliii, viii pp.

丁致聘 中國近七十年來教育紀事

Ting Hsien. Fu-huai Ku-tao T'u-shuo[Illustrated Discourse on Returning the Huai to Its Old Course]. Chung-kuo Shui-li Cheng-pen Ts'ung-shu [Collection of Classics on Water Conservancy in China], I, No. 7. Edited by Hsü Yen-nung. Shanghai, 1936. 66 pp.

丁顯 復淮故道圖說
中國水利珍本叢書 徐硯農

Tseng Yang-feng. Chung-kuo Yen-cheng Shih [History of Salt Administration in China]. Shanghai, 1936. v, 295 pp.

曾仰豐 中國鹽政史

Tso Shun-sheng. Chung-kuo Chin-pai-nien Shih Tzu-liao [Sources for Chinese History of the Last Hundred Years]. Shanghai, 1926. 2 vols.

左舜生 中國近百年史資料

——— Chung-kuo Chin-pai-nien Shih Tzu-liao Hsü-pien [Sources for Chinese History of the Last Hundred Years, Supplementary Volume]. Shanghai, 1933. 2 vols.

中國近百年史資料續編

——— Chung-kuo Hsien-tai Ming-jen I-shih [Anecdotes on Famous Persons of Contemporary China]. Hong Kong, 1951. 109 pp.

中國現代名人軼事

Tung-fang Tsa-chih (*Eastern Miscellany*). Shanghai, 1904– . Semimonthly and monthly.

東方雜誌

Wang Hsin-chung. "Chia-wu Chan-ch'ien Chih Chung-jih Wai-chiao

Cheng-ts'e Kai-shuo" [Summary of Sino-Japanese Foreign Policies Prior to the War of 1894], *She-hui K'o-hsüeh*, II (1936), 149–202.

王信忠 甲午戰前之中日外交政策概說

Wang P'ei-t'ang, ed. Chiang-su Sheng Hsiang-t'u Chih [Gazetteer of Kiangsu]. Changsha, 1938. 596 pp.

王培棠 江蘇省鄉土誌

Wang Shih-chieh and Ch'ien Tuan-sheng. Pi-chiao Hsien-fa [Comparative Constitutional Law]. Shanghai, 1936. 2 vols.

王世杰 錢端升 比較憲法

Wang Tzu-chien and Wang Chen-chung. Ch'i-sheng Hua-shang Sha-ch'ang Tiao-ch'a Pao-kao [Report of a Survey of Chinese Cotton Mills in Seven Provinces]. Kuo-li Chung-yang Yen-chiu Yüan, She-hui K'o-hsüeh Yen-chiu So, Ts'ung-k'an [Academia Sinica, Institute of Social Sciences Series], No. 7. Shanghai, 1935. iii, 224, XLVL pp.

王子建 王鎮中 七省華商紗廠調查報告 國立中央研究院.社會科學研究所.叢刊

Wang Yün-sheng. Liu-shih-nien-lai Chung-kuo Yü Jih-pen [China and Japan during the Last Sixty Years]. Tientsin, 1932–33. 6 vols.

王芸生 六十年來中國與日本

Wen-che (*Quarterly Journal of Liberal Arts*, Wuhan University). Wu-ch'ang, 1930– . Quarterly.

文哲

Wu Ch'eng-lo. Chin-shih Chung-kuo Shih-yeh T'ung-chih [Encyclopaedia of Modern Chinese Industries]. Shanghai, 1929. 2 vols.

吳承洛 今世中國實業通志

Wu Ching-hsiung and Huang Kung-chüeh. Chung-kuo Chih-hsien Shih [History of the Formulation of Constitution in China]. Shanghai, 1936 (?). 2 vols.

吳經熊 黃公覺 中國制憲史

Wu Chün-mien, ed. Li-hsia Ho Shu-t'i Kuei-hai Lun-chi [Collected Articles on the Diking and Opening of the Inner Lower River]. Shui-li Wei-yüan Hui, Shui-cheng Ts'ung-shu [Commission on Water Conservancy, River Administration Series], No. 3. Chungking (?), 1942. 44 pp.

吳君勉 裏下河束隄歸海論集
水利委員會水政叢書

Wu T'ung-chü. Huai-hsi Nien-piao Ch'üan-pien [Complete Historical Tables of the Huai System]. No place of publication, 1928. 4 ts'e.

武同舉 淮系年表全編

Meticulously compiled by the author, this work presents a chronicle of events pertaining to the Huai, and a detailed geography of the Huai valley. Of particular interest is the series of excellent maps showing the historical changes of the Huai. The quality of the maps suffers but little from the fact that they are printed in the traditional manner.

Yang Chia-lo. Min-kuo Ming-jen T'u-chien [Illustrated Compendium of Famous personages of the Republic]. Nanking, 1937. 2 vols.

楊家駱 民國名人圖鑑

Yang Ta-chin. Hsien-tai Chung-kuo Shih-yeh Chih [Modern Chinese Industry]. 2d ed., rev. Shanghai, 1938. 2 vols.

楊大金 現代中國實業誌

Yang Yu-chiung. Chung-kuo Cheng-tang Shih [History of Political Parties in China]. Shanghai, 1936. v, 225 pp.

楊幼炯 中國政黨史

Yen-cheng Tsa-chih [Salt Administration Magazine]. Peking, 1912- Monthly.

鹽政雜誌

Yen Chung-p'ing. Chung-kuo Mien-fang-chih Shih-kao [Draft History of the Chinese Cotton Textile Industry]. Peking, 1955. vii, 384 pp.

嚴中平 中國棉紡織史稿

A revised edition of the work cited immediately below, this book has been made to conform to the Communist ideological line. Of particular interest is the deletion of the entire section describing Chang Chien's difficulties in establishing Dah Sun.

——— Chung-kuo Mien-yeh Chih Fa-chan [The Development of Chinese Cotton Industry]. Chungking, 1943. 305 pp.

中國棉業之發展

A classic study, this work traces the growth of the cotton industry, taking into account all the factors involved. Chang Chien's contribution is placed in its proper perspective.

Yen-wu Yüeh-pao [Salt Affairs Monthly]. Nanking, 1941– . Monthly.

鹽務月報

B. *Western Language Materials*

Biggerstaff, Knight. The Earliest Modern Government Schools in China. Ithaca, N.Y., 1961. xi, 276 pp.

Bland, J. O. P. and E. Backhouse. China under the Empress Dowager: Being the History of the Life and Times of Tz'u Hsi, Compiled from State Papers and the Private Diary of the Comptrollers of Her Household. 2d ed. Peking, 1939. xxiii, 470 pp.

Boardman, Mabel Thorp. Under the Red Cross Flag at Home and Abroad. 2d ed. Philadelphia, 1915. 333 pp.

Brunnert, H. S. and V. V. Hagelstrom. Present Day Political Organization of China. Shanghai, 1912. iv, 572, lxxxi pp.

Still the most authoritative and handy reference to late Ch'ing official ranks and titles.

Bush, Vannevar. "John Ripley Freeman, 1855–1932," *National Academy of Sciences, Biographical Memoirs,* XVIX (1937), 171–87.

Cameron, Meribeth Elliot. "The Public Career of Chang Chih-tung 1837–1909," *Pacific Historical Review*, VII (September, 1938), 187–210.

——— The Reform Movement in China, 1898–1912. London, 1931. 223 pp.

Chang, Chung-li. The Chinese Gentry: Studies on Their Role in Nineteenth-century Chinese Society. Seattle, 1955. xxi, 250 pp.

——— The Income of the Chinese Gentry. Seattle, 1962. xvii, 369 pp.

Ch'en, Jerome. Yuan Shih-k'ai 1859–1916: Brutus Assumes the Purple. Stanford, Calif., 1961. 290 pp.

Ch'ien, Tuan-sheng. The Government and Politics of China. Cambridge, Mass., 1950. xviii, 526 pp.

China, Imperial Maritime Customs. Decennial Reports on the Ports Open to Foreign Commerce in China and Corea; and on the Condition and Development of the Treaty Port Provinces, 1882–1901. Shanghai, 1893–1904. 2 vols.

Chinese Recorder and Missionary Journal. Shanghai, 1869–1941. Monthly.

Chinese Social and Political Science Review. Peking, 1916– . Quarterly.

Chow, Tse-tsung. The May Fourth Movement: Intellectual Revolution in Modern China. Cambridge, Mass., 1960. xv, 486 pp.

Ch'ü, T'ung-tzu. Local Government in China under the Ch'ing. Cambridge, Mass., 1962. xiv, 360, 1 pp.

Dewey, John. Impressions of Soviet Russia and the Revolutionary World: Mexico—China—Turkey. New York, 1929. 270 pp.

Djung, Lu-dzai. A History of Democratic Education in Modern China. Shanghai, 1934. xxxiii, 258 pp.

Dollar, Robert. Private Diary of Robert Dollar on His Recent Visits to China. 2d ed. San Francisco, 1916. 210 pp.

Fairbank, John King and Kwang-ching Liu. Modern China: a Bibliographical Guide to Chinese Works, 1898–1937. Cambridge, Mass., 1950. xviii, 608 pp.

Feuerwerker, Albert. China's Early Industrialization: Sheng Hsuan-huai (1844–1916) and Mandarin Enterprise. Cambridge, Mass., 1958. xii, 311, xxxii pp.

Fitkin, Gretchen. "The Model City of China, A Visit to Nantungchow: Mr. Chang Chien, His City and the People; the Changing Yangtze and How to Control It," *North China Herald*, (May 7, 1921), 406–7.

Fong, H. D. [Fang Hsien-t'ing]. Cotton Industry and Trade in China. Nankai University, Nankai Institute of Economics, Serial Bulletin No. 4. Tientsin, 1932. 2 vols.

Freeman, John Ripley. "Flood Problems in China," *American Society of Civil Engineers*, *Transactions*, LXXXV (May, 1922), 1405–60.

Gale, Esson McDowell. Salt for the Dragon: a Personal History of China, 1908–1945. East Lansing, Mich. (?), 1953. 225 pp.

Gregg, Alice Henrietta. China and Educational Autonomy: the Changing Role of the Protestant Educational Missionary in China, 1807–1937. Syracuse, 1946. xiv, 285 pp.

Harvard University. Committee on International and Regional Studies. Papers on China. Cambridge, Mass., 1947– . Annual.

——— Research Center in Entrepreneurial History. Change and the Entrepreneur. Cambridge, Mass., 1949. vii, 200 pp.

Ho, Ping-ti. The Ladder of Success in Imperial China. New York, 1962. xviii, 385 pp.

——— "The Salt Merchants of Yang-chou: a Study of Commercial Capitalism in Eighteenth-century China," *Harvard Journal of Asiatic Studies*, XVII (1954), 130–68.

——— "Weng Tung-ho and the 'One Hundred Days of Reform,' " *Far Eastern Quarterly*, X (1951), 125–35.

Hsiao, Kung-chuan. Rural China: Imperial Control in the Nineteenth Century. Seattle, 1960. xiv, 783 pp.

——— "Weng T'ung-ho and the Reform Movement of 1898," *Tsing Hua Journal of Chinese Studies*, New Series I, No. 2 (April, 1957), 111–243.

Hsiao, Theodore E. The History of Modern Education in China. Peiping, 1932. xvi, 164 pp.

Hsieh, Pao Chao. The Government of China (1644–1911). Baltimore, 1925. 414 pp.

Hsüeh, Chün-tu. Huang Hsing and the Chinese Revolution. Stanford Studies in History, Economics, and Political Science, XX. Stanford, Calif., 1961. xi, 260 pp.

Hu, Ch'ang-tu. "The Yellow River Administration in the Ch'ing Dynasty," *Far Eastern Quarterly*, XIV (August, 1950), 505–14.

Hummel, Arthur W., ed. Emminent Chinese of the Ch'ing Period (1644–1912). Washington, 1943. 2 vols.

Jansen, Marius B. The Japanese and Sun Yat-sen. Cambridge, Mass., 1954. viii, 274 pp.

Kann, Eduard. The Currencies of China: an Investigation of Gold and Silver Transactions Affecting China, with a Section on Copper. Shanghai, 1926. xviii, 374 pp.
Contains a good description of the various types of taels used in China.

King, S. T. and D. K. Lieu. China's Cotton Industry: a Statistical Study of Ownership of Capital, Output, and Labor Conditions. Shanghai (?), 1929. 51 pp.

Kuo, P. W. The Chinese System of Public Education. Teachers College, Columbia University, Contributions to Education, No. 64. New York, 1915. xii, 209 pp.

Levenson, Joseph Richmond. Liang Ch'i-ch'ao and the Mind of Modern China. Cambridge, Mass., 1953. xii, 256 pp.

Levy, Marion Joseph and Kuo-heng Shih. The Rise of the Modern Chinese Business Class. New York, 1949. viii, 64 pp.

This is a useful pioneering study, but it must be used with caution because the authors based their interpretations and conclusions upon only a limited number of sources.

Li, Chien-nung. The Political History of China 1840–1928. Translated and edited by Ssu-yü Teng and Jeremy Ingalls. Princeton, 1956. xii, 545 pp.

Translation of Chung-kuo Chin-pai-nien Cheng-chih Shih, with certain passages abridged.

Li, Tien-yi. Woodrow Wilson's China Policy, 1913–1917. New York, 1952. 268 pp.

Life of the Honorable Chang Chien: with an Account of the Enterprises Inaugurated by Him. Shanghai, 1915. 67 pp.

An illustrated pamphlet showing many of Chang Chien's industrial enterprises.

McCall, Davy H. "Chang Chien and the Establishment of the Tungchow Cotton Mills." Unpublished paper, Harvard University, 1948.

——— "Chang Chien—Mandarin Turned Manufacturer," *Papers on China*, No. 2 (May, 1948), 93–102.

MacMurray, John V. A., ed. Treaties and Agreements with and concerning China, 1894–1919. New York, 1921. 2 vols.

Murphey, Rhoads. Shanghai, Key to Modern China. Cambridge, Mass., 1953. xii, 232 pp.

North China Herald.

Odell, Ralph M. Cotton Goods in China. Department of Commerce. Bureau of Foreign and Domestic Commerce. Special Agents Series, No. 107. Washington, 1916. 242 pp.

P'an, Wei-tung. The Chinese Constitution: a Study of Forty Years of Constitution-making in China. Washington, 1945. 327 pp.

Reinsch, Paul Samuel. An American Diplomat in China. Garden City, N.Y., 1922. xii, 396 pp.

——— Intellectual and Political Currents in the Far East. Boston, 1911. viii, 396 pp.

Remer, C. R. Foreign Investments in China. New York, 1933. xxi, 708 pp.

Schumpeter, Joseph A. Capitalism, Socialism, and Democracy. 3d ed. New York, 1950. xiv, 431 pp.

Sites, Frederick R. "Chang Chien," *Asia*, XVIII, 587–92.

Steiger, George Nye. China and the Occident: the Origin and Development of the Boxer Movement. New Haven, 1927. 349 pp.

Sun, E-tu Zen. "The Chinese Constitutional Missions of 1905–1906," *Journal of Modern History*, XXIV (1952), 251–68.

——— Chinese Railways and British Interests 1898–1911. New York, 1954. viii, 230 pp.

Tan, Chester C. The Boxer Catastrophe. Columbia University Studies in the Social Sciences, No. 583. New York, 1955. ix, 276 pp.

Teng, Ssu-yü and John King Fairbank. China's Response to the West. Cambridge, Mass., 1954. 296 pp.

——— Research Guide to China's Response to the West. Cambridge, Mass., 1954. 84 pp.

Tsiang, T. F. [Chiang T'ing-fu]. "Sino-Japanese Diplomatic Relations. 1870–1890," *Chinese Social and Political Science review*, XIII, No. 1 (1933), 107–69.

Tsing Hua Journal of Chinese Studies. Taipei, 1956– . Semiannually.

United States. Department of State. Papers Relating to the Foreign Relations of the United States, 1883. Washington, 1884.

——— Papers Relating to the Foreign Relations of the United States, 1914. Washington, 1922. cxv, 1132 pp.

Vinacke, Harold Monk. Modern Constitutional Development in China. Princeton, 1920. ix, 280 pp.

Wong, King-kung. Chang Chien, a Case Study of Attempts at China's Modernization by the Traditional Gentry. Unpublished Masters thesis, University of Washington, 1957.

Yen, Hawkling L. A Survey of Constitutional Development in China. New York, 1911. 136 pp.

Index